MW01133716

Walt Disney's Imagineering Legends

and the Genesis of the Disney Theme Park

Jeff Kurtti

NEW YORK

A Camphor Tree Book
Design by Bruce Gordon

Disney Editions
Wendy Lefkon, Editorial Director
Jody Revenson, Senior Editor
Jessica Ward, Assistant Editor
For information address Disney Editions
114 Fifth Avenue
New York City, New York 10011-5690

Printed in Singapore

First edition

10 9 8 7 6 5 4 3 2 1

Library of Congress Cataloguing-in-Publication Data on File
ISBN 978-0-7868-5559-9

Celebrating the Memory of
Peggy Van Pelt, PhD
The Inspirational Imagineer
"Her medium was people, her art everlasting"

Also by Jeff Kurtti

The Great Movie Musical Trivia Book
Since the World Began: Walt Disney World—The First 25 Years
The Art of The Little Mermaid
The Art of Mulan
A Bug's Life: The Making of an Epic of Miniature Proportions
A Bug's Life: Special Collector's Edition
Walt's Time: From Before to Beyond (Co-editor)
Dinosaur: The Evolution of an Animated Feature
The Mythical World of Atlantis
Subterranean Tours Atlantis: A Traveler's Guide to the Lost City
Milo's Journal: Atlantis, the Lost Empire
Treasure Planet: A Voyage of Discovery (with Jody Revenson)
The Art of Disneyland (with Bruce Gordon)
The Disney Villains: The Top-Secret Files
Disney Insider Yearbook 2005 (Content Editor)
Disney Dossiers: Files of Character from The Walt Disney Studios
The Art of Walt Disney World (with Bruce Gordon)
Walt Disney World: Then, Now, and Forever (with Bruce Gordon)
How Does the Show Go On? (with Thomas Schumacher)
What the Sea Teaches Us

TABLE OF CONTENTS

Foreword — **Growing Up With Imagineering** by Martin A. Sklar — *page v*

What is Walt Disney Imagineering? — *page vii*

The First Imagineer: Walt Disney — *page viii*

Chapter One — **The Prototype Imagineers** — *page 1*
Harper Goff ✶ Ken Anderson ✶ Herbert Ryman ✶ Sam McKim

Chapter Two — **The Executive Suite** — *page 19*
Richard F. Irvine ✶ Bill Cottrell

Chapter Three — **The Place Makers** — *page 33*
Marvin Davis ✶ Bill Martin

Chapter Four — **The Story Department** — *page 47*
Marc Davis ✶ Claude Coats

Chapter Five — **Masters of Mixed Media** — *page 61*
Morgan "Bill" Evans ✶ Roland "Rolly" Crump ✶ Yale Gracey ✶ Blaine Gibson

Chapter Six — **The Model Shop** — *page 79*
Fred Joerger ✶ Harriet Burns ✶ Wathel Rogers

Chapter Seven — **The Machine Shop** — *page 93*
Roger Broggie ✶ Bob Gurr

Chapter Eight — **The Music Makers** — *page 107*
Richard M. & Robert B. Sherman ✶ Buddy Baker ✶ George Bruns ✶ X Atencio

Chapter Nine — **The Unofficial Imagineers** — *page 121*
Ub Iwerks ✶ Bill Walsh ✶ James Algar ✶ Ward Kimball

Chapter Ten — **The Renaissance Imagineer** — *page 135*
John Hench

Bibliography and Acknowledgements — *page 142*

Index — *page 144*

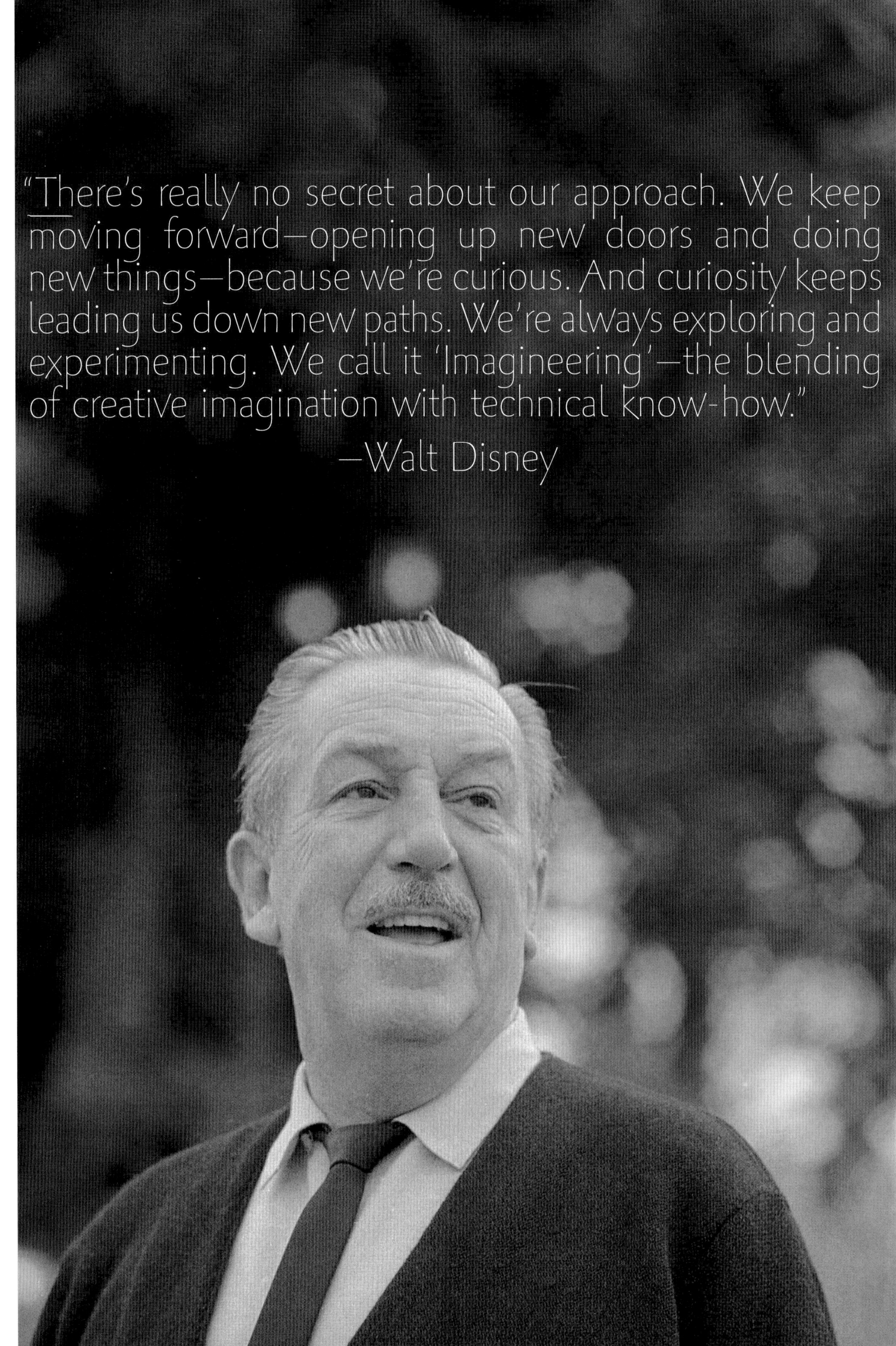
"There's really no secret about our approach. We keep moving forward—opening up new doors and doing new things—because we're curious. And curiosity keeps leading us down new paths. We're always exploring and experimenting. We call it 'Imagineering'—the blending of creative imagination with technical know-how."
—Walt Disney

Foreword

It's not often that a single phrase captures the essence and spirit of an entire organization. I thought I had accomplished it in the early 1960s with a description Walt Disney really liked: "Imagineering is the blending of creative imagination with technical know-how."

Yes, but: in the quintessential book about the Imagineers entitled *Walt Disney Imagineering—A Behind the Dreams Look at Making the Magic Real*, writer Kevin Rafferty really took home the prize. "Question:" Kevin wrote, "How many Imagineers does it take to change a light bulb? Answer: Does it have to be a light bulb?"

It's the kind of answer Imagineers have given to countless challenges in the more than half a century since WED Enterprises was created by Walt Disney in December, 1952, to work with him on the development of his "dream project," Disneyland. The list of "original answers" the Imagineers have come up with has turned on almost as many light bulbs around the world as Thomas Edison did: a litany of "firsts," "never befores," and "one of a kinds" that are so signature Disney that they no longer surprise the more than 2.1 billion people who have visited the eleven Disney parks around the world since Disneyland opened in July 1955.

It might never have happened if Walt Disney's friend and neighbor, Los Angeles architect Welton Becket, had coveted the design job. For when Walt approached him about designing Disneyland, and explained the concept brewing in his head, Mr. Becket gave his friend this advice: "You'll use architects and engineers, of course, but Walt—you'll really have to train your own people; they are the only ones who will understand how to accomplish your idea."

It was, of course, storytellers in the broadest sense of the word Walt Disney needed for his "new concept in family entertainment." And so they came, from Hollywood motion picture and television studios, from Disney and Twentieth-Century Fox especially: art directors, set designers, special effects wizards, writers, production designers, model makers. And they were joined by a new breed of designer such as Bob Gurr, trained to design cars, but more significantly smart enough to know that "no" and "it can't be done" were never answers you gave to Walt Disney's dreams. Harrison (Buzz) Price, who did the original site and economic feasibility studies for Disneyland, put it this way: "Yes, if. . ." is the language of the enabler. You never wanted to tell Walt "No, because. . . ."

I had the privilege (as my own career grew from staff writer, to Vice President of Concepts and Planning, and then to President and Vice-Chairman and Principal Creative Executive of Imagineering) of working with all of the amazing talents you will read about in this volume. They were my mentors, my friends, and in their golden years, my staff. As you will discover, they were "the best of the best." They defined Imagineer and Imagineering. They developed and led the 140 disciplines that form Imagineering today. Their passion for going beyond what they had done the time before was unbounded. Their dedication to Walt, and their belief in his passion for excellence, truly knew no bounds. They were true believers, followers, and leaders. Walt created Imagineering, but Imagineers made it sing and dance. And created, designed, and built as no one had ever done before them.

And they received very clear direction from their boss. "I don't want the public to think they are in the 'real world' when they visit Disneyland," Walt Disney said. "I want them to know they are in another world."

Only the team leader has his name on the front door, but Walt Disney knew who designed and built the house. So the next time you visit Disneyland, take a few minutes for a leisurely stroll down Main Street, U.S.A. Look up at the windows above the shop fronts. There you will find their names. They were the generals and admirals, and it was an army and navy like no other. They are Walt Disney's Imagineering Legends.

Martin A. Sklar
Executive Vice President
Imagineering Ambassador
Walt Disney Imagineering

ABOVE: Marty Sklar and John Hench discussing models and concepts for Epcot, circa 1980.

ABOVE: Walt Disney showcases the progress of construction of Disneyland, just a month before the Park's Opening Day of July 17, 1955.

What is Walt Disney Imagineering?

Walt Disney Imagineering was, in its first iteration, Walt Disney, Incorporated, created in 1952 by Walt to manage his personal assets and to develop plans for what became Disneyland. But as his brother, Roy, felt strongly that there might be a conflict of interest between that new entity and Walt Disney Productions, he quickly suggested that Walt change the name. Later that year it became WED Enterprises (an acronym for Walter Elias Disney).

Out of WED's "brain trust," Disney historian Tim Hauser reflects, "came the theories, aesthetics, design, and engineering of Disneyland; the advancement of three-dimensional storytelling; the development of robotic techniques in Audio-Animatronics; and the perpetuation of an 'architecture of reassurance' as inspired by Walt Disney's personal sense of optimistic futurism." Walt used the word "imagineering" to describe the blending of imagination and engineering in their work.

"As these endeavors unfolded," explains author Steven Watts in *The Magic Kingdom: Walt Disney and the American Way of Life*, "Walt developed a special fondness for WED. He spent many hours roaming its premises, inspecting mock-ups in the model room, tossing around ideas, and brainstorming with the staff about potential projects. The pressures that attended the Disney Studio's extensive production schedule of movies and television shows had become overwhelming, and Walt found a kind of respite by escaping into this smaller, more innovative group."

Walt further elucidated, "Well, WED is, you might call it my backyard laboratory, my workshop away from work. It served a purpose in that some of the things I was planning, like Disneyland for example. It's pretty hard for banking minds to go with it, so I had to go ahead on my own and develop it to a point where they could begin to comprehend what I had on my mind."

More bluntly, as Walt once told artist and designer Marc Davis, "Dammit, I love it here, Marc. WED is just like the Hyperion Studio used to be in the years when we were always working on something new."

As the holding company for Walt's personal projects and royalties for the Walt Disney name, WED became a divisive business point between Walt and Roy, as their small operation grew into a larger enterprise beholden to investors, so in 1965, WED Enterprises was sold to Walt Disney Productions (now The Walt Disney Company).

Walt then formed Retlaw ("Walter" spelled backwards) as his private company and for royalties for the Walt Disney name, as well as his personal ownership of two Disneyland attractions, the Disneyland Railroad and the Disneyland Monorail. Retlaw paid rent for the attractions' rights-of-way and employed the attraction administrators. It also owned the small apartment atop the fire house on Main Street, U.S.A.

In 1982, the Disney family sold the name and likeness rights and the rail-based attractions to Walt Disney Productions. In 2005, the remaining divisions of Retlaw officially became part of the Walt Disney Family Foundation, a non-profit organization led by Diane Disney Miller and her son, Walter Elias Disney Miller.

Since 1987, WED Enterprises has been known as Walt Disney Imagineering (WDI), Disney Imagineering, or simply Imagineering. Imagineering currently has a manufacturing division known as MAPO (Manufacturing and Production Organization); a construction entity known as PICO (Project Installation and Coordinating Office); and a division called Theme Park Productions (TPP), which produces film and video elements for the theme parks and resorts.

Walt Disney Imagineering remains the design, development, and master planning branch of the company, employing a multitude of disciplines utilized in places all around the world. So far, Imagineers have been responsible for the creation of eleven theme parks (two in California, four in Florida, two each in Japan and France, and the newest in Hong Kong, China); three cruise ships; more than twenty resort hotels; and several water parks, sports, and entertainment complexes, among many other creative projects.

The First Imagineer

More than fifty years ago, Walt Disney utterly transformed the concept of outdoor entertainment venues. Gone were the tawdry carnivals and seedy amusement piers that had come to be called "amusement parks." In their place was an entirely new destination that would come into common vernacular as the "theme park."

To Walt Disney, Disneyland was a logical step in a lifelong career of storytelling. It was an opportunity for him to take the characters and stories he had introduced in animated shorts, feature-length films, and television, and bring them to three-dimensional life. At the same time, he was taking cinema and television audiences out of their seats and giving them the chance to step through the screen and live these adventures firsthand. From the very beginning, Disneyland visitors were both spectators and participants. They encountered each scene as if they were part of the show, experiencing not just sights and sounds, but also tastes, smells, and touches.

For Walt,[1] Disneyland was a world seen through fantasy, a place of warmth and nostalgia, full of "illusion and color and delight." A 1953 proposal for Disneyland promised, "Like Alice stepping through the Looking Glass, to step through the portals of Disneyland will be like entering another world."

The result was the first total theme show, a designed entertainment experience in which every element—the architecture, landscaping, attractions, entertainment, colors, sounds, employees' costumes, and even the food and merchandise—were carefully orchestrated to tell a three-dimensional story. All elements of the design worked together in a harmonious relationship, keeping contradictions to an absolute minimum.

Disneyland immersed guests in familiar genres popularized in motion pictures—from jungle exploration and adventure in the Old West, to storybook-inspired settings and futuristic science-fiction worlds. In a sense, the Park is a form of "virtual reality," because it is a place that, although not real, creates its own reality.

To this end, Walt sought to create a "storybook realism," an essence of genuineness and authenticity that is more utopian, more romanticized than the actual environments could ever be. All the negative, unwanted elements have been carefully designed out, while the positive elements are not only retained, but also embellished to heighten their value. Many critics denounce Disneyland for this created reality, confusing it with cynical imitation (or even fraud), but Tom Carson, longtime writer on pop culture and politics for *The Village Voice* and *LA Weekly*, understood the Park's intent and execution when he succinctly commented, "Nothing looks fake. Fabricated, yes—fake, no. Disneyland isn't the mimicry of a thing. It's a thing."

If there is a global thematic motif to Disneyland, it is an "architecture of reassurance,"[2] a message that things will be all right, that people are innately good, and that as a society, we can handle any problems that arise.

Disneyland has sometimes been called "a road map of Walt Disney's life." This is because many areas and themes in the Park reflect an experience in his life, a three-dimensional illustration of his work, his fascination with a particular time period or location, or a realization of a lifelong avocation. For instance, Main Street, U.S.A., recalls his boyhood in Marceline, Missouri; Fantasyland features the characters and stories he popularized in film; and the Disneyland Railroad reflects his lifelong love of trains. The concepts for Tomorrowland were guided by Walt Disney's own optimistic belief that the future was filled with remarkable possibilities that emerging technologies could provide

THIS PAGE: Walt Disney, dreamer and doer.

OPPOSITE: Walt surveys his Magic Kingdom during the final stages of construction in 1955.

1 Throughout this text, the use of the familiar "Walt" to indicate the man is employed to differentiate the creator from the cultural and business institution he created, and not to indicate informality or intimacy.

2 A favorite notion of Imagineer John Hench, this term came into popular use as the name of a 1997 exhibition organized by the Canadian Centre for Architecture, Montreal (University of Minnesota professor of art history and American studies Karal Ann Marling, curator).

to centuries-old problems. Disneyland became a mirror of Walt's interests—his sense of nostalgia for his formative years, his fascination with the future, and his vision for family entertainment.

For the sake of illuminating the collective that created and contributed to Disneyland (and other Disney theme parks), it's best to begin with the originator of the idea, Walt Disney himself. The story of the creation of the Park has become enveloped in dramatic myth for more than a half-century that correctly places Walt at its center, but often neglects both the fascinating personal history that led Walt to Disneyland, and the individuals who shared his vision. In order to relate its creative and logistic origins to the realities of the procedural events, contributors, and their contributions, it is helpful to have an understanding not simply of the legend, but the factual details of the chronology and logic of its origin.[3]

Walt had always been a fan of circuses, carnivals, and fairs. His father, Elias, had been a laborer on the famous "White City," the World Columbian Exposition of 1893 in Chicago, and he must certainly have shared tales of its wonders with his young son. Walt had created a custom Mickey Mouse cartoon for the 1939 New York World's Fair, and had been an enthusiastic visitor to the "other" 1939 Fair, the Golden Gate International Exposition in San Francisco.

One of the things Walt saw there, and returned with, was a collection of meticulous handcrafted miniatures. He loved their detail, their workmanship, their nostalgia; and a few years later, when Disney's doctor advised him to find a hobby, Walt began to design and hand craft miniatures of his own.

Having grown up in the American Midwest, Walt was always entranced by the power, romance, and the very culture of railroading. As a boy, he had been a "news butcher," selling newspapers, peanuts, and candy on the Santa Fe Railroad out of Kansas City. He attended the Chicago Railroad Fair in 1948, and soon after his return combined his miniature-making hobby with his love of trains.

He began building a 1/8-scale model of a Central Pacific Locomotive of the 1870s to circle his Holmby Hills property. Dubbed the Carolwood Pacific, the train had its first trial run in December 1949 on the Studio lot, and soon it was taken home, where it circumnavigated twenty-six hundred feet of track, including a forty-foot timber trestle, two tunnels, and a perfectly scaled and manicured landscape. This new hobby helped him escape the pressures of the Studio.

However burdensome it might have been for him at times, the Studio he had completed in Burbank in 1940 had been another unexpected creative blessing for

3 Much of this account was written for the introduction to *The Art of Disneyland* (Disney Editions, 2005).

Walt. He threw himself into every detail of its design and execution just as he had with his filmmaking endeavors. Everything from building siting to floor finishes saw Walt's influence and approval.

He was very proud of his new Studio; the Kem Weber–designed buildings and furniture and pristine landscaping made his "movie campus" the envy of the moguls. He contemplated Studio tours, but couldn't imagine anything duller than watching people make movies, especially animated ones. Still, he kept receiving requests from children who wanted to visit and see where Mickey Mouse and Snow White lived.

Disneyland, however, did not start out as the ambitious new kind of outdoor entertainment it eventually became. As early as 1940, the combination of available property adjacent to the Studio and the intellectual property of his motion pictures led Walt to mention to animator Ben Sharpsteen that he was thinking of creating an attraction on land adjacent to the Studio, so that visitors might see something more than "just people working."

The "magical little park" was going to be built on an eleven-acre site across from the Walt Disney Studios in Burbank (an area now occupied by the Feature Animation Building, the headquarters of ABC, and a busy branch of the Ventura Freeway). At that time, it was called "Mickey Mouse Park" and was going to include stagecoach and pony rides, "singing" waterfalls, a train, and statues of Mickey Mouse, Donald Duck, Snow White, and other famous Disney characters. Longtime Disney employee John Hench remembers looking out the window and seeing Walt, a lone figure in the distance, pacing off the wasted sliver of land between the Studio and the Los Angeles Flood Control Channel.

In the late 1940s, all of these concepts began to amalgamate as Walt began yet another, separate project, known variously as "Walt Disney's America" and "Disneylandia," which would tour the country, featuring fully dimensional, animated miniature scenes of America's nostalgic past, including a vaudeville hoofer and a barbershop quartet.

For some time, work progressed on the mechanized miniature scenes and the "magical little park" in separate, locked rooms at the Studio, Walt the only connection between them, pondering them as he chugged along on his backyard scale railroad.

On March 27, 1952, the *Burbank Daily Review* printed the first public announcement of Walt's plans to build this park, which was now called "Disneyland." However, Walt was already thinking about making his park more "magical" and less "little." In fact, his ideas rapidly outgrew any available land near the Studio.

He hired the Stanford Research Institute to find the best location for his new project. The institute found an orange grove in the then-sleepy town of Anaheim, California. In August 1953, Walt purchased 160 acres (at about $4,500 per acre)—which was all the land his limited budget could afford. With key backing from the American Broadcasting Company (ABC), in return for a weekly television show from Walt called Disneyland and a stake in the new park, construction began on Disneyland on July 16, 1954.

Almost exactly one year later, on July 17, 1955, at 10:00 a.m., Walt presented Disneyland to a live audience of about 28,000 in-park visitors and the largest television audience to date. By the end of that first summer, after solving some initial problems, the Park was running smoothly—and more than a million satisfied guests had visited Walt Disney's Magic Kingdom.

Everything—from his first visit to the circus as a child to his most recent trip around his backyard railroad—had, at last, culminated in the undertaking that Walt would call Disneyland.

The core of Disneyland, and of nearly every successful Disney creative project, is the story it tells. The language of storytelling that Walt had created and used for more than

THIS PAGE: Walt Disney, media innovator.

twenty-five years in the motion picture business naturally translated to the untried medium of the theme park. Just as naturally, Walt called upon proven talent from his movie studio in creating Disneyland, because of their innate understanding of that language. They may not have been "story men" in the filmmaking sense of the term, but a variety of filmmaking abilities played significant roles in shaping the Disneyland story through the application of their specific talents.

Over a quarter century of transforming his storefront animation studio into the world-renowned cultural powerhouse of "Disney," Walt set in motion a well-known and well-documented escalation of creative, commercial, and technological successes. Less well-known and well-documented is Walt's concurrent evolution in team-building. As a creative leader, it was essential to form an organization of individuals who understood his professional desires and project needs as well as his own often-mercurial temperament.

Many an organization, however, has foundered by the establishment of an employee body whose understanding goes no further. Walt knew that although he was inarguably the visionary of his organization, his goals would require the employment of people of greater talents in specific areas than those he possessed. Fortunately, Walt seemed quite able to establish a boundary to his ego that enabled him to maintain absolute authority while drawing the very best out of the myriad talents surrounding him.[4]

Walt knew that his team needed to be comfortable with their environment and challenged and rewarded by the projects and personalities around them. They received the best in tools, materials, and technology to contribute to their efforts. They required stimulation, encouragement, and persuasion to attain their best work. The one key leadership attribute that Walt seemed to lack was praise. A direct compliment from Walt to an individual was a rare (if not unheard-of) reward. Oddly, it was this lack of verbalized reassurance and acceptance of their work that may have been one of the most effective stimuli to many of the Disney creative and executive group.

"Disney Imagineering evolved into an environmental art form that includes the art of building, but also encompassed human cultural dynamics. While the first Imagineers had no formal training in urban design, the nature of the animator's art made them natural systems architects. As storytellers, they 'wrote' the park, giving it consistency of narrative that is matched by few other public spaces. Animation is an act of pure creation. Unlike filmmaking that involves turning a camera on human beings and physical locations, the art of animation process parallels natural creation systems. Like the universe before the big bang, information exists only as unrealized potential, requiring a burst of energy to transform it into a visible, coherent reality."

—J. G. O'Boyle,
"Mindsetter: A Cultural Analysis of Disney's Main Street, U.S.A."
Persistence of Vision Issue 10 (1998), page 86.

Was this behavior calculated? Doubtful. Any student of effective organization would certainly look on Walt's managerial style with disdain. He was prone to egomania, could be insensitive to a fault, and was often dismissive of ideas that did not follow his overall lead. Longtime animator and animation director Jack Kinney recalled that Walt would often pat a guy on the back one day, and ignore him on the next—thus keeping the employee in a state of confusion and emotional subservience.

Was this behavior destructive? Obviously not. For all the fear, resentment, or hostility Walt's perceived egotism, occasional thoughtlessness, and unpredictable behavior might have engendered in his staff, for many it was this peculiar confluence of traits that made him the creative touchstone that he was, and a daily challenge to their personal best. "There was just something about him that made you want to please him," artist and Imagineer Herb Ryman recalled, "and gaining his confidence was better than payday."

Although stinting with praise, Walt's employees knew when their ideas were discussed, implemented, or elevated, they had been accepted. At the same time as Walt surrounded himself with people who understood him (and therefore created comfort for him), they also tended to be people who challenged his ideas, using Walt's initial inspiration and ongoing input as points of departure for evolving, improving, or spinning off these core notions into new regions or finished products.

As Disney biographer Steven Watts noted in his 1998 book, *The Magic Kingdom: Walt Disney and the American Way of Life*: "Disney functioned brilliantly in the hard-to-define role of artistic visionary at his studio. Those who tried to define what he did kept coming back to the same words: 'intuition,' 'instinct,' a feel for the 'essence of things,' a 'creative catalyst.'" Watts encapsulates that Walt "kept the creative process moving with critical acumen and enthusiasm. The staff saw it again and again and never ceased to be amazed. Disney, as director Jack Cutting concluded simply, 'made it all work.'"

4 It is reported that Walt once met with an enthusiastic Orson Welles about the "boy genius" joining the Disney team for a project. After Welles's departure, Walt ostensibly quipped, "There's only room for one genius at this studio."

In addition, Walt often spotted abilities within his employees that they had little or no notion of, encouraging them to take creative and artistic risks and expand their own aptitudes and skills. Longtime Disney story man Joe Grant affirmed, "He always encouraged your personal originality. Always. And he always had the feeling that there was something more there—and we were always willing to give what we had."

"It always seemed to me," Roy E. Disney—nephew to Walt, and Director Emeritus of and consultant to The Walt Disney Company—says, "that the notion of art in Walt's mind, and in his way of dealing with people, was broader than, say, the guy who came in from Chouinard[5] and said, 'My specialty is this.' I never knew anyone at the Studio who was a one-trick pony."

In this sense, Walt was like the (rather overused) analogy of the symphony conductor—selecting his musicians, creating careful collaborations and tensions, supervising the body and its work, and pulling forth the best possible performances from the individuals and the whole.

However present the possessive term "Disney's" in the history of the organization, Walt was keenly aware that he owed his final success to the talents of a team. "It seems shallow and arrogant," he said, "for anyone in these times to claim that he is completely self-made and that he owes all his success to his own unaided efforts. While it is true that it is a basic Americanism that a man's standing is, in part, due to his personal enterprise and capacity, it is equally true that many hands and hearts and minds generally contribute to anyone's notable achievements."

A few of Walt's loyal animation talents managed to form a creative enclave that, over time, became well known by a larger public, albeit those already inclined to an interest in the art and culture of Disney. These were the "Nine Old Men," Walt's de facto animation "board of directors"—John Lounsbery, Woolie Reitherman, Frank Thomas, Ollie Johnston, Ward Kimball, Eric Larson, Marc Davis, Milt Kahl, and Les Clark—whose individual talents, styles, and contributions to Disney projects elevated their status with Walt, and allowed their identities and efforts to become known outside the walls of the Studio.[6]

Other talent, such as Mary Blair and Eyvind Earle, earned their wider reputation both through their distinctive visual styles—Blair is probably best remembered for

5 Chouinard Art Institute was founded in 1921 and provided Disney with a fair number of artists over the years. In 1961, Walt and Roy Disney merged Chouinard and the Los Angeles Conservatory of Music (founded in 1883), to create California Institute of the Arts (CalArts), the first U.S. higher educational institution to offer undergraduate and graduate degrees in both visual and performing arts.

6 John Canemaker's excellent chronicle of this group, *Walt Disney's Nine Old Men and the Art of Animation* (Disney Editions, 2001), was an inspiration for this book and is an exceptional resource and fascinating document of the creative workings of the Disney Studio in its heyday.

the graphic and colorful whimsy of "it's a small world," Earle for his stylized gothic tapestry in *Sleeping Beauty*—and for the fact that they left the protective creative palisade of Disney and were able to elevate their personal artistic identities in other media. Others, such as Herbert Ryman, Carl Barks, Joe Grant, Bill Justice, and Peter Ellenshaw, became more publicly known either because of sheer longevity or the active pursuit and encouragement of loyal fans of their art.

Beyond the Nine Old Men, there was another creative team, today known as Walt Disney Imagineering, the creative arm of Disney parks and resorts worldwide. For although Disneyland was the inspiration of one man, Walt did not achieve this history-altering concept on his own. Using his innate talent for combining disparate skills and personalities, he assembled a creative team that would blend "creative imagination with technical know-how"—the "Imagineers."

From the beginning, this group of varied talents—culled from the Walt's and other motion picture studios, Chouinard Art Institute and Art Center College of Design, and throughout Hollywood's design community—explored, experimented, and expanded Walt's ideas, creating a new dimensional and immersive entertainment form that has since expanded to the four corners of the world.

Through the span of their careers, these highly skilled artists, with widely differing artistic gifts, viewpoints, personalities, and degrees of ambition and competitiveness, exhibited a loyalty to one another and their employer unparalleled in most professions.

Within these pages is an effort to chronicle some of the "many hands and hearts and minds" of the pioneering and influential theme park designers—the prototype Imagineers—in terms of their personal backgrounds, artistic perspectives and styles, and careers; then to address their relationship with and work for Walt Disney Imagineering during their time there. It introduces a core group of the originators of Disneyland and the other Disney parks, and illustrates why, half a century later, their work continues to be vital and important to millions of people every day, and all over the world.

This story is also an attempt to examine how art influenced the artists, how their experience informed their world view, and how the artists were influenced by Disney (the man and the organization)—and in turn, contributed their own inflection to the vernacular of Disney theme parks.

If nothing else, it will create a record of a group of immensely talented and interesting people, and introduce their lives and works to a new generation of Disney aficionados and theme park fans.

"You see, I'm not Disney anymore. I used to be Disney, but now Disney is something we've built up in the public mind over the years. It stands for something, and you don't have to explain what it is to the public. They know what Disney is when they hear about our films or go to Disneyland. They know they're going to get a certain quality, a certain kind of entertainment. And that's what Disney is."
—Walt Disney

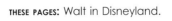

THESE PAGES: Walt in Disneyland.

"The way to get started is to quit talking and begin doing."
—Walt Disney

The Prototype Imagineers

As Walt began to evolve his thinking about Disneyland, he needed to bring his concepts into a visual reality, much as he did with film projects. This process began with a select group of initial team members, whose primary roles extended well beyond simply being artists-for-hire. Walt seems to have chosen each of them for a number of reasons: their confidence in his ideas, their ability to voice and substantiate their opinions, their varied and disparate artistic styles, their regional backgrounds, their points of view, and their character traits. This group of artists is representative not only of a body of rich and diverse talent, but also of the team-building alchemy that was so much a part of Walt Disney's great skill in realizing new and unusual ideas.

Harper Goff: The Second Imagineer

Aristotle suggested that the traditional idea of friendship has three components: friends must enjoy each other's company, they must be useful to one another, and they must share a common commitment to the good.

It is fairly simple to observe that Walt was naturally drawn to spend more time and attention (and expend greater respect) to those with whom he shared a common interest. In Walt's case in the 1950s, model railroaders were in vogue, and it was this interest that brought him together with one of the primary designers of Disneyland, Harper Goff.

"My wife Flossie and I went to England in 1951," Goff recalled, "and I went into a place where you got miniature trains . . . steam trains . . . a company called Basset-Lowke." Goff saw a locomotive he wanted, but was told by the shopkeeper that there was another man who had expressed an interest in the locomotive, and would return that afternoon. If he didn't take it, Goff could have it. "We came back that afternoon and we saw this fellow in the store," Goff recalled, "and he had purchased the locomotive." The man turned and introduced himself to the startled Goff—it was Walt Disney. "He asked me what I did for a living," Goff continued, "and I told him I was an artist. He said, 'When you get back to America, come and talk to me.'"

Goff was born March 16, 1911, in Fort Collins, Colorado, a former military reservation that became a thriving railroad hub in the 1870s, and by the time of Goff's youth was an archetypal American small town, with a bustling seventy-six-acre central business district and nearly 10,000 citizens.

"My dad owned a newspaper there," Goff recalled, "the *Fort Collins Express Courier*, and I grew up there. It was a very prosperous town. We had banks that looked like banks, you know, and there was a Victorian city hall. These buildings were around when I was a kid."

In the late 1920s, Goff and his family moved to Santa Ana, a similarly bucolic southern California agricultural town with a population of about 25,000, famed for fruit orchards, strawberries, and other seasonal crops.[1] Artistic since his youth, Goff soon began attending art classes at the Chouinard Art Institute in Los Angeles. In the mid-1930s, Goff briefly lived in New York City, where he executed paintings for *Colliers, Esquire, National Geographic,* and *Coronet* magazines.

Back in California, he worked for several years under art director Anton Grot at Warner Bros., designing settings for *Captain Blood, A Midsummer Night's Dream, The Charge of the Light Brigade, Anthony Adverse, The Life of Émile Zola, Sergeant York, Casablanca, Destination Tokyo, Objective Burma,* and *The Adventures of Don Juan*. During World War II, Goff worked on a motion picture series called Air Views for Douglas Aviation Company, showing their planes in various battle configurations.

By the time of his 1951 meeting with Walt, Goff had left Warner Bros., but he said to Walt, "I'm not an animator. What can I do here?" (At the time of their first meeting, Walt Disney had released only one live-action feature, *Treasure Island*, in July 1950.) Walt was aware of Goff's experience as a magazine illustrator and film designer, and he knew he needed to add to his staff for his recent entry into the live-action motion picture field. "This fit in with my experience at Warner Bros.," Goff said.

Goff quickly fell into place at Disney. In addition to the mania for model railroads that he shared with Walt and others

ABOVE: Harper Goff with one of Captain Nemo's dive crew on the set of *20,000 Leagues Under the Sea.*

BELOW: "Father" Goff (center) makes a cameo appearance with Harry Harvey (left), Paul Lukas, and Peter Lorre (right) in *20,000 Leagues Under the Sea*.

OPPOSITE: The sinister squid lurks outside a porthole of the Nautilus in Disneyland's *20,000 Leagues Under the Sea* attraction.

1 And just a few miles from the future Anaheim site of Disneyland.

at the Studio, Dixieland music was his lifelong hobby. Goff soon became the banjo player for the Firehouse Five Plus Two, the famous jazz band led by Ward Kimball and composed of Disney animators and designers.

Walt asked Goff to execute storyboards for a True-Life Adventure short, tentatively titled *20,000 Leagues Under the Sea*, while Walt went on a business trip to Europe. "It happened that *20,000 Leagues Under the Sea*, the silent version, was my favorite movie as a kid," Goff said. Instead of the nature film that Walt wanted, Goff filled eight four-foot by eight-foot storyboard panels with designs and sketches for a potential live-action feature based on the classic Jules Verne book. "He was kind of angry since all that time I hadn't made the sketches that he'd asked me to do." Goff chuckled. But Goff's distinctive visual styling of the Verne tale won Walt over, and he finally acquiesced to produce *20,000 Leagues Under the Sea* as his first all-live-action film made in the U.S. Goff became well-known for his designs of the iron-plated sharklike submarine *Nautilus*, with its luxurious Victorian interiors as described in the Verne novel.[2]

Grudgingly, it seems, Walt had become convinced both by Goff's persistence and the communicative skill of his artwork. "Harper had a way of placing you inside the environment he created in a piece of art," Marty Sklar says. Both Goff and his ideas were very persuasive.

It was during the preproduction for *20,000 Leagues Under the Sea* that Walt assigned Goff to another project, this one known as "Disneylandia," or "Walt Disney's America," which was planned as a national touring exhibit. The display was intended to feature fully dimensional animated miniature scenes of America's nostalgic past in a precursor to Walt's Audio-Animatronics technology. Goff claims that he suggested the barbershop quartet scene, and made a model of the proper scale, but not a very careful model, he admitted. Walt liked the work Goff had executed, especially the sense of place he had established in the setting, and according to Goff, "took it and had other people work on it." (Goff is probably referring to Ken Anderson and Roger Broggie, who were most closely associated with the project at this point.)

The ideas that Walt had for these displays were really the "ramp up" to Disneyland. He wanted to evoke the fun and nostalgia of a developing craze for Victoriana that would reach its zenith in the mid-1950s, but he also wanted to create and showcase a new entertainment medium that would use the blooming technology derived from wartime applications and the burgeoning field of electronics.

For a time, "Disneylandia" was planned as a major exhibition that would tour on a private railroad train. "This traveling show would come to everyone's hometown," Goff recalled. "Walt's train would be there on the railroad tracks, and it would be a special event in Chicago or St. Louis or wherever." In this scheme, a special twenty-one-car train would be accessible on a siding with public access. Visitors would enter the train from the rear and proceed through a series of cars, each containing miniatures, animated displays, and artifacts related to a Disney view of American history and culture. The size of the displays was not only dictated by Walt's interest in miniatures (the exhibit was planned to contain Walt's personal collection) but due to the fact that he wanted to adapt existing railroad cars rather than customizing or widening cars.

2 Goff makes a cameo appearance in *20,000 Leagues Under the Sea*, as a passenger in the San Francisco Steam Packet office.

The railroad idea moved onto the siding for several reasons, chief among them being the decline of the American rail lines—routes to reach many cities had become confusing and indirect. Goff remembered, "In order to get to Denver, for instance, a train would first have to go to Cheyenne, Wyoming. Then it would have to turn around on a different railroad, the Colorado and Southern, and go back south to Denver." Many of the railroads had expanded or contracted to the degree of accommodation required to conduct business efficiently—a public access attraction and excursion train just couldn't be accommodated by many railroads. Finally, word of Walt's "train idea" leaked within the tight-knit railroad business, and suddenly, "everyone began planning to make a lot of money just to let Disney in," Goff said. Plainly, the idea had simply outgrown its logistic constraints and its ability to pay for itself, let alone turn a profit.

There was briefly a plan to create the displays in such a manner that they could tour department stores across the country, with twenty animated dioramas operated by inserting coins. Imagineer Randy Bright wrote, "Even had it proved successful, a cost analysis revealed that twenty scenes of similar scope, with people constantly putting quarters in every coin slot, would not take in enough money to pay for maintenance." Walt concluded that his idea of a Studio tour park and his ambitious miniature automaton plans could be combined to create a single major project at a permanent location. "Disneylandia" became "Disneyland."

Having grown up in a small town, Goff was no stranger to Walt's concept of a typical small-town Main Street. His initial designs reflected a more rustic, rural town, with clapboard false fronts and wooden sidewalks more akin to his Colorado roots than the Midwest of Walt's memory. Although Disneyland's City Hall bears a striking resemblance to that of Fort Collins, the rest of the street design became more urban, with two- and three-story facades and Victorian architectural embellishment.

In Adventureland, Goff developed the nascent concept of a river ride into the familiar and beloved Jungle Cruise. Initially, the ride called for the river launches to be powered by a moving current in the river, for Walt wanted to avoid the noise, smell, and insurance liability of gasoline engines. The boats would drift around show scenes set up on a central island. Goff took this concept and added the element of African adventure, inspired by a popular film of the day. He eliminated the central island, creating a winding waterway to better enhance the feeling of exploration, with show action on both sides of the launch.

The designers found that they could not accurately plan the ride length, capacity, and show elements on paper to the satisfaction of the engineers and contractors, so Goff created the "Jungle Jeep." This was a dummy ride launch mounted on a jeep. Goff and his crew could drive it on the site and stake out just what kind of room was needed for turns and curves, site the show scenes, and time the ride length. (Walt was so charmed by this that he used the idea to show the attraction in progress on the February 9, 1955, episode of the *Disneyland* TV show. The jeep was replaced by a Rambler Cross-Country station wagon, since American Motors was a sponsor of the show.)

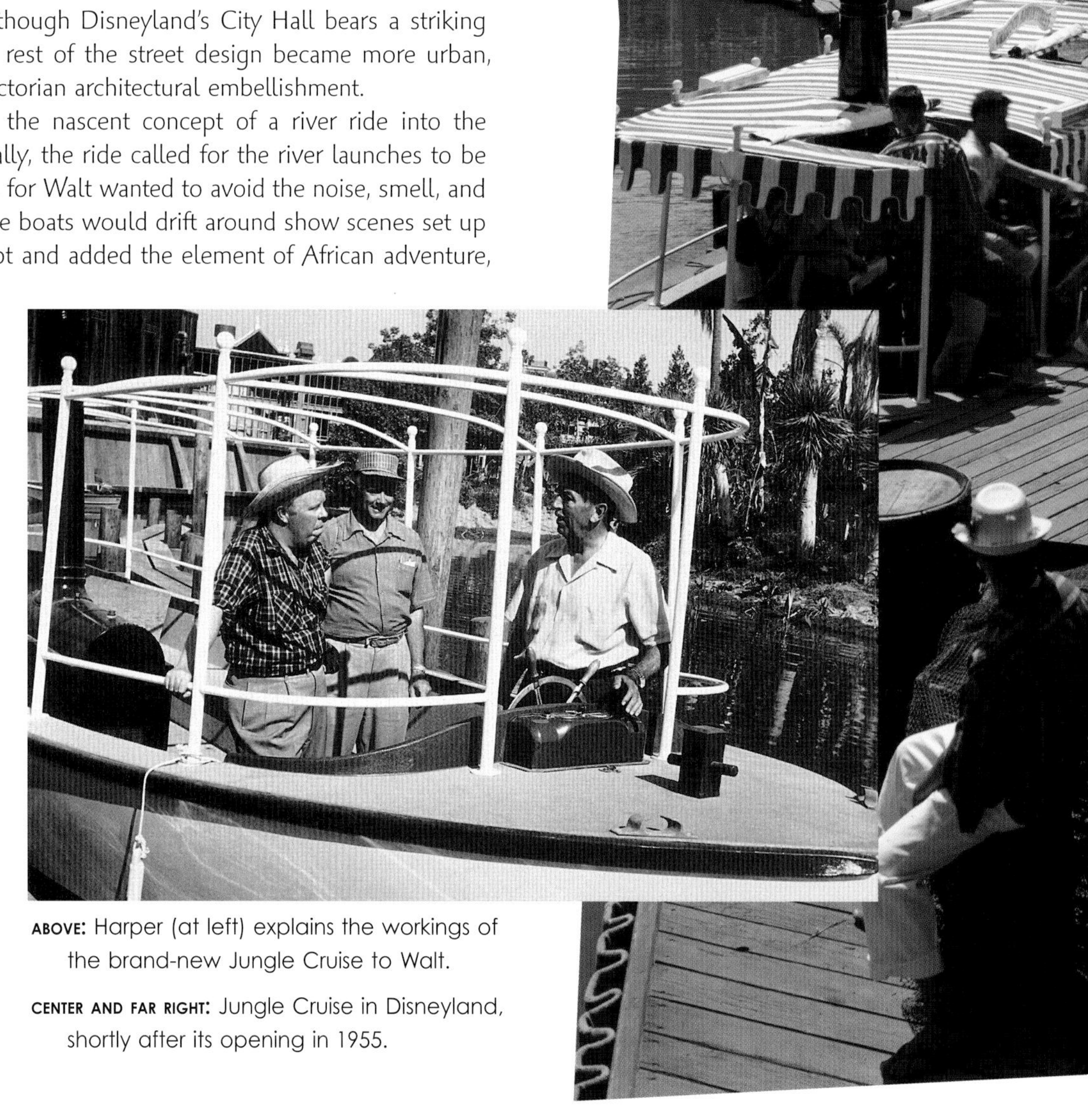

ABOVE: Harper (at left) explains the workings of the brand-new Jungle Cruise to Walt.

CENTER AND FAR RIGHT: Jungle Cruise in Disneyland, shortly after its opening in 1955.

Goff spent a great deal of time during Disneyland's construction in the field, mainly focused on Adventureland and Jungle Cruise. He remembered that he spent a lot of nights and weekends at the site, and that Walt was frustrated with the slow progress of the construction. "So I'd take him over and show him the concrete forms which were in place for the waterfall, and then we'd walk around and do 'questions and answers' on all the work going on." This kind of hands-on, in-the-trenches approach was much more satisfying to Walt; it hearkened to days at the Studio going through dozens of storyboards with "the boys" until late in the evening.

In the 1960s, Goff returned to film design. His final credits were *Fantastic Voyage* and *Willy Wonka and the Chocolate Factory*. A degree of Goff's "theme park logic" can be seen in his *Wonka* designs: the Chocolate Room has elaborate layers of fantastic decor, but a closer look reveals the infrastructure of a factory building, including elements of cast iron and brick.

Goff returned to Walt Disney Imagineering in the late 1970s as a conceptual consultant for Epcot, where he devised the layout for World Showcase. "We were working on a plan where each pavilion occupied uniform floor plans with equal 'street frontage,'" Marty Sklar recalls. Goff thought the idea seemed too mundane and sterile, and drew up a concept that addressed the square footage issue but brought fantasy and showmanship to the pavilion ideas by bringing iconic architecture and landscaping to the exteriors.

Goff worked on concepts for the Japan, Germany, and United Kingdom pavilions. Curiously, he worked extensively on components of these pavilions that were never built in Epcot. These included the Rhine River ride for Germany (the huge closed door once in the back right-hand corner of the Biergarten was the entrance to the show building), a Thames River ride for the United Kingdom pavilion, and Meet the World (with Claude Coats and Herb Ryman, among others), which went to Tokyo Disneyland. Goff continued to serve as a consultant in Disney's parks up until his death on April 1, 1993.

"I was an illustrator and I could make drawings that would sell," Goff said in a 1992 interview with *E-Ticket* magazine. "We had ideas, but Walt would say, 'When you get something drawn and I can see what you mean, then I'll talk to you about it.' If somebody asked how to make it so that it works, I'd say, 'I don't know—I'm not an engineer, I'm a dreamer.'"

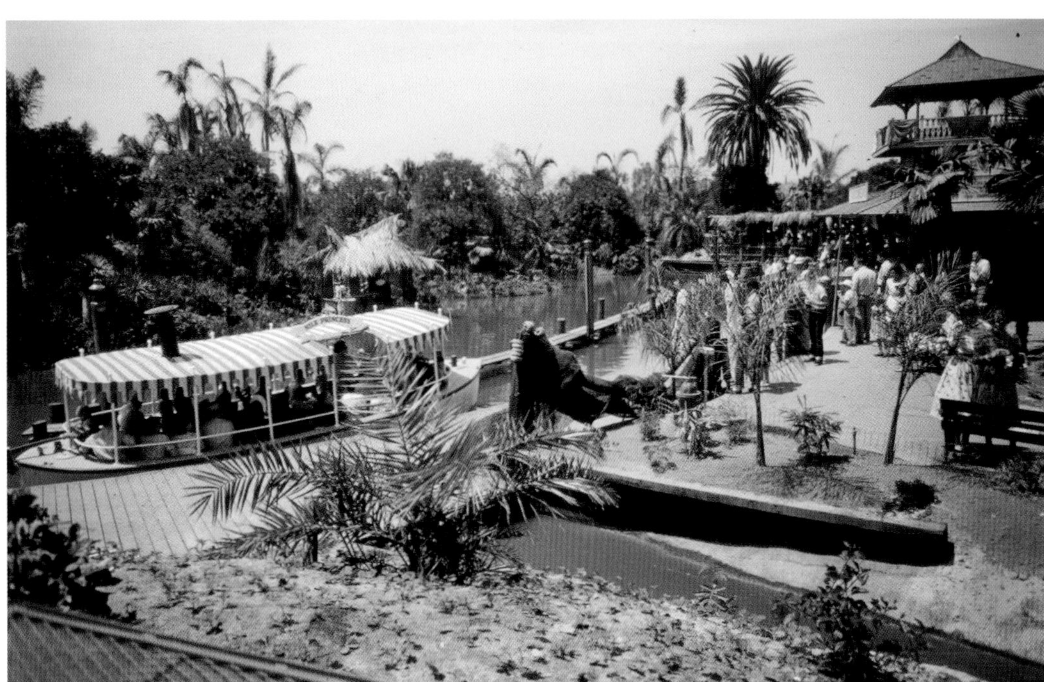

Ken Anderson: Architect of Character

Ken Anderson began his Disney career in 1934, contributing to many of the animated classics as an art director, beginning with *Snow White and the Seven Dwarfs*. Since he had an architectural background, he came up with innovative perspectives and camera angles on such Silly Symphony short cartoons as *Goddess of Spring* and *Three Orphan Kittens*.

"It was Ken who helped establish Disney as the world leader in animation," Disney Publicity vice president Howard Green says. "However, throughout his forty-four years with Disney, Ken was invaluable to more than just the animation facets of the Studio." Ultimately, his blend of talents bridging animation, character, story, and architecture made Ken a perfect candidate for Imagineer. Often referred to by Walt as his "jack-of-all-trades," Anderson used his skills as an architect, artist, animator, story man, and designer to pioneer many different areas of the Disney entertainment spectrum during his association with the Studio.

A native of Seattle, Washington, Anderson received an architecture degree in Europe before returning to California to work as a sketch artist at MGM, where he contributed to such films as *The Painted Veil* and *What Every Woman Knows*. Anderson lost his job in 1934, and although his MGM bosses had assured him that the layoff was temporary, he and his new bride, Polly, found themselves smack in the middle of the Great Depression. "We spent the week—or the month, really—living on the beaches on the canned beans and whatnot," Anderson said in a 1984 interview for *Disney Family Album*.

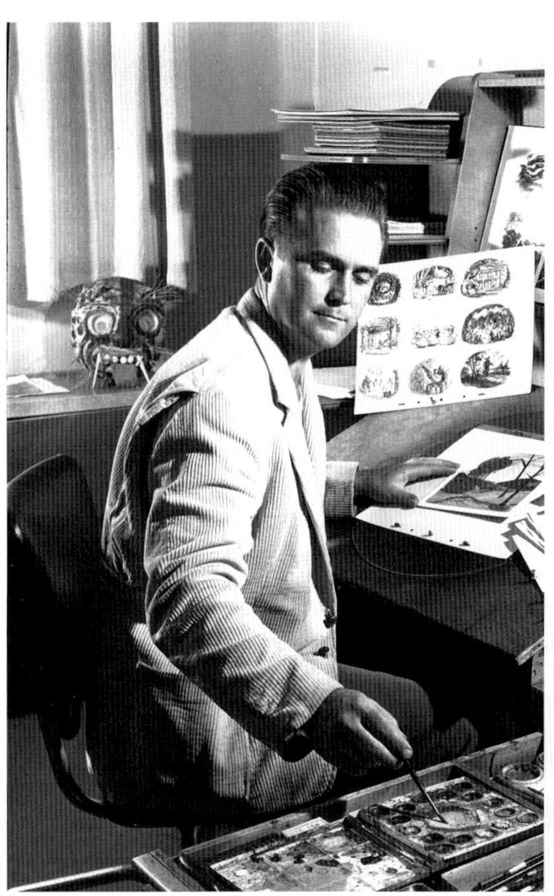

ABOVE: Ken Anderson brought a variety of talents to his work at Disney. Here he paints a study for *Song of the South* (1946).

Driving past the Walt Disney Studio on Hyperion Avenue one day, Polly encouraged Ken to apply for a job. Ken felt that his experience as an architect, painter, and sketch artist would be wasted in a cartoon studio, but he had no notion of Walt's ambitious plans for the animation medium. Ken was hired.

Anderson's experience as an architect was almost immediately employed on *Three Orphan Kittens*, on a vast panning shot in which a kitten chased a feather through a series of rooms with the moving backgrounds in perspective. "It jittered like crazy," Ken chuckled, "but [Walt] loved it." So did audiences and the Motion Picture Academy voters—the short won an Academy Award for its innovative artistry.

Anderson's first feature assignment was as art director on *Snow White and the Seven Dwarfs*. He built scale models of the dwarfs' cottage to help the other animators visualize the settings dimensionally, and even inspired Dopey's characteristic ear wiggle with his own unique talent to do so. Like the rest of his colleagues, Anderson found himself inspired by the enthusiasm of his boss. "He lit a fire under all of us," Anderson said. "Every one of us worked Saturdays and Sundays, nights, everything else—we just loved it. Everything was new."

Anderson went on to serve as art director on *Pinocchio, Fantasia* (the "Pastoral Symphony" sequence), and *The Reluctant Dragon*; and contributed to story on *Melody Time, So Dear to My Heart*, and *Cinderella*. As a color stylist, he had a great influence on *Alice in Wonderland*, and his layouts were pivotal to the staging and design of *Peter Pan*.

For *Song of the South*, he contributed technical and procedural innovations to the combination of animation and live action. Anderson served the vital role as a key liaison between the lead animators and the live-action unit, developing staging and interaction between the live-action Uncle Remus and the animated characters so that the two elements would merge seamlessly on the screen. It is inspired work that is still admired today, both for its technical and storytelling virtuosity. As for Anderson, he was glad to be challenged, and delighted to have Walt's regard as a versatile and handy talent.

"I didn't want to be stuck in animation," Anderson recalled. "I wanted to do story, I wanted to do painting, I wanted to do everything, be involved in everything. I loved being close to Walt—because Walt was where everything started."

With his knowledge of architecture, perspective, art direction, and story, it was natural for Anderson to be tapped by Walt to become one of the initial designers of Disneyland. In 1951, Walt approached Anderson and told him that he wanted to take him off the Studio payroll and pay him out of his own pocket. He had a special room on the third floor of the Animation Building that he and Ken would have keys to, and where Ken could work in relative seclusion on an idea Walt had for a series of dimensional animated dioramas, which Walt likened to Norman Rockwell magazine covers. "Not that good," Anderson recalled, "but that kind of Americana." The result was drawings for the prototype of Audio-Animatronics called Project Little Man, a miniature vaudeville hoofer on a stage setting, executed as a mechanical figure. Anderson also worked on a barbershop quartet (the one that Harper Goff also had a hand in), and "Granny's Cabin," a dimensional miniature set based on one of the principal settings of *So Dear to My Heart*.

ABOVE: Anderson at WED in 1984, working on the proposed Africa pavilion for World Showcase in Epcot.

Happy to be versatile and in demand, Anderson returned to animation for his work on layout in *Peter Pan* and *Lady and the Tramp* (the new wide-screen CinemaScope aspect ratio demanded his expertise with perspective) but was pulled back to WED as Disneyland came closer to reality.

Anderson's varied talents again led to his becoming a "jack-of-all-trades," designing many parts of Disneyland, some at the very last minute. His concept drawings and design work were employed in Fantasyland attractions that brought to life many of the films Anderson and his colleagues had originally created: Snow White's Adventures, Peter Pan's Flight, Mr. Toad's Wild Ride, and Storybook Land. In several cases, Anderson himself painted sets and show elements for the attractions (as did Eyvind Earle, Claude Coats, and John Hench).

In addition to those major portions of Fantasyland, Anderson art-directed the old Pirates Lagoon area adjacent to the Chicken of the Sea Pirate Ship restaurant and the last-minute installation of sets and props from the feature film *20,000 Leagues Under the Sea* into a Tomorrowland walk-through exhibit just barely in time for the Park's opening.[3]

In 1957, Anderson returned to the Studio as an art director on the final push to complete *Sleeping Beauty*, which had been in production for more than five years. Anderson later recalled having found great satisfaction in working with the opulent and complex production designs by Eyvind Earle. The geometric precision and unique perspective (or lack thereof) must have provided the artist with daily challenges.

Back in the animation business, Anderson was given a complete about-face with his next major project, *One Hundred and One Dalmatians*. Anderson worked with Ub Iwerks and the new Xerox drawing-transfer technology, which eliminated the complex and expensive production step of hand-inking all of the animation cels. This process saved time and money, and preserved much more of the vigor of the animators' drawings, but it left a coarse black outline around the characters. Anderson solved this stylistic discord in what today seems a fairly simple way. "Just about every ingenious act of innovation makes you think, 'Well, of course!'" Roy E. Disney says. "But Ken's bold design idea was truly original."

Anderson abandoned the painterly and deeply dimensional settings that had been the Disney hallmark for years, and instead created backgrounds that were executed in the same unpolished outline style on cels, then placed over backgrounds that were in many cases simple planes of solid colors.

3 Intended as a temporary display, the attraction did not close until 1966.

The result was an amazing confluence of the modern style of contemporary print graphics and the UPA[4] cartoons, as well as the burgeoning design styles coming into the mainstream through TV animation. The animators loved it, because the new technology and Ken's design staging showed off the nuances of their animation drawing as never before. Audiences loved it because it looked so modern. Walt didn't love it.

Anderson began to specialize in character design, and was focusing on development of *The Sword in the Stone* when he underwent a debilitating health crisis, suffering a massive stroke at the age of fifty-two. For a time, it appeared as though the artist would not recover. "I was practically given up for dead," Anderson recalled—the stroke had left him blind and unable to move. But with the encouragement of his wife and daughters, and the therapeutic surroundings of his favorite stand of California Live Oaks in Descanso Gardens Park, he began to take remarkable steps toward recovery.

Anderson was able to return to the Studio in time to begin work on *The Jungle Book*, where Walt charged him with creating the physical look of the villainous tiger Shere Kahn. He created a smooth, supercilious-looking cat, based to a large degree on the portrayal of such villains by character actor Basil Rathbone. Walt loved this design approach, and immediately suggested suave British actor George Sanders as the voice.

After Walt's death, Anderson continued to contribute layouts, color styling, story sketches, and character design to *The Aristocats, Robin Hood*, and *The Rescuers*. (An extensive sequence where the secret agent mice Bernard and Bianca check out their mission equipment from a sour old mouse in the supply room was abandoned after Anderson worked on it for several weeks.) His final Disney animation project was creating a design for the title character, Elliott, for the live-action musical fantasy *Pete's Dragon*.

Like so many Disney veterans, a life of leisure was ill-fitting for Anderson. "So he and Polly traveled," John Canemaker reported in his book on Disney story artists, *Before the Animation Begins*. "To Antarctica, to Africa, around the world—and everywhere they went, Anderson filled sketchbooks with line drawings of the people they met and the flora and fauna they saw." He came back to Imagineering a few years after his retirement at the behest of a new generation of Imagineers, led by show producer Tony Baxter, who wanted the benefit of his expertise for a complete renovation of Fantasyland.

"Ken Anderson was my sage," Baxter (now senior vice president of Creative Development at Walt Disney Imagineering) says. "I knew he had been so much involved in the first Fantasyland that in 1982 I called and said, 'It would be wonderful if you could come and give us some help on the new Fantasyland.'

"Ken was great because he was someone who had been there the first time, with Walt. So, all of us 'new kids' had a father. When someone wanted it this way and others that way, Ken would be able to come and say: 'No—this is what we need to do in here.' Ken would soothe everybody's egos, and do a quick little sketch of what it should look like, and that would be it. So much of the architecture on Snow White and Mr. Toad is from Ken. He was very strong on those two designs, he had a very strong influence on the rest of us during that whole process."

"The first painting I ever did, when I was twelve or so, was of one of the buildings that Ken designed in the Castle Courtyard," Imagineering show producer Tom Morris recalls. "He was a great production designer, of course, but also a great architect who knew story."

ABOVE: Over the years, Anderson's style continually evolved to suit the needs of projects.

ABOVE CENTER: Storybook Land in Disneyland.

RIGHT AND ABOVE RIGHT: Anderson had been an art director on the original film, so it made sense that he contribute to the visual design of the Disneyland version of *Snow White*.

4 United Productions of America animation studio, known as UPA, was founded in the wake of the Disney animators' strike of 1941, which resulted in a number of longtime employees leaving the Studio. Many of these outcast artists disagreed with the hyperrealistic style of animation that Disney had developed and promoted. UPA put forward a graphic and stylized animation design that was the reverse to a design philosophy of a painstakingly realistic imitation of life, but rather defied logic and realism for the sake of the art itself.

Based on his extensive world travels, Anderson was called upon for input to Epcot, especially the World Showcase area. Along with Herb Ryman, he worked on a proposed African pavilion in collaboration with *Roots* author Alex Haley. He contributed an amalgamated design for the pavilion exterior, especially designed not to reflect any single African nation or region. "Anybody from any part of Africa, from sub-Sahara to South Africa, could claim at least one of these buildings as having been inspired by his area," Anderson said.

Anderson remained active in all areas of his art, and in 1992 published his first children's book, *Nessie and the Little Blind Boy of Loch Ness*. He died on December 19, 1993, after suffering another stroke.

"Ken was big almost from the start," his longtime colleague Frank Thomas told John Canemaker. "Way back, he was recognized as a special talent."

Herbert Ryman: The Master

In the early fall of 1953 the not-yet designed Disneyland already faced its first crisis. Roy Disney, Walt's brother, was due to travel to New York to convince a group of bankers to invest in the new venture. With only a few days left before the trip, a master plan for Disneyland existed in only Walt Disney's mind. Walt called his friend; a painter and sketch artist named Herbert Dickens Ryman. "Herbie," Walt said, "I'm working on an idea for a new kind of park we're going to build."

"That's great," replied Ryman, "I'd like to see what it looks like."

"Good," said Walt, "because you're going to draw a picture of it for us."

On September 26 and 27 of 1953, with Walt Disney by his side, Herb Ryman created the first detailed map of Disneyland, the beginning of an ongoing association with the Imagineers in which he would often play integral roles at key moments in the Park's history.

Ryman was not even working for Disney at the time, but he had been involved in several of Walt's projects in years past. Ryman first went to work for Disney in 1938, a time when several full-length animated films were in the planning stages. He contributed to *Pinocchio* and served as an art director on *Dumbo, Fantasia,* and *Victory Through Air Power.*[5] He was credited as "art supervisor" on *Saludos Amigos* (in which he also appeared) and as a layout artist on the legendary propaganda short *Education for Death* and the feature film *The Three Caballeros*.

Ryman's road to the Walt Disney Studio began in Vernon, Illinois, on June 28, 1910. The son of a surgeon who was killed in battle during the second Battle of the Marne during World War I, young Ryman was expected to follow in his father's vocational footsteps. "But I loved to draw, and everyone looked upon it as a harmless hobby," Ryman wrote. He briefly attended Milliken University in Decatur, Illinois, then studied for four years at the Chicago Art Institute, where he graduated cum laude in 1931.

In 1932, Ryman came to Southern California, where his sister Lucille was living. He cast about for work as an artist, and enjoyed a somewhat enchanted life of early Hollywood. Ryman lived in the Alto Nido Apartments on Ivar Avenue in the heart of the town (this is the building where Joe Gillis, the unemployed screenwriter played by William Holden, lives in the classic film *Sunset Boulevard*). For a few short months, Ryman had an art studio and gallery in the famous Olvera Street[6] enclave, but the artist claims that during that time "not one single customer ever came in to browse, much less purchase one of my art treasures."

Ryman then traveled through the Southwest, enthralled by the beauty of its landscapes. "Everywhere I looked, the variety of nature's forms and materials excited and fed the soul of this anxious artist." Through friends of his sister, Ryman was surprised to learn that there was employment to be had for fine artists, at the major movie studios. There, artists created scenic designs, prop paintings, layout settings, and what Ryman called "artistic, sensitive illustrations." In the MGM art department from 1932 to 1935, under the legendary Cedric Gibbons, he worked on the classic films *Mutiny on the Bounty, David Copperfield, The Barretts of Wimpole Street, The Good Earth, Tarzan and His Mate,* and *A Tale of Two Cities*. The story for *The Late Christopher Bean*, the last film of the beloved character actress Marie Dressler, required two dozen original oil paintings,

OPPOSITE: Herb Ryman at work on his moody painting of the interior of the Mexico pavilion in World Showcase in Epcot.

BELOW: Walt and Ryman review concept paintings for the Ford Wonder Rotunda at the 1964-1965 New York World's Fair.

BOTTOM: Ryman's concept art for the entrance to Epcot, May 1981.

5 *Victory Through Air Power* is a combination live-action/animated propaganda feature advocating the use of strategic bombing in warfare, and based on the best-selling book by Major Alexander de Seversky, who also hosts and narrates the film.

6 Olvera Street (c. 1877) is in the oldest part of downtown Los Angeles, California. After years of decline, a public campaign in the 1930s built up Olvera Street as "a center of Mexican romance and tourism." Olvera Street remains a popular destination today.

created by the never-seen title character, an artist who becomes prominent after his death. The very-much-living Ryman took care of Bean's brushwork.

Weary of what he called "the phoniness of the pictorial qualities" of the motion picture, and frustrated by his own lack of worldly travels, Herb took up an invitation from a cousin in Bangkok and set off on an around-the-world trek that would consume his next two years. This journey created an appreciation of world cultures and a lifelong interest in Oriental history, a result of a year spent in Peking from 1936 to 1937 at his journey's end. "I'm inordinately infatuated with the world," Ryman later wrote, "its people, history, and geography. These elements are inseparable, and one lifetime is far too short to even grasp an infinitesimal phase of it."

Ryman had created dozens of art pieces during his travels, and upon his return to Los Angeles, Verne Caldwell, the head of Chouinard Art Institute, suggested that Ryman mount an exhibit there. The exhibit led to an invitation to the Walt Disney Studio, where he was offered a staff position, and where Ryman encountered his old pal Ken Anderson, with whom he had worked at MGM.

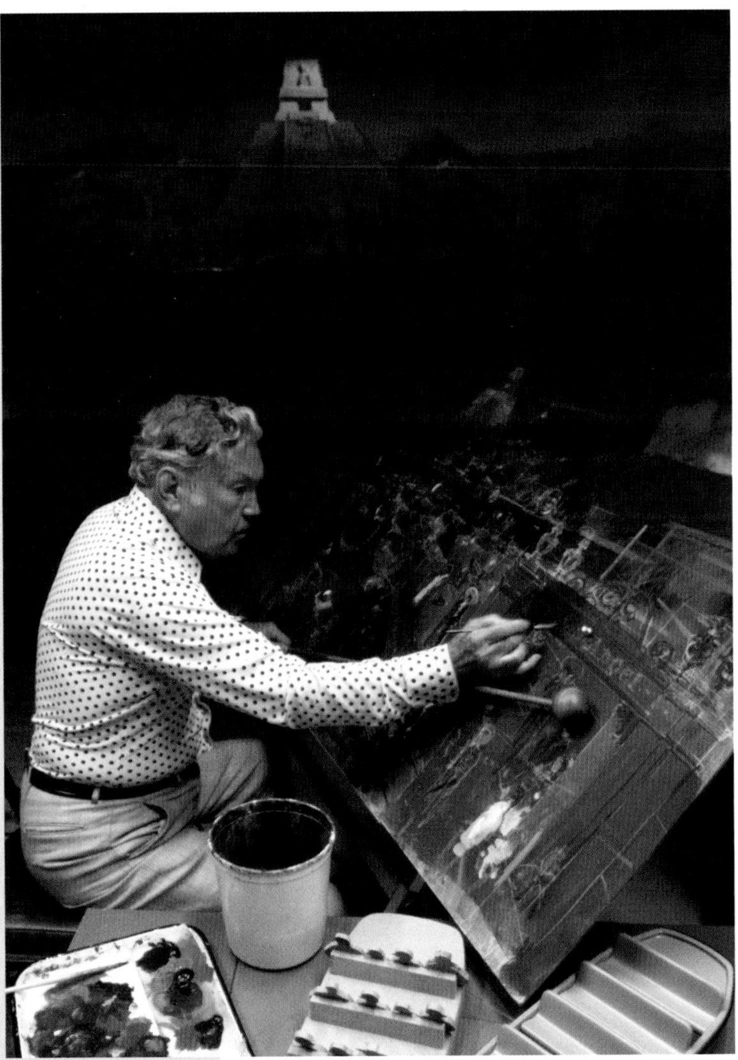

Ryman found the environment at the Studio difficult in many ways. Where MGM had been strictly hierarchical and formal, "Mr. Ryman" found himself being addressed as "Herb" and "Herbie" by colleagues with short-sleeved open-collar shirts and even a few bare feet. Where at MGM, his art informed other artisans, at Disney, his art was the product. But he loved the work. "It was more difficult to work with a Disney script. In the animated films each frame had to be drawn and each and every frame had to be illustrated."

After eight years at Disney, Ryman took the opportunity to join the art department at Twentieth Century Fox, where the film *Anna and the King of Siam* was beginning preproduction. During his trip to Asia, he had personally known the Siamese royal family and spent time with the author of the book on which the film was based. The artist never had a formal contract with Disney. "We were friends, and my being employed there was on a friendship basis," Ryman said. So, with Walt's blessing, Ryman finished up his work and went across town to the Fox lot. For nearly four years, Ryman remained at Twentieth Century Fox, contributing his art and vision to films such as *Forever Amber, Down to the Sea in Ships, David and Bathsheba,* and *The Black Rose*.

Although Ryman had found a way to make a profession of his art, he never seems to have been overly concerned with the mundane act of "having a job." In the summer of 1948, he was invited by Bill Antes, the advance man for Ringling Brothers Circus (it had yet to merge with Barnum & Bailey) to join them on the road and do a series of documentary paintings. He joined the circus in Chicago the following spring, and spent the summer of 1949 traveling cross-country with the big top by train. "To my knowledge, I was the only artist that was ever invited to travel with the Ringling Brothers Circus." He was so enthralled with this life that he joined the circus again in the summer of 1951—the last year the Circus performed "under the big top," before the merger of the circus titans. The result of these journeys was possibly the most famous of Ryman's non-Disney artistic career, an exceptional series of sketches and paintings of circus life so evocative that the famous clown Emmett Kelly said, "Herb Ryman put the smell of sawdust into paint."

Ryman also loved the pictorial inspiration of the Pacific Ocean shores, and he often painted watercolors of the California coastline, as well as portraits and other paintings that became part of many of Hollywood's most prominent collections. The Disney family, John and Lionel Barrymore, Thomas B. Costain, Mrs. William Guggenheim, and Cecil B. DeMille were some of the famous collectors of Ryman's art.

Then in September of 1953 came that legendary phone call from Walt Disney. Herb hustled over to the Studio to see what was up. "We went into the Zorro building," Ryman later wrote. "Bill Cottrell, Dick Irvine, and Marvin Davis were there." It was early Saturday morning, and Walt wanted Ryman to draw an aerial schematic illustration of his proposed park, based on a footprint executed by Marvin Davis, and several vignettes already developed by Davis, Cottrell, and Harper Goff—by Monday morning.

"When Walt had [an] idea, and whoever he called in, it was instantaneous—you were supposed to be instantly useful and instantly productive and kind of 'instant genius.'" Ryman's initial reaction to Walt's request was refusal. "You're not going to call me on a Saturday at 10:00 a.m. and expect me to do a masterpiece that Roy could take and get the money," Ryman pleaded, "It will embarrass me and it will embarrass you." Walt asked the others to leave the room and appealed to Ryman personally. The artist acquiesced, with the promise that Walt would stay himself to guide the drawing. By Monday morning it was finished. "Just a carbon pencil drawing with a little color on top of it," Ryman said. "But Roy got the money—so I guess it turned out all right."

Later, Walt called Ryman and told him the news, and asked the artist if he was interested in continuing to help out on the project. Ryman replied, "Sure, of course I am." He also made Walt a promise: "I'll work on this thing as long as it's interesting and exciting, and when it ceases to be interesting I'll go back to my work. And Walt said, and I remember very well, he said, 'Well, Herbie, I'll try to keep it interesting.' And of course, he did!"

In the ensuing decades, Ryman's brush and pencil touched every corner of the Magic Kingdom. Like his colleague Harper Goff, Main Street, U.S.A., was a vision Ryman and Walt shared. Where Goff's imaginings tended toward a rough-hewn Western character, Ryman shared a more urbane memory of the Midwest. "Walt was a product of Illinois," Ryman said, "as was I, so we had a lot in common while discussing and developing Main Street."

Ryman's tender pastel fantasies of the palace Courtyard of Sleeping Beauty Castle were never executed with the grace and detail of his intent. Schedule and budget dictated another, simpler design approach. He created interiors and backgrounds for Snow White's Adventure, and worked on the visualization of the Chicken of the Sea Pirate Ship restaurant for Fantasyland. He also did paintings and sketches of Jungle Cruise, Frontierland, and the Rivers of America, and several concepts for the Tomorrowland entrance plaza.

Ryman's art helped visualize attractions for the 1964–1965 New York World's Fair, an especially important task since WED was venturing into a new arena of show design that would have a significant impact on the future of Disney. For the fair, Disney was interested in designing Disneyland-style attractions for corporate and government sponsors. (Thus, Disney could expand their R&D in public recreation, showmanship, and the attendant technical expertise at the expense of a third-party financier.) Presenting ideas to corporations and government entities—not exactly renowned as hotbeds of creative discourse—required exactly the kind of visual story impression Ryman could create in a single image. He created renderings of "it's a small world" and the Ford Wonder Rotunda featuring the Magic Skyway, including a scheme for its planned relocation to Disneyland that never happened. In the late 1950s, Ryman also created streetscapes for Liberty Street and Edison Square, both intended to run behind the East Block of Main Street next to Tomorrowland, both never built.[7]

As Disneyland continued to grow and develop, Herb continued to bring ideas to visual life with Walt. He envisioned the Tyrolean Chalet at the Fantasyland end of the Skyway, the Swiss Family Treehouse, River Belle Terrace, Matterhorn Bobsleds, the Monorail Station, Submarine Voyage, Flight to the Moon, and the New Tomorrowland of 1967.

Ryman's most prolific and enthusiastic work in Walt's lifetime was arguably the sketches and paintings he created for New Orleans Square and its centerpiece show, Pirates of the Caribbean. "We made many, many trips to New Orleans to get inspiration," Ryman said. In addition to Park guests, Herb Ryman featured many habitués of New Orleans old and new in his studies for New Orleans Square, including sailors, artists, clergy, and the Sisters of Charity. "I always think if I can put something in that really belongs there, people will be deceived into thinking I knew what I was doing," Ryman joked.

"He was just a guy who saw the picture of everything," Roy E. Disney says. "Maybe he didn't see the philosophy of it, or the operation of it, but he was able, in his work, to create a visualization of an idea that would give it life and momentum."

After Walt's death in 1966, Ryman worked on Magic Kingdom Park in Walt Disney World, painting the ubiquitous icon of Cinderella Castle, as well as concept renderings for Liberty Square and The Hall of Presidents.

Ryman retired from Walt Disney Imagineering after the opening of Walt Disney World in 1971 and spent the next several years painting his beloved landscapes and portraits, and traveling. He returned in 1976 to work on Tokyo Disneyland and Epcot, on projects such as The American Adventure, the entrance to Epcot, the China pavilion, numerous conceptual renderings, and the Meet the World attraction for Tokyo Disneyland. Herb also created evocative art of the rugged Maine coast for the title sequence of the 1977 Disney musical fantasy film *Pete's Dragon*.

He continued to work with Disney, adding his expert touch to Main Street, U.S.A., in Disneyland Paris and the Indiana Jones™ Adventure in Disneyland, both as an artist and an inspiration to new generations of young artists.

---

7 Like all Disney concept design, however, no good thought or creation is ever wasted. Many of Ryman's 1956 designs were used in the development of Liberty Square in Walt Disney World Magic Kingdom Park. The 1958 Edison Square concepts evolved into the Carousel of Progress.

ABOVE: One of Ryman's most famous and beloved paintings, for the China pavilion in World Showcase in Epcot, benefited from the artist's extensive travels there in 1936–1937.

Herbert Dickens Ryman succumbed to cancer on February 10, 1989, at his home in Sherman Oaks, California. He was seventy-five years old. Lucille Ryman Carroll, Herb's sister, had been told by her mother in 1930 to promise that she "would forever be there to help her brother, as an artist surely could not survive merely on his art." She took this advice to heart, and the two were lifelong friends.[8]

After Ryman's death, Carroll worked diligently to preserve the memory of both his physical works and his ideals. "It was agreed by family and friends that the most positive way to commemorate the life of Herb Ryman was to carry on his philosophy and commitment to teach and encourage young artists to reach their full potential," Marty Sklar says.

It was in this spirit that the Ryman-Carroll Foundation was created in 1989 as a living tribute to Herbert Dickens Ryman. Its founders were Lucille Ryman Carroll, Sklar and his wife, Leah R. Sklar, Sharon Disney Lund (Walt's second daughter), and Harrison A. and Anne Shaw Price. The foundation was renamed Ryman Arts in 2005. (Carroll died on October 23, 2002.)

This legacy was especially appropriate for Ryman. Because he exuded an eccentric charm and a depth of experience, young people were drawn to him, curious to learn from him, and to learn more about him.

As for Ryman, he treasured a blessed life where he found a truly joyous balance between art and commerce, and he never took for granted the audience his art had reached. "I'm most proud that I had the privilege and the opportunity to participate in the development of Walt's dream," Herb said, "because I would have had a very limited audience. But here in Disneyland, it's a world audience. So what better showcase could an artist have?"

---

8 Carroll had a life as fascinating as her brother's. She had formed and become director of the MGM Talent Department under Louis B. Mayer from 1941 to 1954. She helped boost the careers of Marilyn Monroe, Lana Turner, June Allyson, and Janet Leigh, and was one of the few women to reach a real position of executive power during the heyday of the studio system.

Sam McKim: The Detail Guy

Sam McKim didn't get the first Disney position he wanted. Of course, he wasn't applying for an artist's job—he was a twelve-year-old child actor auditioning for the voice of *Pinocchio* in 1937. Although Dickie Jones ended up with the coveted part of the little wooden boy, McKim came back to the Studio seventeen years later, and utilized a whole different skill set to cast an even larger shadow in the history of Disney, as one of the original Disneyland designers.

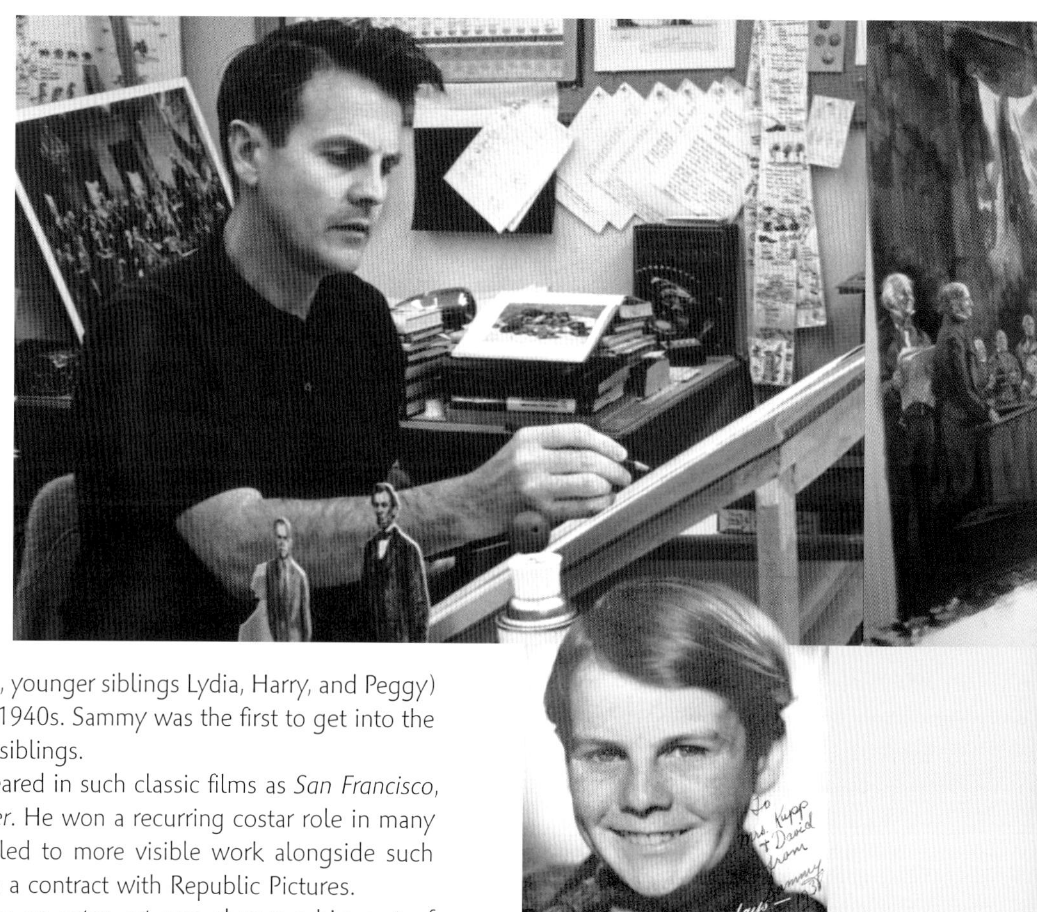

John Samuel McKim was born in Vancouver, Canada, on December 20, 1924. The family moved to Seattle, Washington, when Sam was quite young, and settled there for a time. Sam's father was in ill health, and the family moved to Los Angeles in 1935 for its warmer desert climate. Unfortunately, their father's health worsened, and he died in 1938.

With his beaming freckled face, unruly hair and a sunny disposition, Sammy McKim was discovered by a relative who was a casting agent at MGM. He was the second in a family of five children (older brother David, younger siblings Lydia, Harry, and Peggy) who all became child actors in the 1930s and 1940s. Sammy was the first to get into the movies, and blazed the trail for the rest of his siblings.

He started working as an extra, and appeared in such classic films as *San Francisco*, and the 1938 serial version of *The Lone Ranger*. He won a recurring costar role in many of the "Three Mesquiteers" Westerns, which led to more visible work alongside such cowboy stars as Hoot Gibson, and landed him a contract with Republic Pictures.

Even though he was enjoying success as an actor, art was always a big part of Sam's world. He told *Storyboard* magazine in 1987: "In 1935 I was working on a picture called *The Frisco Kid* with Jimmy Cagney. I did a caricature of him and asked him to sign it." Cagney said that when he was a boy he had wanted to be a political cartoonist for a New York daily newspaper, and encouraged McKim's drawing. "For the rest of the film, during breaks, we would sit in his dressing room, both of us drawing."

In the late 1930s, while still in high school, Sam submitted drawings to the Studio, and was offered a job in the Traffic Department (the Studio's mail delivery and messenger area), with an explanation that "the breaks would happen . . . later." In 1942, both he and brother David tried to enlist in the U.S. Army but were turned down for not being American citizens. The two Canadians gained their citizenship the following year, and signed up for duty, putting their acting careers on hold. After serving in the Army, Sam McKim enrolled in Art Center College of Design. He continued to accept small film roles, in pictures such as *The Adventures of Mark Twain* (as the Cub Pilot), *The Hucksters*, and *Flamingo Road*. The day after he graduated from Art Center in 1950, he was called back into the Army to serve in Korea, where he earned several medals and honors, including the Distinguished Service Cross and the Bronze Star. Upon returning to the States, he took advanced art classes at the Chouinard Art Institute, and continued in occasional film roles, including *The Story of Will Rogers*. During his acting career, McKim appeared in films with John Wayne, Spencer Tracy, James Cagney, Rita Hayworth, and Gene Autry. He remained a Western fan and celebrity for the rest of his life.

In 1952, McKim faced a crossroads. He had taken a job in the art department at Twentieth Century Fox, and was working on early CinemaScope trailers, when he got a call that a script was waiting for him over at Columbia Studios. "John Ford offered me a supporting role in *The Long Gray Line* with Tyrone Power, Maureen O'Hara, and Ward Bond," Sam recalled. "Would you believe I turned it down to become an artist?" McKim stayed in the art department at Twentieth Century Fox, and left acting behind for good.

Content in his artistic endeavors at Fox, Sam's art director asked if he'd be interested in being "loaned" to Disney for a couple of weeks to work on sketches and designs to help visualize "something called Disneyland." McKim reported to work the following Monday. He stayed for thirty-two years.

TOP LEFT: McKim working on designs for Great Moments with Mr. Lincoln, 1963.

ABOVE: Sam working on one of the epic paintings that appears in The Hall of the Presidents.

LEFT: Sammy McKim began his career as a child star in Westerns in the 1930s—until a new artistic calling beckoned.

BELOW: Sam McKim's emotional and inspiring production and concept paintings for Great Moments with Mr. Lincoln.

Sam joined WED Enterprises six months before the opening of Disneyland. His initial assignments included sketches for attractions, shops, and restaurants for Main Street and Frontierland, including Swift's Red Wagon Inn and the Golden Horseshoe Revue, although every land in Disneyland eventually benefited from his touch. McKim recalled, "WED always did everything they could to make your current job interesting—they always wanted you to do your best. Many studios wanted the art 'quick and dirty,' Disney didn't. There wasn't anyone over your shoulder, waiting to 'pull your boards.' Many times we were given the very basic idea of what was wanted and then were allowed to play with it, turn it over, create something unique."

Sometimes these unique design demands of developing Disneyland called for clever solutions. For the shoreline of the Rivers of America, McKim and landscape designer Bill Evans took photographs of the barren shoreline. Sam then created an overlay of opaque watercolor on acetate showing the location and scale of water features, boulders, trees,

outcroppings, bushes, and ground cover. "Bill later told me that he carried those paintings in the trunk of his car for years to use for reference," McKim said.

During downtime at WED, McKim would occasionally be called back to his old role as an art director and production artist. He worked on live-action Disney projects such as *Zorro*[9]; *Johnny Tremain; The Shaggy Dog; The Gnome-Mobile;* and *Nikki, Wild Dog of the North*.

For the 1964–1965 New York World's Fair, Sam contributed sketches for all four Disney attractions: "it's a small world," Carousel of Progress, Ford Magic Skyway, and Great Moments with Mr. Lincoln. "I did a series of thirty-some paintings for the pre-show, and figure close-up and pan paintings of Lincoln for the press previews," McKim recalled.

Since the Lincoln figure was not ready to perform prior to his debut (nor did Walt want to lose the "premiere" impact of the unique Audio-Animatronics presentation), Walt and James Algar presented the Lincoln show to Fair officials and dignitaries from the State of Illinois just as they would "walk through" the story of an animated feature—as a series of storyboards, with McKim's drawings of Lincoln "performing" his speech in lieu of the mechanical figure.

For the pre-show of the attraction, McKim's painterly skills and attention to minute detail were the keys to success. "Sam's attention to the tiniest details in his paintings was really extraordinary," Marty Sklar says. While an artist such as Herb Ryman could render his art in a fairly loose manner in order to communicate a tone or environment, nothing delighted McKim so much as working out detailed story elements and including them in his vision. "He was a master of detail." Roy E. Disney agrees.

The paintings were created for an eight-foot by twenty-eight-foot wide-screen presentation; McKim's originals were eight inches by twenty-eight inches. McKim, Algar, and Walt determined that there would be thirty key paintings, some used for panoramic camera moves, some for close-ups. "The next step was simple," McKim said with a chuckle, "divide the number of paintings into the number of days until deadline, and we knew what we had to do."

After Walt's death, McKim stayed on at WED. His paintings helped introduce the public to The Haunted Mansion in Disneyland, and The Hall of Presidents in Magic Kingdom Park.

"In the early days, everybody was trying to please Walt," McKim said. "He was the conductor of the orchestra. We all worked with each other; the good ideas that someone came up with, you tried to be faithful to those. Where necessary you added your own little bit, but the ultimate decision was with Walt. After his death, his key lieutenants did their best to keep that Disney teamwork and spirit intact."

In his later Imagineering work, McKim's art contributed to the story development of Epcot pavilions, including the Universe of Energy, and the then named Disney-MGM Studios, including The Great Movie Ride.

While McKim produced key designs and illustrations for many projects during his WDI career, he was perhaps most famous for his fantasy souvenir maps that were sold in the parks. Sam's "fun maps" charted the layouts of Disneyland, Magic Kingdom Park in Walt Disney World, Pirates of the Caribbean, and Tom Sawyer Island. (In 1992,

9 *Zorro*, a kind of Robin Hood in the pueblo days of Los Angeles, was created in 1919 by author Johnston McCulley. More than sixty-five *Zorro* books and short stories followed. Douglas Fairbanks, Sr. portrayed Zorro in a 1920 silent film; Tyrone Power played him in a 1940 remake.

McKim was asked to create his first new "fun map" in more than a decade for the about-to-open Euro Disney, now Disneyland Paris.) Following his retirement from Imagineering in 1987, McKim remained connected with WDI and Disney.

McKim's two sons both worked for Disney—Matt for Imagineering and Brian for Feature Animation. In addition to appearances at Disney fan events and consulting work, Sam also continued to be active in the arts. His work can be found in the U.S. Air Force and L.A. County Sheriff Department Collections, as well as in private collections.

"I worked with Sam on many projects, and you always knew you were in good hands," Marty Sklar says, "not only because of his drawing skills, but because he was the quintessential researcher. You could bank on Sam digging out the real meat of any subject, and offering a gem everyone else missed. His early black-and-white sketches of Main Street and Frontierland are inspirational—still among the very best ever drawn for Walt Disney theme park attractions. He was also as fine a gentleman as you would ever want to know," Sklar adds.

John Hench said of him, "Sam was the greatest to work with. He loved this Company, and his enthusiasm was always contagious. Once he got involved in anything, no matter how problematic, you always knew everything was going to be okay." Hench also valued McKim's candor: "If I ever needed to hear the truth about something, I always went to Sam."

McKim died of heart failure on July 9, 2004, at Providence Saint Joseph Medical Center in Burbank. He was seventy-nine years old.

Looking back on his many years with Imagineering, Sam once said, "For me, happiness in one's career is the measure of success. I've had a lot of happiness, so I should know."

OPPOSITE: A concept sketch for the never-realized Edison Square in Disneyland.

BELOW: Classic Sam McKim concept art, painted during the development of the Ford Wonder Rotunda pavilion in the 1964-1965 New York World's Fair.

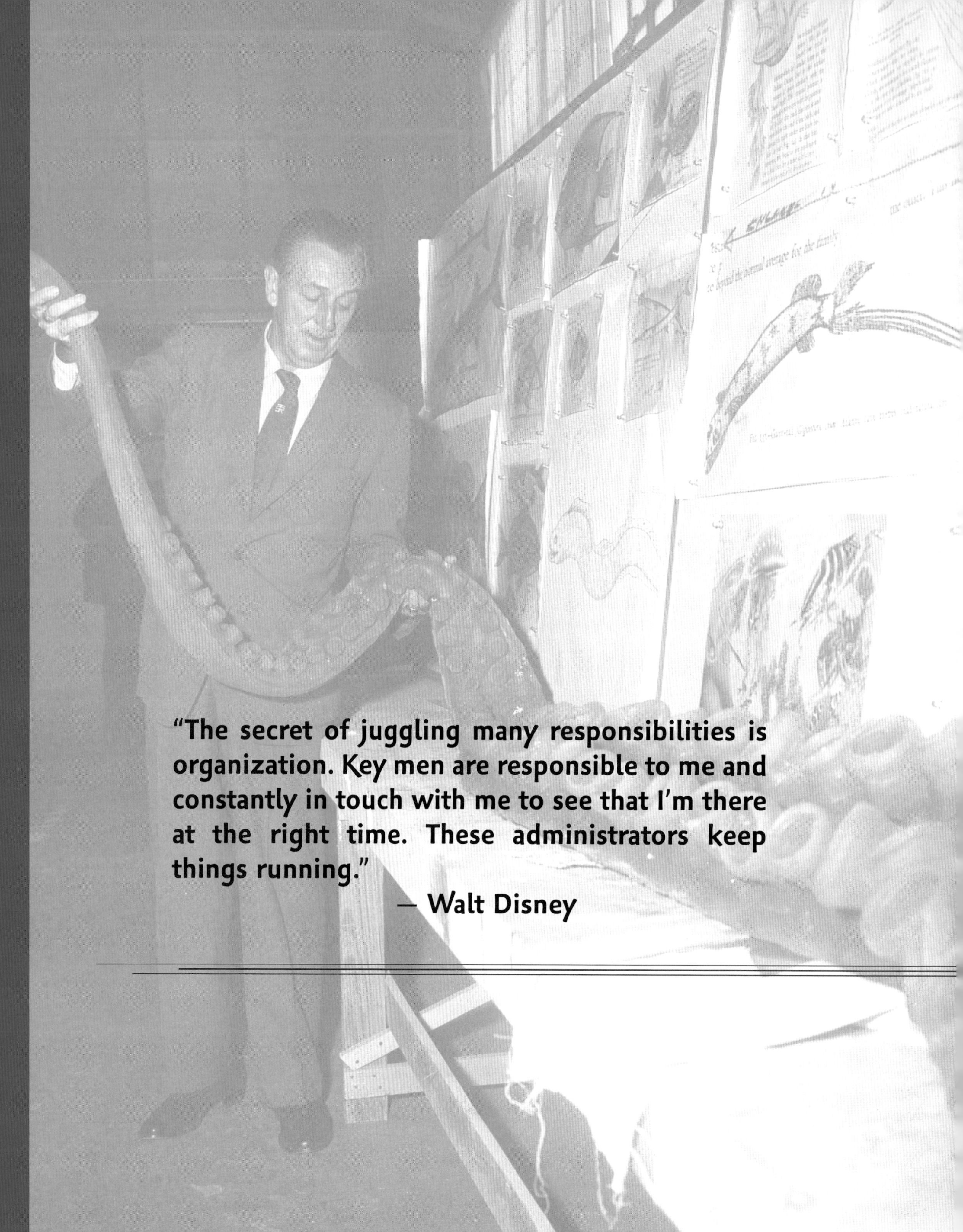

"The secret of juggling many responsibilities is organization. Key men are responsible to me and constantly in touch with me to see that I'm there at the right time. These administrators keep things running."

— Walt Disney

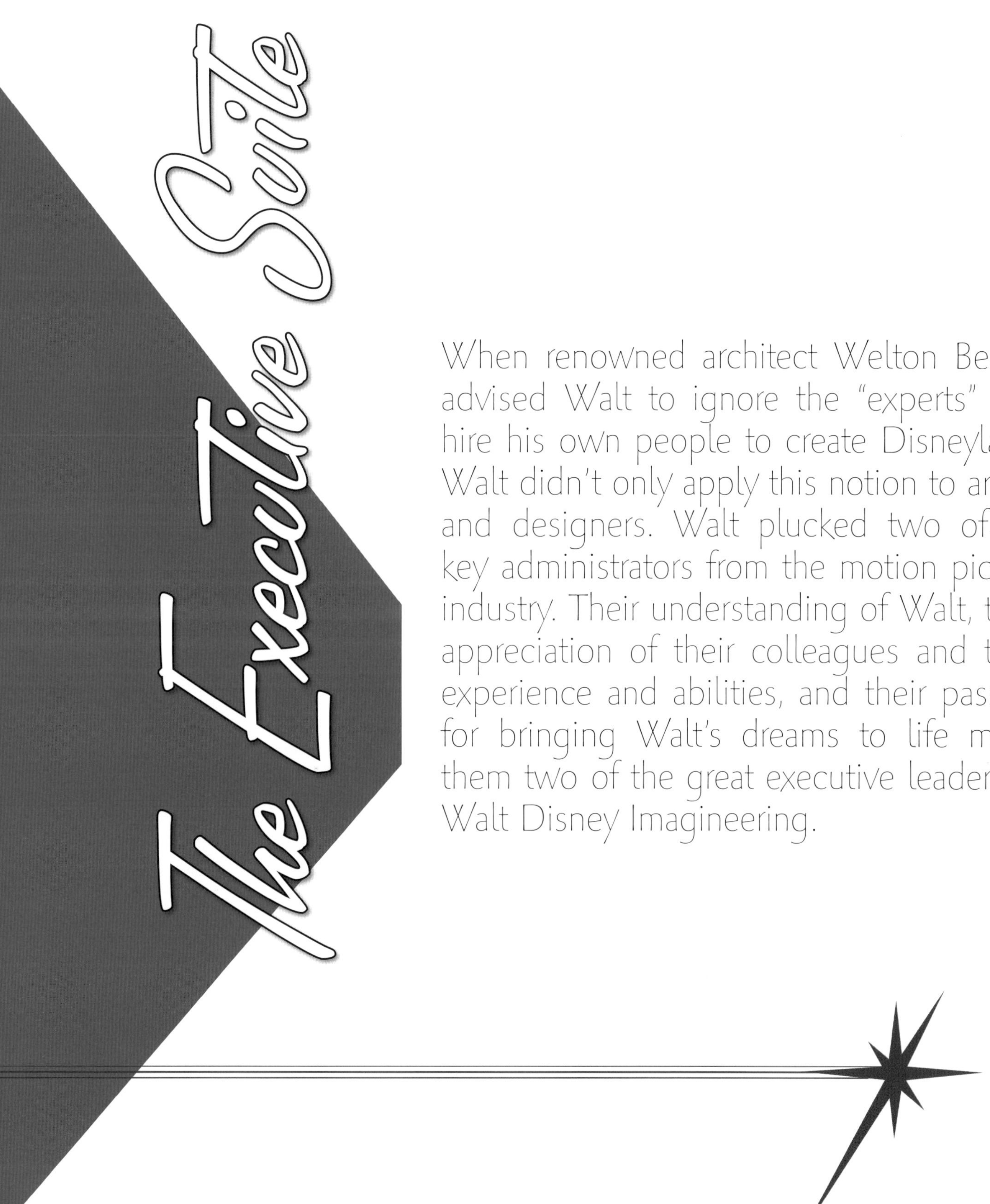

The Executive Suite

When renowned architect Welton Becket advised Walt to ignore the "experts" and hire his own people to create Disneyland, Walt didn't only apply this notion to artists and designers. Walt plucked two of his key administrators from the motion picture industry. Their understanding of Walt, their appreciation of their colleagues and their experience and abilities, and their passion for bringing Walt's dreams to life made them two of the great executive leaders of Walt Disney Imagineering.

Richard F. Irvine: A Creative Executive

"I think it was 1952 or 1953. I was called to come out and interview with [Walt Disney] . . . supposedly it was going to be on *Zorro*. He had that in his own company, WED, as opposed to the Studio having it.[1] And I had lunch with him that day and then we spent the rest of the day together. And he told me about his dreams for Disneyland at that point in time. And he wanted me to start working with him on it."

Born in Salt Lake City on April 5, 1910, Richard F. Irvine moved to Los Angeles in 1922 with his father, Dr. A. Ray Irvine, Sr., a prominent Los Angeles ophthalmologist.[2] Irvine, Jr., attended Stanford University and the University of Southern California, followed by professional training at Chouinard Art Institute,[3] now part of the California Institute of the Arts. In 1940, he married the former Ann Nerney of Los Angeles.

Irvine had already been associated with Walt Disney during World War II, working as an art director. He reminisced in a 1968 interview with Richard Hubler, "I first met him back in 1942 when I went to work on *Victory Through Air Power*. I was there as a live action art director, and stayed on through *The Three Caballeros*, which was the first show in which he combined live action with cartoon action. After that stint was finished, things became slow and I was let go. I went out to Twentieth [Century Fox Studio]."

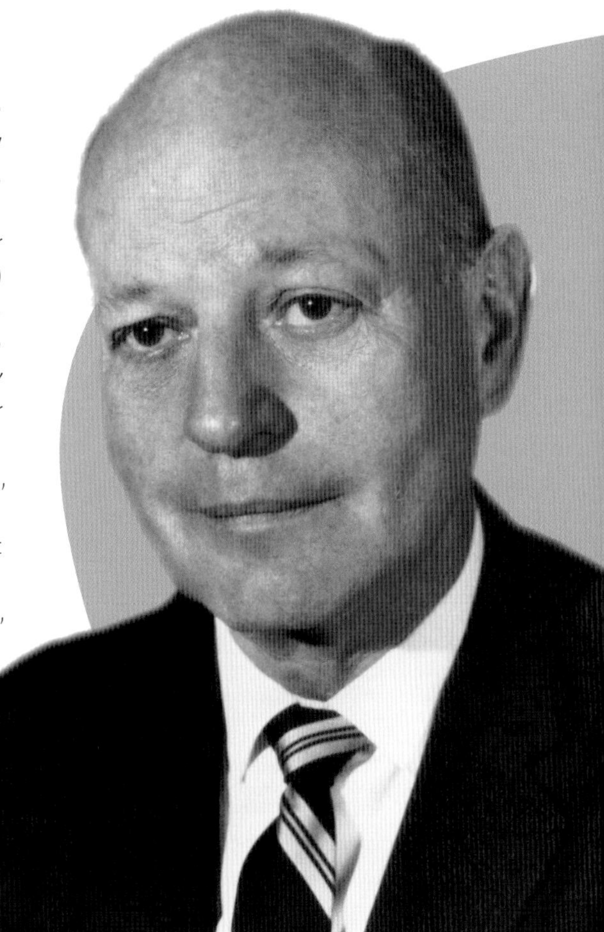

"He's most noted for his work on *Miracle on 34th Street*," (1947), Irvine's daughter (and former senior vice president of Creative Administration at Walt Disney Imagineering) Maggie Elliott said fondly in a 2004 presentation. "And he worked very closely with Herb Ryman and Lyle Wheeler,[4] who was a very famous motion picture art director in the 1930s through the 1950s." Some of Irvine's better-known film work includes *Eternally Yours* (1939), *Sundown* (1941, Academy Award nomination, Best Art Direction-Interior Decoration, Black-and-White), *The Brasher Doubloon* (1947, based on the Raymond Chandler novel), *Apartment for Peggy* (1948), *Mr. Belvedere Goes to College* (1949), *Follow the Sun* (1951), *Don't Bother to Knock* (1952), and *O. Henry's Full House* (1952).

"In the early fifties," Maggie Elliott continued, "about the time I was born, Walt decided he was going to do this wonderful thing. Wasn't quite sure what it was. And, I'm sure you've heard this story a million times, where he talked to architects and they said, 'Use your motion picture people because they really understand what you want to do a lot better than architects will.' And so Walt called around and talked with Lyle Wheeler at Twentieth and said, 'Who have you got available?' And Lyle said, 'I've got this guy, he's perfect. He's got an architectural background from USC. He studied at Chouinard Art Institute. He's a great combination of architect/artist. Dick Irvine.' And Walt said, 'Well, I know him. I worked with him on a few films during the war.' Dad thought that this was kind of a neat thing, so he gambled and left Twentieth and went to work for Walt to do this thing called Disneyland."

"When I was asked to come over here by Walt," Dick Irvine told Hubler, "he already had the stagecoaches built, he had the 'little man'[5] on display. He had a little concept sketch of a little park done over there for the

1 Irvine would have been brought to the Studio under cover of *Zorro* in 1952 since it was that year that Walt had licensed the rights to the Zorro stories.

2 One of Dr. Irvine's patients was a filmmaker named Walt Disney.

3 Irvine had also studied at Stanford University, where his classmate was Morgan "Bill" Evans.

4 Lyle Wheeler (1905–1990) created sets for more than three hundred fifty motion pictures, including *Gone with the Wind* (1939), *The King and I* (1956), and *The Diary of Anne Frank* (1959).

5 "Project Little Man," developed for the Americana project, was a nine-inch-tall cam-driven mechanical figure of a dancing/talking man; it became the prototype of Audio-Animatronics technology.

Studio, and he was working on a deal with the L.A. Park Association whereby he could run his train down along the river into Griffith Park. Before the freeway went in, he had that corner property, which is part of the back lot. It wasn't needed at that time for production, so he was thinking of building a little entertainment center there. Well, when Walt hired me, they had retained Pereira & Luckman as architects to work on the concept for Disneyland. And he asked me to be his liaison at the architectural office. They were looking at a site down at Palos Verdes, and Walt went out there and looked at it. He decided that if he were really going to do his ideas and get them developed that he probably could start out with his own staff, so that we could jell the ideas before he could go with an architect. And then, finally, when he started to jell the ideas, the momentum started to build and he got excited about it, and went ahead and did it in-house, so to speak."

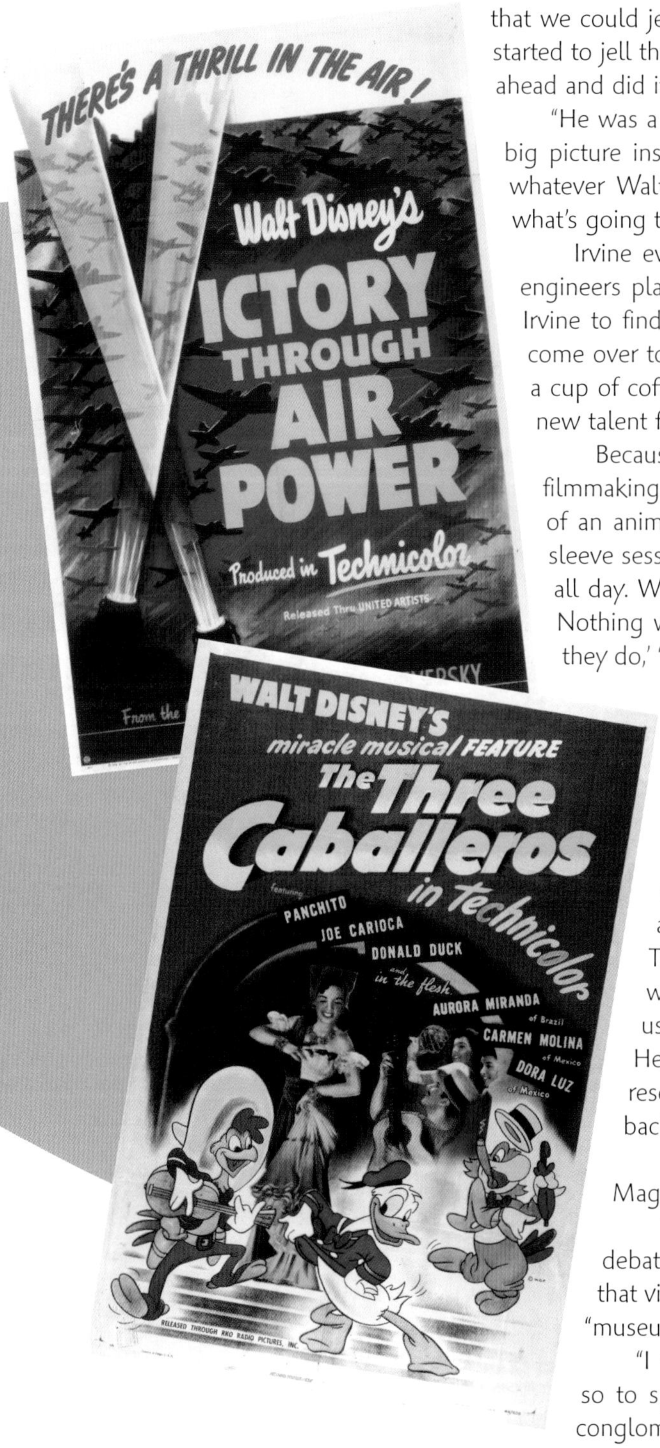

"He was a crucial guy," WED engineer Bob Gurr says of Irvine, "and he understood the big picture instantaneously, and he never explained anything to anybody. But it was like whatever Walt started to say, Dick understood it instantly, and could read back to Walt what's going to work, what's not going to work."

Irvine eventually became the leader of the team of designers, artists, architects and engineers planning and developing the original Magic Kingdom. Walt Disney looked to Irvine to find the people and resources to make his dreams come true. "Every time he'd come over to WED," Irvine said, "he'd come over to my office first and sit down and have a cup of coffee, and explain things that he wanted. And he would use me to try and get new talent for him. Sort of a casting director, I guess."

Because of their concept of storytelling in a real place, and their shared experience in filmmaking, the Disneyland design process was not too different from the development of an animated feature. "The way we'd work is that we would get together at a shirt-sleeve session and kick ideas around," Irvine explained, "from four hours, to six hours, to all day. We used to have storyboards and we would make a list of ideas and concepts. Nothing was really pinned down except that 'what would people need,' 'what would they do,' 'what kind of entertainment would they have'—all the needs for the public that would have to be contemplated going into this park. We would write our ideas out on squares of paper, put them up on a board, and Walt'd come down in the afternoon and sit there and look at them and juggle them around. And eventually it evolved.

"[Walt] wasn't anxious to get it to sketches and visualization, he wanted to get a plan for circulation. However, we had to do a bird's-eye view of it for Roy to take back to New York, so we got Herb Ryman in on a Saturday, and Herbie did the first bird's-eye view of Disneyland by Monday, and I think Tuesday morning Roy took them to New York with him. And that first concept was the one that was taken from a plan[6] and Walt was over there working with us and researching and giving his thoughts—what he saw, and working over Herbie's shoulder, so to speak, and making this thing come off. He was gathering research so that he could interpret it, and that first plan was the one that Roy took back with him."

"Daddy was one of the people who helped color it in after Herbie drew it," Maggie Elliott adds with a laugh.

Walt's interest in the "plan for circulation" caused a lot of research, discussion, debate, design, and redesign. Advisors told Walt he couldn't have a single entrance, that visitors wouldn't walk that far, and Walt himself wanted to avoid what he called "museum feet." This led to the creation of a radial "hub and spoke" plan.

"I would say it evolved," Irvine explained, "It was a series of cleaning it out, so to speak. We had Main Street, and off of Main Street we had an area with a conglomeration of ideas. Gradually it was simplified down to the point where it

6 The plan footprint had been developed by Marvin Davis and was located for reference on the lower right-hand corner of Ryman's bird's-eye-view drawing.

became the radial plan, or the hub plan, for moving people. The thing that we learned as we'd go to The Pike[7] or another park, was that the main drag always gets the traffic. Anything off the main drag suffers. So we were trying to think of Main Street as a main drag with people going down to a hub, and from that they could see other areas that would attract them. Then they would come back to the hub, and be oriented by coming back to the same spot they started."

Irvine's recollections reinforce the oft-echoed notion that most of the big ideas—and a lot of the tiny details—had their origins with Walt. "Walt had that wonderful capacity, or instinctive intuitiveness, of knowing what felt right and what was wrong," Irvine said. "We talked a long time about what would be the symbol of Disneyland. Of course, the concept of Fantasyland suggested the castle [but] the castle wasn't necessarily the symbol of the whole thing. In our first plan, you went through the courtyard in the castle, which of course was the back of it, and then as we studied The Pike, Knott's Berry Farm, and others, we realized that, as we looked down the Main Street, that we had to have a "marquee," a "wienie" [Walt's term]—to draw people down it. So that's how the castle got located where it is."

ABOVE: Richard Irvine's daughter, Maggie, began her career at WED while still in high school. She headed up the model shop during the design and construction of Epcot, then became Senior Vice President of Creative Administration for Imagineering prior to her retirement.

Irvine recalled another idea that Walt simply "tossed out" at a planning session for the 1967 Tomorrowland renovation. "He had a lot of fun in the story conferences. I'll never forget when we were planning Tomorrowland. This was early spring before he passed away and we were talking about this dance area. What could you do with a bandstand? 'Well, let's put it on an elevator,' he said. 'An outdoor bandstand looks like the devil when it doesn't have people in it, so let' s get rid of it, go underground and have a waterfall on top of it. So when the band isn't playing you have a beautiful waterfall. But when the band starts to play, up comes the bandstand and all the activity.' He threw out the idea and all of us started to chime in. .And it turned out to be a terrific thing in Tomorrowland."

At the Walt Disney Studio, no idea is ever thrown away, no notion ever wasted. Walt developed *Peter Pan* and *Alice in Wonderland* as animated features at least three times before they were finally made. *Mickey and the Beanstalk* was planned as a feature in 1940, and made its public debut as half of the 1947 release *Melody Time*. The same notion held true for WED.

"You never know when you start down another road," Irvine said. "that one of these ideas won't come back and be used in a different manner. In other words, there were story ideas that you could change and they would not be the same, but the philosophy behind them would be the same."

Irvine continued in charge of planning and design of all new attractions in Disneyland, and the four Disney shows at the 1964–1965 New York World's Fair. When WED Enterprises became a subsidiary of Walt Disney Productions in 1965, Irvine was appointed vice president, design, and vice chairman of the WED board of directors.

A big part of Irvine's job was interpreting Walt's desires, and much of their exchange of information took place on frequent walks through the Park itself. "Saturday morning, we'd get in there early. Later on we started going Monday and Tuesday when nobody was in the Park.[8] Walt used to get annoyed at the public coming up and wanting his autograph, but of course, he was always very gracious. He'd pre-write his notes and have them stuffed in his pocket, with 'Walt Disney' on it, so if some kid wanted an autograph he'd say, 'Here, take it!' and give it to them."

7 The Pike was an amusement park and arcade near the beach south of Ocean Boulevard in Long Beach, California. Started in 1902, The Pike ran until 1979. It was most noted for its large wooden roller coaster.

8 Difficult as it is to believe today, Disneyland was, for many years, closed to the public on most Mondays and Tuesdays. It did not become a 365-day-a-year operation until 1985.

Maggie Elliott recalls, "I can remember as a little kid coming down with Dad on weekends, because he worked seven days a week, walking the Park during construction. So, I had what I call a fairy-tale life. You know, Walt would call on the phone and 'Daddy, Walt's on the phone and he wants to talk to you.' So I knew him from a very different perspective. He was Dad's boss and I didn't think anything about it."

"We were sitting at lunch [in the Studio Commissary]," Irvine recalled, "and he walked in and sat down with us. Joe Fowler was there, Mel [Melton],[9] myself and he said, 'The doctors say that I can't do any work. That I can only come visit.' He said, 'See, I can't put my arms up.' He told us that they had taken out his lung, and that he couldn't talk business. Then he turned to Joe Fowler and said, 'What's wrong with the submarine ride? When will we get it back working?'

"During the course of conversation we talked and I said that we had some sketches of Mary Blair's murals in Tomorrowland. Marc [Davis] had some wonderful ideas for the Bear Band. We were programming the Pirate ride at WED. So as we finished he said, 'Dick, would you drive me over to WED?' I said I'd be delighted to. On the way over, we were talking about Tomorrowland building finishes and Mary Blair's murals; we were looking for new materials that would be maintenance-free. I recommended that we go with the mural in tile, and he said, 'Good, that's the way to go.'

ABOVE: The *Richard F. Irvine* riverboat was the second riverboat in Walt Disney World Magic Kingdom Park; it opened on May 20, 1973, just eighteen months after its counterpart, the *Admiral Joe Fowler*, which sailed from October 2, 1971, through 1980. (Admiral Fowler oversaw the original construction of both Disneyland and Walt DIsney World.) The *Richard F. Irvine* was completely refurbished and returned to service in 1996, but rechristened the *Liberty Belle* riverboat. Today, one of the "friend ships" that transports Magic Kingdom visitors across the Seven Seas Lagoon has been named in Irvine's honor.

"He came in [to the WED headquarters] and saw Marc's concepts on the Bear Band. He just wanted to chat. He said that he was terribly disappointed that the Pirate [Audio-Animatronics] figures were down. We didn't realize that Walt was coming over, so we had taken them down for some minor adjustments. We had the mock-up on the Moon ride pre-show, with scanning station, and he discussed ideas. And finally he said, 'Well, maybe you'd better take me back.'

"So I took him back, and as we got to the Studio gate, someone put their head in the car as we went through the gate, and he said, 'I'm sorry that you've been sick, Walt, I'm glad to see you back,' or something like that. And Walt said afterward, 'I don't want anyone to ask me how I feel.' That was typical. He never wanted to think of himself, I think, in relation to people that felt sorry for him or anything like that. I dropped him off and he said, 'I'm going down to Palm Springs for the week, and I'm going to have some checkups, and then I'll be back to see you.'

"That was the last time I saw him."

"He always seemed to like it over here," Irvine remembered. "This place sort of grew into a favorite spot of his, and it was a way that he could escape from motion pictures. It was something that he could build and change. When a motion picture was finished it would go out and he couldn't change it, or improve it. That's better than change it—make it better."

Following Walt's death in December 1966, Irvine was given the primary responsibility for the master planning, design, and show development of Walt Disney World. He was appointed executive vice president and chief operations officer of WED Enterprises in July 1967. As he and Roy O. Disney tried to follow the path of Walt's desire, they faced

9 Orbin V. (Mel) Melton joined Walt Disney Productions in 1942 and, except for a period of military service, remained until his retirement in 1975. During his 33-year career, Mel served as president of WED Enterprises (1965–1972). Subsequently he served as vice president, finance, and until his retirement, vice president and treasurer of Walt Disney Productions.

challenges and course changes. "I often wonder what would have been done differently if Walt had been alive," Irvine admitted to Walt biographer Bob Thomas in 1973. "You know darn well it would have been entirely different from what we did do."

Without Walt, Irvine had to make decisions that may not have been the ones Walt would have made, but rather decisions made the way Walt would have made them. Before his death, Walt had Marvin Davis assemble the information and give some initial form to his EPCOT concept, Irvine told Thomas. Walt knew that Davis was the right man for the project's needs at that time, but he realized that Davis alone couldn't work it through to the final vision while also overseeing all the ancillary and resort amenities, including a whole new Magic Kingdom. "That was when he started pushing to get somebody else," Irvine said, "and let the WED group stay with the theme park and [Walt] would develop this other group to develop the EPCOT concept. That was why when we did Walt Disney World, I felt that I could go to [Welton] Becket and get Becket to do the hotels as opposed to try and do them in-house, because we needed the expertise. Becket had worked with Walt and we had worked with Becket at the New York World's Fair. He did the facilities for Ford Pavilion and also the General Electric Pavilion. He was sympathetic to Walt and Walt's ideas and Walt's way of working. Roy backed us up on that, too. Roy knew that we couldn't do it all. We had to get some expertise."

Irvine's longtime dedication to achieving Walt Disney's dreams and his personal interest as an alumnus of Chouinard Art Institute were reflected in his interest in the nascent California Institute of the Arts project. "We started out in WED, [Walt] had a 'City of the Arts' concept, a community of the arts, which basically would be like the Bauhaus,[10] where the students would not only have a lot of motivation, they would see the practical experience and application as well as all the theory. We laid out preliminary ideas of what Walt's City of Arts might be, in relationship to the art school, the residences, etc., again, thinking of a place where the public and the students could be exposed to each other. It was difficult [to find] someone strong enough to help him get it off the ground, with looking for the site and going through preliminary concepts and ideas, like we did originally for Disneyland.

"I think it was always in the back of his mind that it would be all of the arts put together and that's why we called it the City of Seven Arts. That was the name of the project when we started working on it. That grew when Mrs. Von Hagen[11] came into the picture and they were trying to merge with the School of Music [Los Angeles Conservatory of Music]." Dick and Ann Irvine played a vital role in the formation of "Disney Artists for CalArts," whose annual art show raised substantial funds for scholarships and student loans at California Institute of the Arts in Valencia, California.

Richard F. Irvine retired from WED Enterprises in 1973 as a result of a heart condition. He passed away on March 30, 1976. "Unfortunately, my father never got to see Walt Disney World open due to a long illness," says Maggie Irvine Elliott, "which was really sad. But lots of people gave him wonderful reports on how well it did. Of course, his first love was Disneyland."

"Strictly Disneyland," Irvine said. "As a matter of fact, when I went to work for Walt on Disneyland that was it. I left the motion picture business. I never went back to it. Never regretted it, either."

OPPOSITE: Irvine spent many years bringing Walt's dreams into reality. Even after Walt's passing, Irvine's determination and loyalty lay behind the realization of two of Disney's greatest dreams: Walt Disney World in Florida (here, Walt explains that in scale to the map behind him he is "six miles tall"), and California Institute of the Arts in Valencia.

10 Bauhaus (1919–1933) was a progressive, influential school of architecture and applied arts founded by Walter Gropius, with the ideal of integrating art, craftsmanship, and technology.

11 Lulu May Von Hagen was then chairman of the Los Angeles Conservatory of Music (founded 1883). A 1961 merger of the Chouinard Art Institute (a professional art school founded in 1921 in Los Angeles) with the Conservatory to create the California Institute of the Arts was spearheaded by Walt and Roy Disney, along with Mrs. Von Hagen, due to concerns over Nelbert Chouinard's age and health, and fears that both institutions faced imminent demise. CalArts was the first degree-granting institution of higher learning in the United States created specifically for students of both the visual and performing arts.

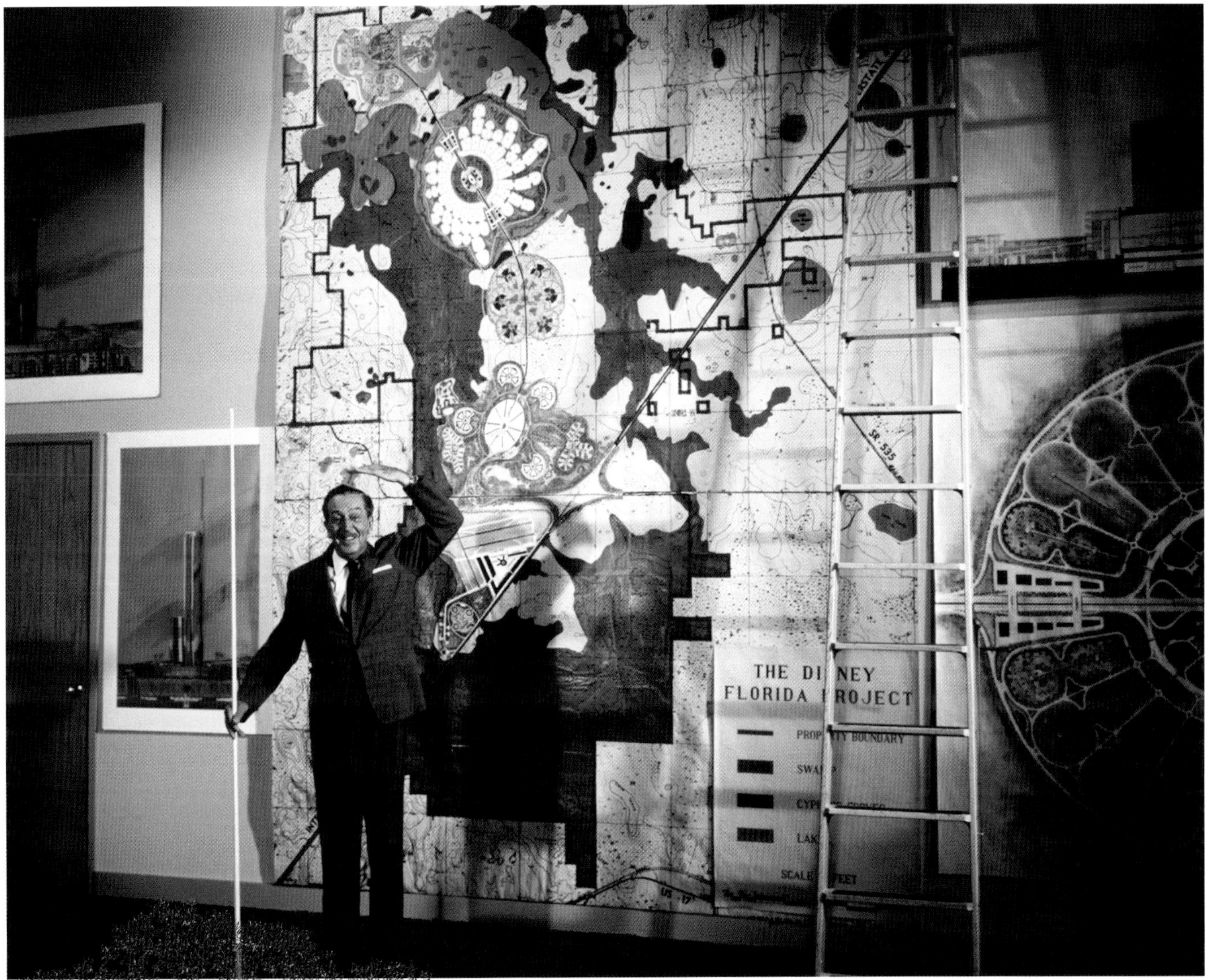
FLORIDA
SR-535
US 17
SCALE

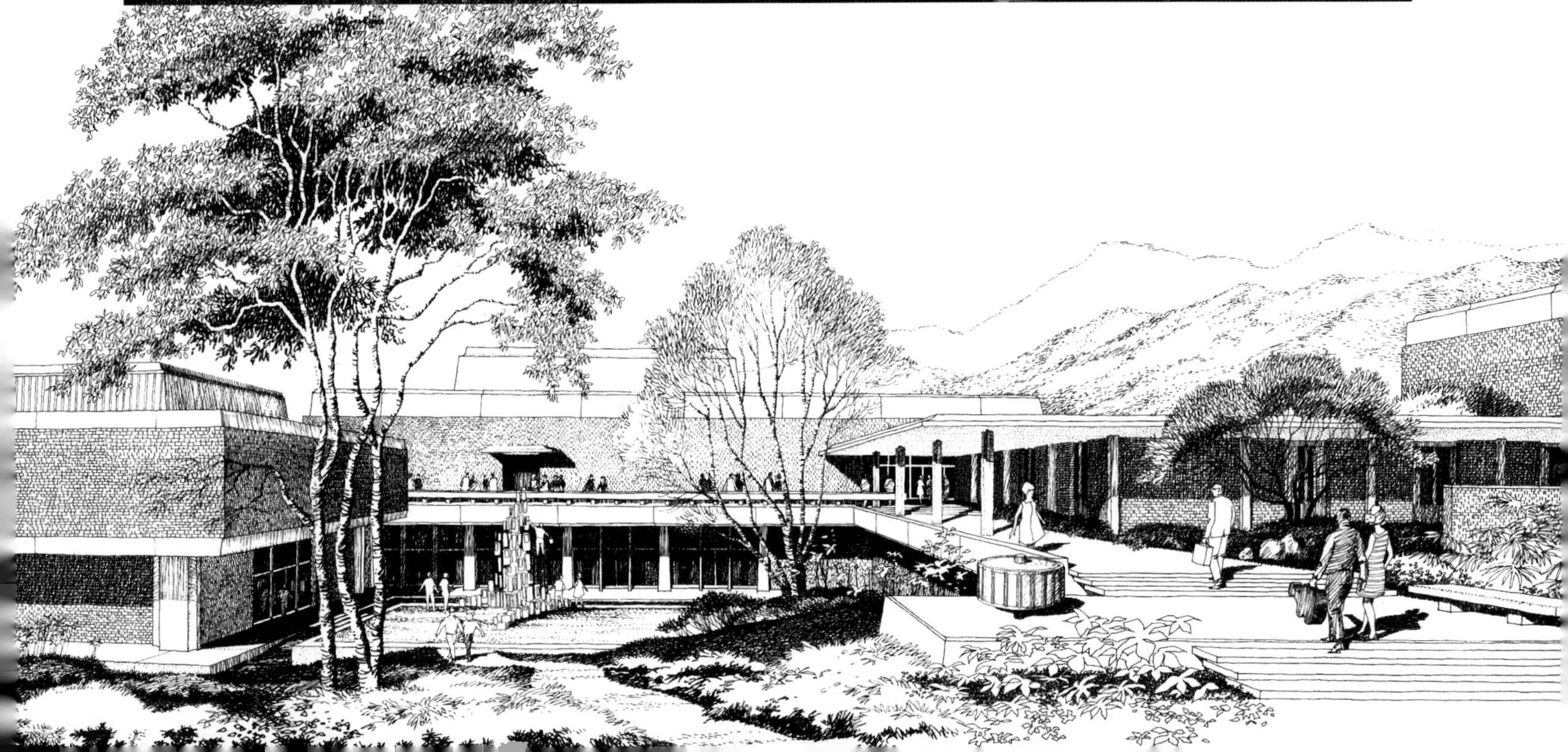

RETLAW ENTERPRISES, INC.

1333 FLOWER STREET, GLENDALE, CALIF. 91201
Telephone (213) 245-0121

Bill Cottrell: Uncle Bill

Imagineer Marvin Davis once said, "It was Walt who said 'Let there be Disneyland,' but it was Uncle Bill who was Walt's counselor and right-hand man."

Born to English parents in South Bend, Indiana, in 1906, "Bill Cottrell's maternal grandfather, Benjamin Davis, was a Shakespearean actor," Disney historian Robin Allan wrote. "His paternal grandfather was Thomas Cottrell, a theatrical scene painter. Cottrell père was a graduate of Birmingham University and emigrated in 1901."

Bill graduated in English and journalism from Occidental College in Los Angeles, and like most college graduates, set out to utilize his hard-earned academic experience in a suitable career. He was hired as a cartoonist and sports writer on Southern California's *Orange County Plain Dealer*, but soon would venture north to Hollywood.

"It came about this way," Cottrell said in a 1983 interview for Walt Disney Imagineering. "Roy Disney knew my sister through the Security First National Bank. My sister worked there, and the Studio used to bank with them. He knew she had a brother, and she said, 'He's just out of school and he's looking for a job,' and Roy said, 'What does he do?' 'Well, he's trying to get on a newspaper as a newspaper writer, sports writer, or a cartoonist.'" So, Roy sent young Cottrell to a Walt—but not Walt Disney.

"'Walter Lantz[12] is looking for someone in animation,'" Cottrell related Roy's reply. "'I'll give you my card, and you can give it to your brother.' So I took a card from Roy Disney and went to see Walter Lantz. But the job had already been taken—it was 1929 and jobs weren't available for very many hours."

"A few weeks later, Roy asked my sister if I got the job, and when she said no, he said, 'Why don't you have him come in and see my brother, Walt?' I got together some drawings—I knew they weren't too good, but I took them along—and I took along things that I'd written for newspapers, and the thing that impressed him more than anything was the stuff that George Herriman[13] used." With an academic background in English and journalism and story work for Herriman, Cottrell was hired by The Walt Disney Studio in the Ink and Paint department.

"I started painting cels, and then inking cels. And then they needed help on camera, so I got on camera, and Johnny Cannon, I think, was doing the camera work, and he went into animation. So I went into [camera]. That was more or less the procedure with inexperienced help. It was a way to learn the cartoon business, you might say."

The Studio was still small, and Walt spent time in every department. His curiosity about technology and advancing the visual sophistication of animation often led him to visit Bill in Camera. "Walt was interested in cameras and practically everything relating to pictures. We had a camera built with a rack and pinion," Cottrell said. "It was on a tube with a rack and pinion gear so that the camera could come down closer and closer. It changed focus all the time, of course. For every frame, practically, you had to change focus. That was a development that was a step ahead. Then there were other things as to sliding cells, and things that could give a dimension by your background, your farthest background would move slower than your front scenes."[14] This innovation fed the excitement of the young Studio, and those men and women who were there at the time became the pioneers of the Disney organization. This experience, much like military service, created a lifelong bond among them.

In the recurring theme of the Disney organization, Cottrell earned his stripes, and in due course, wound up in the story department. "Prior to working at the Studio, I had submitted some continuity dialogue and ideas to George Herriman. He happened to use a couple of my continuities in his Sunday page and gave me credit for them, which helped

---

12 Walter Lantz (1900–1994) was a cartoonist and animator best known for creating Woody Woodpecker. In 1928, Charles B. Mintz hired Lantz as a director on the Oswald the Lucky Rabbit cartoon series for Universal. Earlier that year, Mintz and his brother-in-law, George Winkler, had snatched Oswald from the character's creator, Walt Disney. Universal president Carl Laemmle fired Mintz and Winkler; legend has it that Lantz then won the character in a poker game with Laemmle.

13 George Joseph Herriman (1880–1944) was an American cartoonist, best known for Krazy Kat, and for his illustrations for Don Marquis's archy and mehitabel poems and stories.

14 This camera innovation led to the development of Disney's Multiplane Camera, a device that moves a number of pieces of artwork past the camera at various speeds and at various distances from one another, creating a dimensional effect of depth. William Garity developed the Multiplane at Disney for the production of *Snow White and the Seven Dwarfs*. The camera was completed in early 1937 and tested in a Silly Symphony called *The Old Mill*, which won the 1937 Academy Award for Animated Short Film.

me get a job in the Studio. See, everyone who was in that business had ideas of 'gags' or 'business.' Everybody submitted ideas—you weren't excluded from doing that just because you weren't an animator. So somehow or another I ended up in the Story Department, which I was quite pleased about."

In 1935, Cottrell was teamed with Joe Grant,[15] and formed a working partnership that Grant once called "probably one of the most enjoyable times I had." Together they brought excellent story work to classic short cartoons such as *Three Orphan Kittens, Pluto's Judgment Day, Who Killed Cock Robin?* (1935), and *Three Little Wolves* (1936), and pushed the development of the Eugene Field nursery rhyme "Wynken, Blynken, and Nod" as a Silly Symphony subject. "He brought gentleness and good taste to all his work," Robin Allan said of Cottrell's story work, "a foil to the satirical sharpness of his colleague Joe Grant."

"Bill was far more than a trusted employee; he was also family," say Disney biographers Richard Greene and Katherine Greene. In 1938, Bill Cottrell married Lillian Disney's sister, Hazel Sewell, a marriage that endured until Hazel's death in 1975.[16] "That, in addition to unquestioned integrity, led to Walt's showing an enormous amount of trust in him," the Greenes conclude.

Cottrell moved on to become a sequence director on *Snow White and the Seven Dwarfs*. "I did the Queen and the Huntsman, and the Magic Mirror transformation of the Queen into the witch, and the witch sequences. I did all of the villainous roles," Cottrell said. "Joe Grant and Dorothy Ann Blank and I did the story sequence on that." Much as he had done in film, and would continue to do in designing Disneyland, Walt "cast" the directors

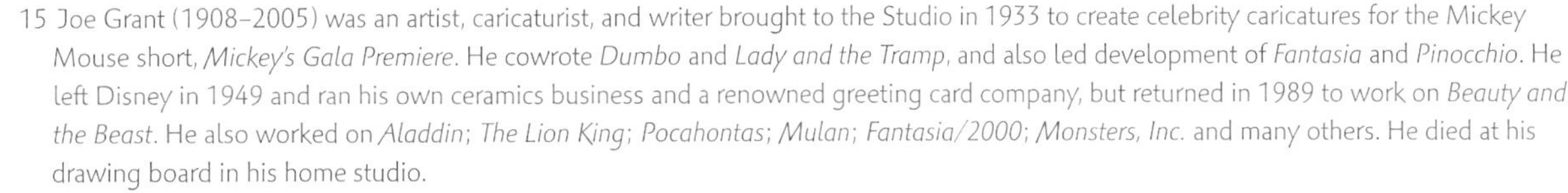

15 Joe Grant (1908–2005) was an artist, caricaturist, and writer brought to the Studio in 1933 to create celebrity caricatures for the Mickey Mouse short, *Mickey's Gala Premiere*. He cowrote *Dumbo* and *Lady and the Tramp*, and also led development of *Fantasia* and *Pinocchio*. He left Disney in 1949 and ran his own ceramics business and a renowned greeting card company, but returned in 1989 to work on *Beauty and the Beast*. He also worked on *Aladdin*; *The Lion King*; *Pocahontas*; *Mulan*; *Fantasia/2000*; *Monsters, Inc.* and many others. He died at his drawing board in his home studio.

16 Hazel Bounds Sewell was the mother of Marjorie Sewell by her previous marriage to Glen Sewell. Marjorie married Marvin Davis making Cottrell Davis's stepfather-in-law, and Davis Walt's nephew.

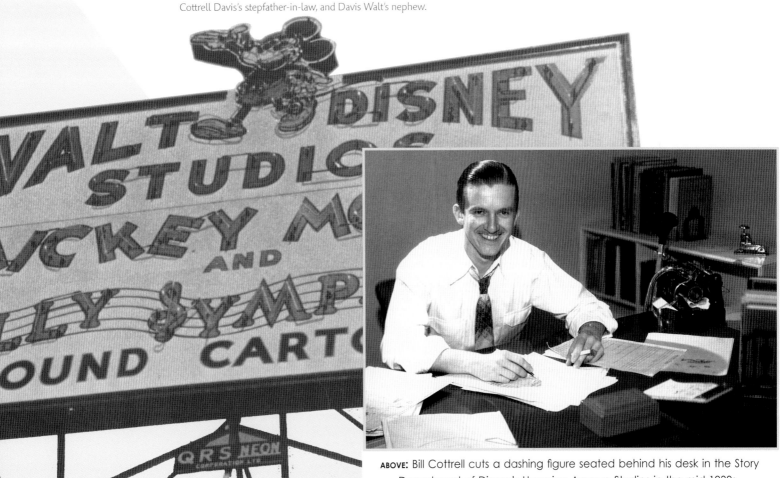

ABOVE: Bill Cottrell cuts a dashing figure seated behind his desk in the Story Department of Disney's Hyperion Avenue Studios in the mid-1930s.

on sequences according to their special talents. "The casting of someone in a role whether it was an animator, a director or sequence director, story man or anything else more or less came in relation to that person's ability or interest in what they could do," Cottrell told Jay Horan.

After the premiere of *Snow White and the Seven Dwarfs* in 1937, Walt split up the Cottrell/Grant team. Grant was asked to form and lead the Character Model Department; Cottrell developed extensive written treatments for stories such as *Cinderella, Sleeping Beauty*, and *Bambi*, among others. Grant saw this separation as the repetition of a lifelong behavioral pattern in Walt. "Disney had something within him," Grant told John Canemaker, "that if we got too chummy, too close, and maybe too successful, he'd break it up."

As a story writer, Bill's next assignment was *Pinocchio*. "I had what I thought was a great ending for this sequence in *Pinocchio*," Cottrell told Richard Greene and Katharine Greene, "and Walt came in and looked at the sequence and suggested changes, but he had a different idea for the ending, quite different from what I had. I tried to convince him that my way was the best. And he said, 'No, I don't think so.' When the meeting was over, I said, 'Now Walt, which way do you want to do this? Your way or my way?' And he said. 'We're going to do it my way.' I replied, 'We'll never know whether my way is better than yours, will we?' And he smiled and said, 'No, I guess not.'"

ABOVE: Bill *(to Walt's right)* joins *(from left)* Claude Coats, John Hench, engineer Don Edgren, and Richard Irvine in a brainstorming session at WED.

Cottrell had found a niche in Animation story, and his contributions continued for more than a decade, influencing the story and characters of films such as *The Reluctant Dragon, Saludos Amigos, Victory Through Air Power, The Three Caballeros, Melody Time, Alice in Wonderland,* and *Peter Pan*. As an admirer of Sherlock Holmes, Cottrell brought up an idea for an animated feature about a dog detective several times. Although nothing came of it, the notion was taken up many years later by the Disney Animation Department when they bought the film rights to the Eve Titus novel *Basil of Baker Street*, which was the inspiration for the animated feature *The Great Mouse Detective* (1986).

In 1948, Cottrell decided to leave Disney. "I wanted the opportunity to be a screenwriter," he told John Canemaker. Live-action films interested him, and he spent the next few years on the Paramount Pictures lot in Hollywood as "Joe Gillis," turning out screenplays that weren't produced. But as always, Walt had plans, and those plans provided Cottrell with a return to Disney for a new venture. On December 16, 1952, WED Enterprises was incorporated to manage Walt Disney's personal assets, and develop personal projects, including plans for an amusement park. Walt called Cottrell back and appointed him vice president (and later, president) of WED Enterprises.

Bill initially helped to develop the *Zorro* television series. Although the program did not air on ABC Television until 1957 (through 1959), Walt used WED Enterprises to license the rights to the *Zorro* stories while looking for a source of financing for Disneyland, planning to produce a number of episodes and use the resulting profits for developing the Park.

In addition, Cottrell served as a right-hand man to Walt in the various projects and activities related to the creation of Disneyland. "We all did a lot of things," Cottrell told Bob Thomas in 1973. "It was the same formula as the early days of the Studio. And I think this was part of the great pleasure at WED."

Cottrell proved to be especially adept on nomenclature, creating a patois for the Disneyland culture that is still in use. John Hench recalled, "He was a talented writer and helped shape how we referred to events and attractions in Disneyland. For instance, he encouraged us to quit using the term 'ride' and refer to attractions as an 'experience,' which is exactly what they are."

THIS PAGE, TOP TO BOTTOM: Three of the important collaborations of Joe Grant and Bill Cottrell during the 1930s: *Three Orphan Kittens, Three Little Wolves,* and *Pluto's Judgement Day.*

After the opening of the park, Walt again had a new assignment for Cottrell, based on a basic and inherent trust, not only of his core values, but his understanding and ability to communicate "the Disney way," that is, a cultural knowledge based on long experience. Walt was typically blunt about what he wanted Cottrell to do. "Walt was president of Disneyland," Bill said, "and he called me in and said, 'I want you to be assistant to the president.'" His first assignment was to review and revise contracts that had been executed for Disneyland in haste, and that held inconsistencies and errors. "When Disneyland opened, we had a lot of contracts with various merchants for their stores or shops, plus exhibitors of national products," Cottrell explained. "At some time or another there were some problems over some of the contracts, not necessarily intentionally, but it became obvious that in the rush to get things done, contracts were possibly negotiated by people who didn't know exactly what the policy of Disneyland might be. Cottrell established a basic tiered approach to contracts with vendors and lessees in Disneyland.

"There were three approvals," Cottrell said, "one was Sales, getting the thing started; and another was Legal, and the final approval was me thinking 'Does this meet all the standards and policies of the Park?' I guess you could call it a kind of a 'watchdog' operation, but policies written down anymore than indicating what kind of policy it was. How do you dictate the nature of a cartoon? It's never been written down. It's something that you either know or you don't know. So that's where I got started in that area. It requires a lot of knowledge of what we're doing, what has been done, and what should be done, and I seemed to fit into that role," Cottrell concluded.

As much as WED had invigorated the collegial culture of the old Hyperion Avenue studio, Cottrell saw Walt's activity continually increase, to the detriment of a kind of personal touch Cottrell had known and enjoyed since the early days. "[His direct involvement in everything] had to diminish as you added more people and more responsibility. Walt was there early every morning, he got in at seven thirty or seven forty-five and he left on average around seven o'clock every night. He put an awful lot of hours in. And Saturdays he would be back a good part of the time, and walk around the Studio and see how things were. He knew everyone. I think he knew almost everyone by their first name. And that's what was greatly missed as things went on—that personal contact on the back lot.

"In the earlier days of the studio, Walt used to come to the shop and if they were building a piece of period furniture, he'd say, 'Who did this?' He'd say, 'Gee, that's beautiful, how do you turn this?' He was interested in knowing how to do it. He eventually had a shop of his own. You'd be surprised at how much that did for morale. To have someone come in and say, 'That's beautiful.' That didn't happen after a while."

In late 1964, Walt had another move in mind for Cottrell, one that took into account his trustworthy status, his family ties, and his understanding of Disney culture. Bill was named president of Retlaw Enterprises, Walt Disney's private family corporation. This new organization originated from the pending sale of WED Enterprises to Walt Disney Productions, and the need to split private family-owned properties, businesses, and assets from those creative assets being sold to WDP.

Walt kept the rights to two Disneyland attractions—the Disneyland Railroad and the Disneyland Monorail. He assigned those properties to the new company and Retlaw paid rent

ABOVE: Bill Cottrell in 1979.

OPPOSITE, TOP: WED's first off-lot home on Sonora Avenue in Glendale, playfully nicknamed "the pancake house" because the triangle awning resembled a nearby restaurant.

OPPOSITE, BOTTOM: The current home of Walt Disney Imagineering, on Flower Street, around the corner from the Sonora Building. In 1962, this building was the corporate headquarters and plant of Studio Girl Cosmetics. For months after they moved in, the Imagineers endured the smell of stale perfume.

for the attractions' rights-of-way and employed the attraction's operators in exchange for a licensing fee and profit participation. Retlaw also owned the apartment above the fire station on Main Street, U.S.A. The other vital asset of Retlaw was the name and likeness of Walt Disney himself, which was licensed to Walt Disney Productions.

"You see, the Studio had the license to use the name Walt Disney in many, many respects, by contract," Cottrell explained. "It always worked out all right, because anytime a contract was sent to the Studio—for merchandise, for instance—it had to go through Legal, and they knew by this time what rights were granted on the use of the name 'Walt Disney,' to affix it to the box of watercolors, or whatever it was that was being sold, and everything was spelled out in that contract. If the contract went over five years, again, it had to have the approval of the family corporation. That was part of the contract between the family corporation and the Studio. I don't know who inserted that, but the purpose of that, of course, was to see that no one signed something up, gave something to someone and it was there for fifty years, and you couldn't do anything about it, so it had to be approved."

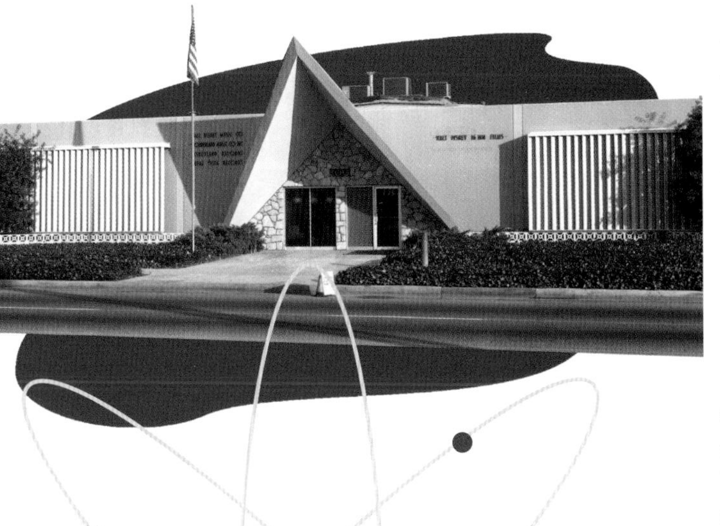

In 1979, Bill Cottrell became the first member of the Disney organization to celebrate fifty years of employment. He retired after fifty-three years of service in 1982, at which time the Disney family sold the name and likeness rights, and the Disneyland rail attractions, to Walt Disney Productions in exchange for 818,461 shares of Disney stock. In 2005, the remaining divisions of Retlaw, several television stations and real estate holdings, were either sold or became part of the Walt Disney Family Foundation, a nonprofit organization led by Walter Elias Disney Miller, Walt's grandson.

WED imagineering

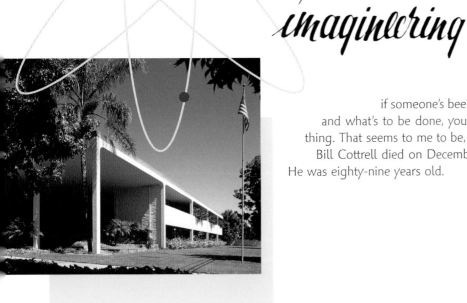

Cottrell said to Bob Thomas of his long career and unique standing with Walt Disney, "I can only think that he had a belief in my integrity and that I would not run away with the job and get him into trouble with . . . things that were beyond our power to deliver. I think he probably respected my judgment. He could have done it with anyone else, I guess, but I don't think he ever worried that I was going to do anything detrimental to the company, or to him, or his family. It's a case of trusting someone—not only their honesty, but their judgment. Once again, I think it's a case of experience, you know, if someone's been around long enough, and seems to know what's wanted and what's to be done, you don't have to worry that they're going to do the wrong thing. That seems to me to be, more or less the explanation of that."

Bill Cottrell died on December 22, 1995, at Saint Joseph Medical Center in Burbank. He was eighty-nine years old.

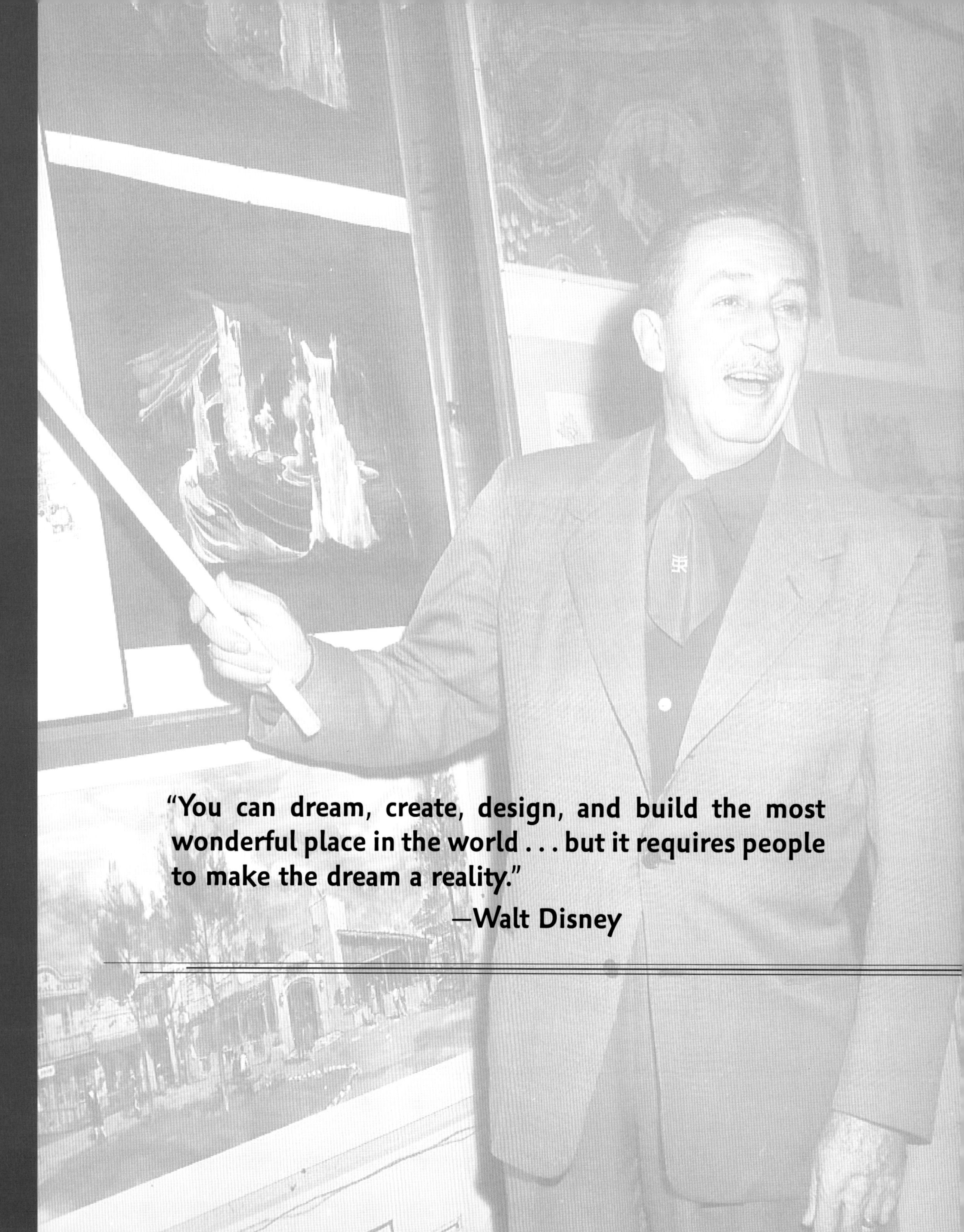

"You can dream, create, design, and build the most wonderful place in the world . . . but it requires people to make the dream a reality."

—Walt Disney

The Place Makers

One of the most curious debts in entertainment history is owed by Disneyland to another movie studio across town: an influx of talented personnel led to WED by Walt's initial call for assistance to Lyle Wheeler at Twentieth Century Fox that resulted in the irreplaceable Disneyland contributions of Dick Irvine, Herb Ryman, and Sam McKim, along with two other unique talents whose spatial perception, sense of place, and ability to communicate those notions brought the park its special efficiency, capacity, and intimacy.

Marvin Davis: A Theatrical Architect

"In addition to being a great site planner," Imagineer Tom Morris says of Marvin Davis, "he was part of the 'Disney-Fox Art Direction Mafia' that gave both studios' live-action films such a great look."

"I joined Disney in 1953. I had been working with Dick Irvine at Twentieth Century Fox," Davis told *The E Ticket* magazine in 1997. "At Fox I worked as an assistant art director on a lot of musicals, the ones with Carmen Miranda,[1] doing everything the art directors did. I was assistant to Joe Wright, who did all the musicals, and such movies as *The Snake Pit* (1948)."

"Because Marvin had a rich background in live-action motion picture design," John Hench once recalled, "he had a strong sense and understanding of theater, and how to give life and meaning to structures, which typically most formally trained architects aren't interested in. He knew how to create architectural form that had a message for people. For instance, his structures on Main Street, U.S.A., are irrepressibly optimistic."

Born in Clovis, New Mexico, on December 21, 1910, Marvin attended UCLA for two years and then transferred to the University of Southern California at Los Angeles, where he graduated with a degree in architecture. As top student in the class of 1935, he also received the prestigious American Institute of Architects medal. Two years later, Marvin landed his job at Twentieth Century Fox, where he worked as an art director on such films as *Gentlemen Prefer Blondes* and *The Asphalt Jungle*.

In 1953, he was invited by Dick Irvine to join WED Enterprises. At the time, WED was located in a ramshackle temporary building on the Studio Lot, referred to as the "Zorro" building. The development of the *Zorro* stories as a television or motion picture project, although legitimate, was also something of a red herring to keep on-lot curiosity about the real purpose of the assembled talent at bay. The Disneyland designers toiled away in their tumbledown digs (furnished with heavy, dark wood furniture that would ultimately be used in the hacienda of Don Diego de la Vega in the eventual TV series), sweltering in summer and freezing in winter, doing their best to bring reality to Walt Disney's vision.

"We were all in one big room," Davis said, "and I had four drafting tables. We had storyboards in there, and little sketches of different scenes within the various rides."

The project wasn't even called "Disneyland" at this point, but was typically referred to as "Walt's park." As such, Walt was the primary visionary and motivator on the project, and Davis and his colleagues saw a lot of him.

"Our building was right there just inside the gate," Davis said, "and Walt would stop by as he came in from the parking lot, on his way to his office. He'd stop in and take a look and come around and see every one of us. I'd be working on the park master plan, trying to get an overall idea of what it might look like for circulation and so forth.

"Walt was very interested in the overall plan of Disneyland," Davis said, "and two or three times he brought in a little scribble on a napkin or a piece of paper. I finally said, 'Walt, if you're going to do this, take a roll of tracing paper with you!' From then on, he'd draw out what he had in mind.

"The back of my neck was red many times from him looking over my shoulder," Davis recalled with a laugh. "He thought I was stubborn, but he was the most stubborn guy. When Walt and I had opposing ideas on things; obviously I couldn't just rear back and say, 'Walt, you're wrong,' you know, but I had my devious ways of getting around, which he understood, or realized." Whatever their day-to-day conflicts, Davis always deferred to the brilliance of Walt's concepts.

"The overall shape of the park, with its single entrance, was Walt's," Davis said. "And that was the key to the whole thing. Walt was very circulation conscious, and he wanted a single entrance, so that they could control the number of people that came in, and know the number that went out, and know what's in the park."

Davis was a vital man in translating Walt's expectations into workable designs, space planning, and

1 Brazilian singer and actress 1909–1955. In the 1930s she was the most popular recording artist in Brazil, where she appeared in five films. Her sister, Aurora Miranda, appeared as "The Brazilian Girl" in the 1945 Disney feature *The Three Caballeros*.

BELOW LEFT: Marvin Aubrey Davis.

BOTTOM: An early concept layout of Disneyland, created by Marvin Davis, is the first to show the Park in its approximate final size and shape on Opening Day.

creating overall layout of Disneyland. As such, he was critically involved with design, planning, and placement of everything within the park. "We owe a lot to Marvin," Tom Morris says, "who had the unglamorous job of laying out the park and making it practical. It was actually he, not Herbie [Ryman], who first arranged the park; Herbie's rendering, beautiful and full of spirit as it was, was based on the early layouts that Marvin was doing. He did such a great job that we have basically stuck to his geometric formulas and distances ever since."

"I guess I must have done, well I know I did," Davis stated. "A hundred and twenty-nine different schemes for the solution of the thing, until finally it developed into the scheme that it is now, with the single entrance and the walk up Main Street to the center of the hub. Walt's idea was to have the whole thing as radials from that hub." The park theme areas were shifted, moved, altered, named, renamed,[2] and rethought over and over again. "We knew we wanted the fantasy rides up at the end of Main Street, once you go through the castle. Then the other lands just logically took their place," Davis explained.

Tomorrowland was positioned as a final "spoke" on the left (west) side of the hub, but it soon became apparent that this plan got in the way of the Rivers of America. For efficiency's sake, Frontierland and Adventureland had to be adjacent, since they both contained enormous water elements, and Tomorrowland did not. Tomorrowland was begun last, finished last, and had less to offer on Opening Day. "That area was the most difficult because everything in it had to be created, while the other lands were the result of research," Davis said.

"This was before they even knew where the Park was going. Before they bought the property," Davis told Richard

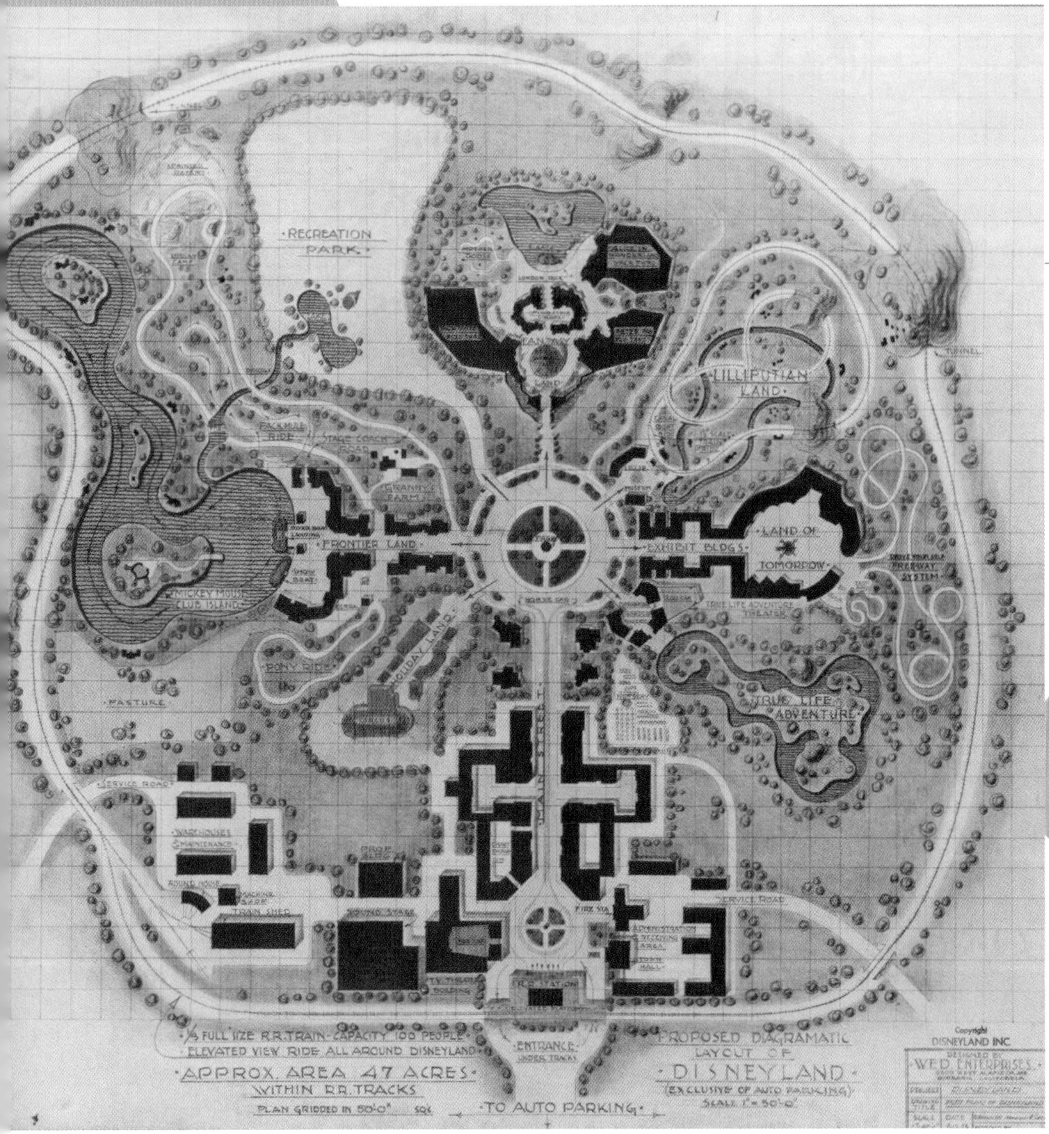

2 Frontierland was "Frontier Country"; "World of Tomorrow" and "Land of Tomorrow" preceded "Tomorrowland"; Adventureland began as "True-Life Adventure Land."

and Katherine Greene. "Buzz Price[3] was a member of Stanford Research. He came in as part of Stanford Research,[4] which we hired for $25,000 in 1953 to recommend a site for Disneyland—anything from San Diego to Monterey—anything between there. Pick the best place for population, for traffic, for atmosphere, humidity, rain, all the things that affect attendance to a Park. Gave them the full range. They studied it and came back after several months with this exact site right near Anaheim. So immediately, in my little plane, I went out and took pictures of everything. Anyhow, they picked that spot, and you can see it turned out pretty good."

In the days when Disneyland was in development, Marvin was an eyewitness to the unique polarity of interests held by Walt and his brother Roy. Although Roy supported the vision of his brother—it had, after all, built the organization that bore his name—he also had a responsibility to shareholders in his role as CEO of Walt Disney Productions, a publicly held company. "Bill Cottrell was the liaison between the two, and a peacemaker," Davis recalled. "It was really amazing how he could do it. Roy would talk to him, even though Bill was definitely with Walt, he was on 'his team.' But [Bill] was able to talk to Roy, and on certain situations where they just had to get together, Bill was the one to do it.

"Actually, when Walt had the idea of Disneyland, Roy didn't want to spend that kind of money . . . but anyhow, toward the end of financing the thing, they were running out of money and Walt said, 'I've got to have some more money, or we can't open the Park.' Roy said, 'Well, I'm just not going to give it to you. You've spent enough, and enough is enough.' Walt said, 'Okay, I'll sell my name to some banks I know, and I will raise my own money, and to heck with you.' Of course, this brought Roy around real quick. Walt hocked everything—including [his wife] Lilly's life insurance. He was the epitome of the showman, and he was always thinking, 'How can I make a good show out of this, not only for kids, but for everybody?'"

Following the opening of Disneyland in 1955, Davis made an easy segue into the Studio side of Disney.[5] Davis became a full-fledged live-action art director on the "Davy Crockett at the Alamo" segment of the *Disneyland* TV series, the third installment of the phenomenally popular serial. He moved on to art-direct eight episodes of the *Swamp Fox* series for *Disneyland*, after which he took the same role on the (at last produced) *Zorro* TV show, starring Guy Williams. That was a lot of fun to do," Davis remembered. "We went on a lot of location trips down in South Carolina [for *Swamp Fox*], and down to Mexico for the *Zorro* series. I designed the Diego de la Vega hacienda set, and of course the whole Pueblo de Los Angeles village, with the jail, the church, and the town square." Davis worked on feature films for Walt Disney Productions, including *Westward Ho, the Wagons!* (1956); *Moon Pilot; Bon Voyage!; Big Red* (all 1962); *Savage Sam* (1963); and *A Tiger Walks* (1964).

A pilot by avocation, Davis often scouted locations for these projects from the air, just as he had zipped down over the Anaheim site for Disneyland to shoot a few pictures when the locale was chosen. Flights over Lake Sherwood in Ventura County, California, near the city of Thousand Oaks, and Harry Warner's 1,100-acre horse ranch determined locations for *Zorro* and the rolling green hills seen in *Westward Ho, the Wagons!* In 1963, Davis also won an Emmy Award for Outstanding Achievement in Art Direction and Scenic Design for *Walt Disney's Wonderful World of Color* television series.

---

3 Research economist Harrison "Buzz" Price helped Walt Disney select the optimum locations for Disneyland in 1953 and Walt Disney World in 1963. Over time, he became one of Walt's most trusted advisors. In all, Buzz conducted over 150 project studies for The Walt Disney Company.

4 Stanford Research Institute, now one of the world's largest contract research institutes and known as SRI International, was founded in 1946 by the trustees of Stanford University as a center of innovation to support economic development in the region. Later it became fully independent and was incorporated as a nonprofit organization.

5 As Davis told *The E Ticket* magazine in 1997, "I happened to be in the men's room in the Animation Building, and Walt came in and went to the next urinal along the wall. While there, he said, 'Hey, Marv, I want you to take over the *Davy Crockett* and *Zorro* shows.' And that's how I got my job."

THESE PAGES: Davis sometimes returned to his motion picture roots, these are some of the Disney films that carry his Art Director credit.

Then, in 1965, Marvin returned to WED to work as a project designer on the concept for Walt Disney World. "Walt came in and said, 'Marv, you've got to quit this and go over to WED,'" Davis explained, "'I want you to work on Disney World just like you did on Disneyland.' I went to Florida with him quite a bit," Davis says of this new venture. "We walked around there, and we flew over it a few times—at one point we rented a helicopter, and that was very exciting." In his master planning role, Davis was one of the select few who truly knew what was going on in Florida, how the property was being acquired, and just what the property was like. "Actually on a scale of ten, that property was a one-plus, maybe. It was just awful. It was a swamp. There was only one high spot in the whole thing. Bay Lake was all swamp, too. It had these cypress trees that, when they come down to the ground, they flare out and then they have 'knees,' which are the roots. They come up and turn around and go back down. Well, these things were all over that area, because the water was knee deep. So, in order to dig out Bay Lake, we had to bring in huge dredger machines and scooper-uppers. The roots would go down thirty feet, and you had to get them out or they'd just keep growing."

Who would want to buy such property, and so much of it? It was imperative that the Disney interest be kept secret. "[If people in the area knew what Walt was up to] then the thing would have gone through the roof," Davis said. "Because they knew what happened in Disneyland.[6] Everybody knew that I guess." Initial approaches to Florida were discreet and well-guarded, public sightings and local interactions were concealed through false identities, diversions, or tales of location scouting for an epic movie.

Traveling in Florida was especially hard for Walt, who was familiar to anyone with a television after hosting a top network series for almost a decade. "It was really classified stuff. It was CIA. His luggage was all [monogrammed] WED. So [when he visited Florida] he called himself 'Walter E. Davis.' That was so cloak-and-dagger."

The acquisition of dozens of parcels of land that comprised the desired property required a monumental effort.[7] To do it secretly was nearly impossible. "We sent an attorney down there," Davis said. "He went down there completely incognito. He couldn't even send any mail to his wife—he had to send it to New York, and they'd transfer it. He had a totally different name. I think there were at least forty different owners he had to round up. This fellow managed to pull it off and rounded up all these guys and got them to put their name on the dotted line before it was announced. I bet they all wanted to kill him after they found out."

Through various dummy corporations, Disney finally secured 27,800 acres of land (twice the acreage of Manhattan) located between the cities of Orlando and Kissimmee. "Here in Florida we have something we've never enjoyed in Disneyland: the blessing of size," Walt said in a 1966 film. "There's enough land here to hold all the ideas and plans we can possibly imagine." And his master planner was Marvin Davis.

Davis was also party to the welcome that Walt received at the headquarters of major corporations. In his business dealings with Disneyland, the 1960 Winter Olympics, and the New York World's Fair, Disney had gained a reputation for his vision in the realm of public recreation, and his interest in future developments was greeted enthusiastically by the corporate world. They had seen what he could do with technology, and what an association with Disney could do for their companies.

"I traveled with Walt to a couple of places, checking out all the research and

6 "We could have made a bloody fortune if I wanted to buy up a lot of property around [Disneyland]," Davis said. "It was selling for $4,000 an acre."

7 Many individual parcels of future Walt Disney World had been sold through a mail-order scheme in the 1920s, many of the owners' heirs had no idea that they were the proud landlords of prime Florida Cypress Swamp.

development labs at RCA, Xerox, and IBM, and that was fascinating. We got to see products and concepts that wouldn't be on the market for five or ten years. When we first worked on Disneyland, I didn't think it would work, but by this time I was a believer. I knew that if Disneyland could work, anything Walt did would work. I knew we'd have no problem in Florida." These corporate ties were even more important because of the vision that Walt had for the Florida project. Not just a resort or amusement park, but a whole new idea of urban planning and design.

As Walt's reputation grew beyond that of just a cartoonist or filmmaker, the innovation and efficiency of Disneyland was not lost on his admirers. Author and optimal behaviorist[8] Ray Bradbury once asked Walt to run for mayor of Los Angeles. Disney replied, "Why should I want to be mayor when I'm already king?"

Joking aside, Bradbury no doubt knew that Walt had begun to worry about the world of the future that his grandchildren would inhabit. He saw modern cities as ill-planned, disorganized, dirty, and unpleasant for the citizens who were supposed to be their raison d'etre. He began to realize that all that had been accomplished in the development of Disneyland could be put to use in urban planning communities.[9] As he had with miniatures and model railroads, Walt began to immerse himself in his newest interest: city planning.

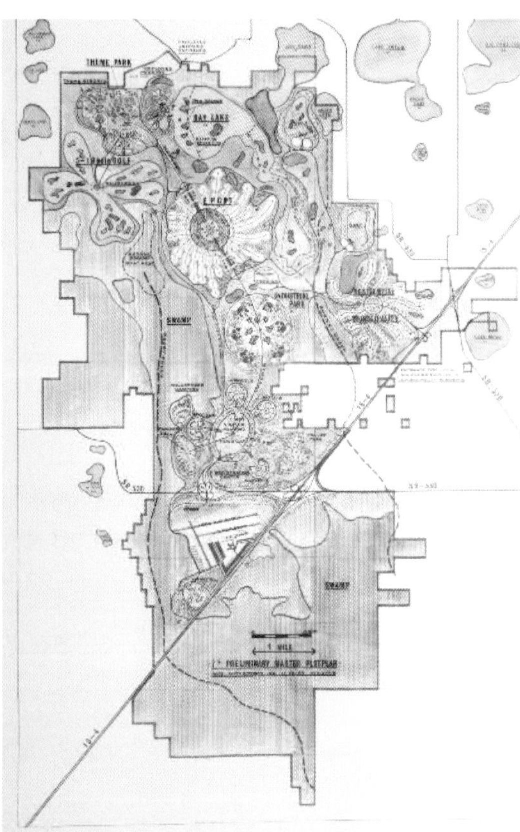

ABOVE: One of Marvin's early layouts for the Florida property that became Walt Disney World.

OPPOSITE TOP: On the Studios soundstage with Walt Disney, early October 1966. Filming his appearance to communicate his vision for Epcot was the very last time he stood before the cameras.

The Experimental Prototype Community of Tomorrow (EPCOT) was to be a "community of the future" that was designed to stimulate American corporations to come up with new ideas for urban living. "EPCOT will take its cue from the new ideas and new technologies that are emerging from the forefront of American industry. It will be a community of tomorrow that will never be completed. It will always be showcasing and testing and demonstrating new materials and new systems."

Walt's passing in 1966 left a beautifully built performance vehicle with no engine. With Walt, colleagues such as Davis knew what to do, and what to expect. "He was a wonderful guy to work for, but he got every ounce of energy and creativeness that you had in you. He would come in and maybe the first scheme that you had, he would just completely tear apart, you know? It might have been something that you thought was pretty good, or you wouldn't have showed it to him, you know. He could just deflate you right down to zero. Then, after you recovered a little bit, you would start right back over. Eventually, you would come up with something better. You'd do this three or four times, or however many times it took, and it was entirely possible that you would come back to the original scheme, the first one that you showed him. But he wanted to see every idea that you could possibly have before he settled on something."

Even worse than the loss of the man, the core of the future plans of Walt Disney Productions, and particularly

8 Bradbury said, "If you behave yourself, and you behave optimally—every day of your life, every week, every month, every year—if you do the thing that you love, up to the optimal mark, at the end of a year of doing what you should be doing, you feel good. I'm an optimal behaviorist, like Disney. With a grand sense of fun and passion, you're going to create something fine. Not always, but Walt was a bursting fountain, always running at full speed. That makes for optimal behavior. Behaving at the peak of genetic madness."

9 In 1963, in his keynote speech before the 1963 Urban Design Conference at Harvard University, developer James Rouse said, "I hold a view that may be somewhat shocking to an audience as sophisticated as this: that the greatest piece of urban design in the United States today is Disneyland. If you think about Disneyland and think of its performance in relationship to its purpose, its meaning to people—more than that, its meaning to the process of development—you will find it the outstanding piece of urban design in the United States."

the EPCOT project were in flux and in doubt. Davis remembered, "He had freedom to do whatever he wanted, and it just about did me in when Walt's plans were changed so drastically when he died. When it happened, there was a big meeting that included [WDP executive vice president and chief operating officer] Card Walker, [de facto Studio Head] Bill Anderson, and [CEO] Roy [O.] Disney. This meeting was in a big room, and to the best of my ability I presented Walt's concepts for EPCOT. I got through, and sat down, and Roy turned around and looked at me and he said, 'Marvin . . . Walt's gone.'

"I'm not complaining about the things that they did, because I think those were probably the best answers. This 'community' thing would have worked only so well without Walt's guidance. Walt wasn't concerned about the Magic Kingdom, so I just did the position of it. His approach was just to do it again. He'd already gone through that planning, solving all the difficulties of planning Disneyland. His attitude was 'I want to do EPCOT!' There was a flaw in that position, and I'll concede that."

Once the Florida project got going again, Davis became the liaison between the three hotels being designed by Welton Becket and Associates and WED Enterprises. "WED switched gears altogether, and we stopped even thinking about EPCOT." Davis retired from the Company in 1975.

"It was quite a departure for me to come with Disney and work on Disneyland," Davis once said. "I was scared to death of the thing, and I was convinced that there was no way it could work. But by God, it did." Marvin Davis died on March 8, 1998, in a Santa Monica, California, hospital after a brief illness. He was eighty-seven years old.

Bill Martin: A Master of Place Design

"My real job as an art director was to meld the actual designs and construction projects with the Disney ideas, stories, and motion picture themes," Bill Martin described his Imagineering role. "I was an artist myself, and architecture was my forté."

Born in Marshalltown, Iowa, on June 15, 1917, Bill Martin and his family later moved to Los Angeles. In 1937, he graduated from Los Angeles Junior College, and continued his studies in architecture at nearby Chouinard Art Institute and the Art Center College of Design. After school, he landed a job as a set designer for Twentieth Century Fox until World War II began; from 1941 to 1945, Bill served in the U.S. Army Air Forces training pilots and bombardiers, and was commissioned a captain. "I didn't leave the country," Bill said in a 2005 interview with Don Peri. "I graduated from Luke Field in Phoenix, and we were divided into three groups. One-third went to Alaska, one-third went to North America, and one-third were made instructors. I lucked out and got that. I was an instructor most of the war."

Following the war, he worked for Panoramic Productions and then returned to Fox as an assistant art director. "I worked on a lot of pictures over there," Martin said. "*The Razor's Edge, How Green Was My Valley*. The last one was *The Egyptian* with George Davis."[10] One day in 1953, while working on *The Egyptian*, Martin received a surprise phone call: Walt Disney was seeking help to create his new theme park, Disneyland. Although official Disney Company bios report Martin at the time as "eager to expand his talent as an art director and set designer" and that he "readily accepted the challenge," he remembers things a little differently. "I thought I was going downhill leaving the [Fox] Studio and going to Disney. But it didn't turn out that way at all. I liked it very much. My wife didn't want me to leave Fox Studio to go to Disney, but I went anyway. I remember we were in [Dick Irvine's] office. Walt was in there and he turned to me and said, 'You know, this is not a lifetime job.' I said I knew it, and at that time, coming in green—this

10 George Davis (1914–1998) was a celebrated art director who began his career at Twentieth Century Fox and won Oscars for his work on *The Robe* (1953) and *The Diary of Anne Frank* (1959).

whole project was green to me—I didn't think it was a longtime job either. But it lasted for about twenty-two years.

"The reason he brought us over [was,] in a way, he didn't trust his animators to design the park. Now, they worked on the rides, that's for sure. But he wanted set designers that were used to building false facades and so forth cheaply, because they would build a set, shoot it three times, and then tear it down." Walt knew how a drawing could sell an idea—after all, he used them to sell Disneyland. But he also knew that he could be sold by a drawing, too. "Walt once said jokingly, 'I don't trust the artists that I've got, because they can exaggerate anything and I don't see what I'm getting.'"

Martin is quick to point out that his Disney colleagues were no less talented, just of a different skill set. He told *The E Ticket* in 1994, "Those guys were great artists and we used them all the time. Ken Anderson was one of them, and Herbie Ryman was a marvelous illustrator. I worked with him very closely and he did a lot of sketches for me. So did Sam McKim, Dorothea Redmond, and Colin Campbell. I knew Marc Davis from way back in the early days. So I was one of the art directors that came from Fox, along with Marvin Davis and his architect, George Patrick. There were art directors for different parts of the park. So that's how we came in from the studio business to the theme park."

Martin brought a useful combination of talents to the project, in a talent to create both the imaginative and the practical, resulting in a place of both timeless fantasy and daily reality. Walt called Martin, Irvine, and Davis 'bricks and mortar men,' based on their ability to create real dimensional places, where his own team of animation artists were more adept in filmmaking. "I had done perspective drawings and back-projections,[11] and being an artist I was able to keep things 'Disney' while keeping these projects moving," Martin explained.

As much as Walt might have insisted that he needed guidance in the new world of architecture and place, he was a quick study, and soon learned how to read a blueprint like an engineer. "He went over my plans with a fine-tooth comb. I'd drawn sidewalks on the blueprints with square corners and Walt said: 'Bill, people aren't soldiers! They don't turn in at sharp angles! Curve the sidewalks! Make the corners round!' He knew from long experience that it was easy to cheat on a drawing and make it look better than it was. He said, 'You can work at set sketches, but you don't know if it's going to look like that once they build it.' He didn't trust them, in a sense. That's why we built so many models. He could see what we were getting with the models."

This model work resulted in the creative use of set designer's methods of forced perspective, an optical illusion where objects appear farther, closer, larger, or smaller than they actually are, through the manipulation of relative scale. It also resulted in the oft-repeated apocryphal tale that Main Street was built to "5/8-scale."

"You've probably heard the 5/8-scale, haven't you?" said Martin. "Well, that was basically from the [model train] engines. Those are 5/8-scale from a real engine. That's where the thing started, and somehow, that got related to everything, all the buildings and everything, but in reality, it wasn't [5/8-scale]. These were scaled down. The ground floors were scaled pretty full size, but there were no [full-scale] second floors on Main Street in Disneyland." Individual buildings were scaled individually, on a case-by-case basis, as Martin and his colleagues saw fit.

Working on Disneyland meant working side by side with Walt Disney on a daily basis. "Walt was in on everything," Martin said. "Nothing was really consummated until he gave the okay. He would come in my office while I was working, and if he didn't like the thing, he wouldn't say he wouldn't do it. He would never say, 'That looks lousy.' It was, 'You know, Bill, let's try something a little different, and let's do it this way.' That

11 Martin is referring to the process of taking a plan drawing and "projecting" it into a more "artistic" concept illustration of the completed structure.

was the comment I got. So we just dropped what I was doing and went off on another track. But he never criticized openly, to me or anybody I know of."

Being a "new guy" held its difficulties for Martin, but he quickly understood the boss's boundaries. "I had been there probably six months or so and I got a raise from Dick Irvine. Walt was in my office at the time, looking over what I was doing, and I told him, 'Thank you, Walt, for the raise.' He was so flustered. He was very embarrassed for some reason. I never did that again. I told Dick about it. There was something about Walt; he didn't like to be complimented or eulogized that way. I thought it was just natural, but he was so flustered he left the office. He didn't expect it, I guess. When I came in over there, I didn't know any of them, and these guys had been with him for so long. They should have told me what not to say and what to do. So I blurted out half the time, which didn't seem to bother him any."

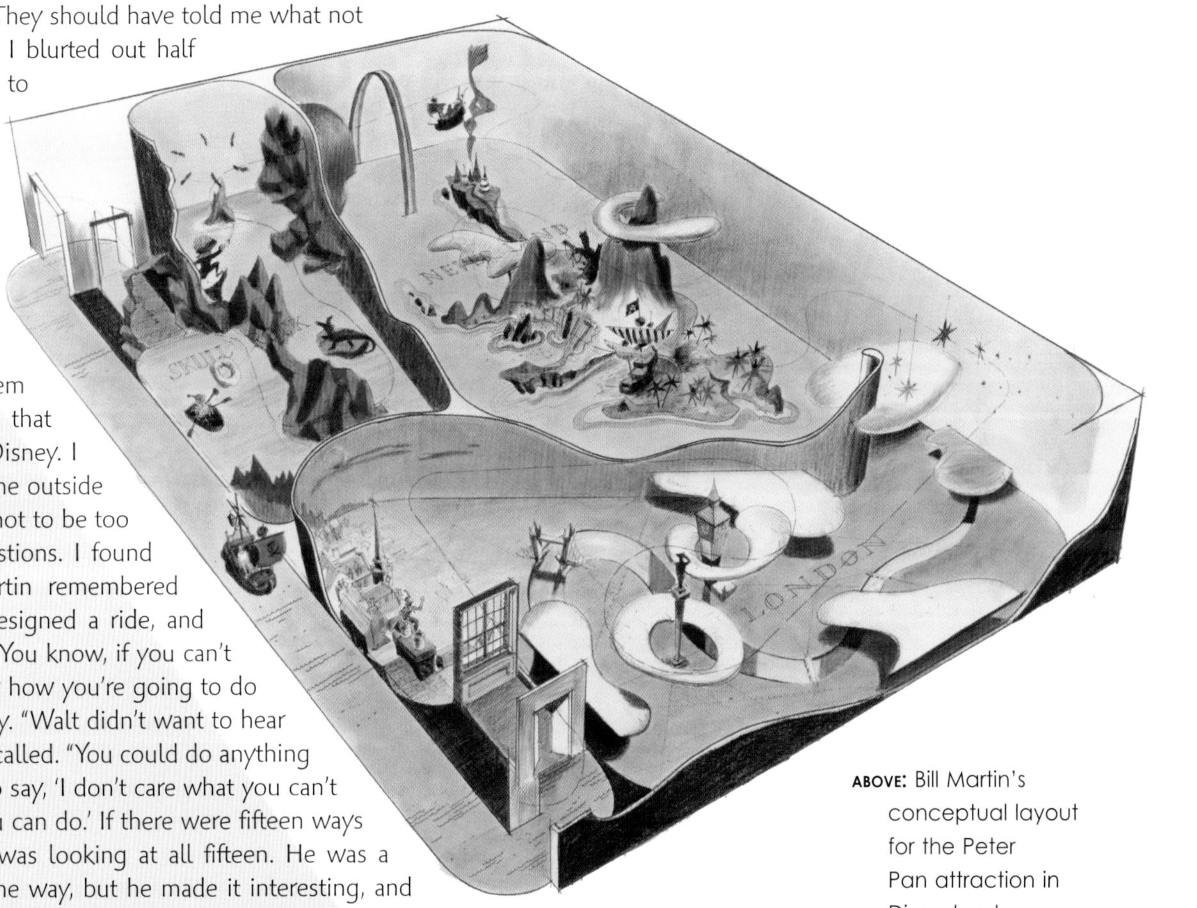

Martin learned that Walt would easily tolerate his "blurting out" if it was creative, collaborative, and most of all, positive. "I came from Fox Studios, and when they asked me a question there, I told them what I thought, so I did that when I went to work for Disney. I guess Walt appreciated some outside thinking. He did teach me not to be too dogmatic about my suggestions. I found that out in a hurry." Martin remembered a certain artist who had designed a ride, and when the artist told Walt, "You know, if you can't do it this way, I don't know how you're going to do it," he was fired the next day. "Walt didn't want to hear that kind of talk," Martin recalled. "You could do anything if you wanted. Walt used to say, 'I don't care what you can't do. I want to hear what you can do.' If there were fifteen ways to solve a problem, Walt was looking at all fifteen. He was a taskmaster, let's put it in one way, but he made it interesting, and he'd give you a little charge to go ahead and do it the way you liked it best. Then he would comment on that."

ABOVE: Bill Martin's conceptual layout for the Peter Pan attraction in Disneyland.

OPPOSITE: Bill and his trademark pipe at Imagineering in 1977.

The Disney Animation Library provided rich resource for the Fantasyland attractions, especially the "dark rides," with vehicles on tracks traveling in darkened buildings past animated tableaux lit with ultraviolet "black light." "Snow White was the scariest, and Peter Pan had the most wonder," Martin said. "I really think Mr. Toad is probably the most exciting of the dark rides. I think it was Walt [who] chose the specific ride concepts from his movies. These themes had to include something that could be used as a ride vehicle. Snow White, for instance, had those carved wood cars. They weren't exactly mine cars, but they were something like that."

Dick Irvine remembered, "We were talking [about] what things we could use for Fantasyland, for one of the rides. We kidded, 'Well, we could do a Peter Pan fly-through.' [While Walt was] in Europe in 1952 or '53, Bill Martin came up with an idea. Bill made a little schematic bird's-eye view of where you would go, and that became the ride."

"We worked on Disneyland until it opened in 1955," Martin recalled, "and we were still working on it after it opened." Disneyland's opening-day problems were many, and have been well documented. Martin remembers that there were several things left undone that became the first post-opening WED projects. "The big pirate ship in Fantasyland was only half completed opening day. It was no more than an empty shell and we only had time to paint half of it, the half facing the public. The rest remained bare wood. At that point we had offices upstairs in the Main Street City Hall. For the next twelve years, from when Disneyland opened until the work began in Florida, I worked on just about every project in Disneyland.

ABOVE: Bill's conceptual layout for Fantasyland in Disneyland.

"I did most of the planning for Rainbow Caverns Mine Train, right after the Park opened. We put in the Painted Desert, Cascade Peak, and Rainbow Caverns. I worked on laying that out from the very beginning, including the miniature buildings in Rainbow Ridge. They were a favorite of Lillian Disney, and I remember that Walt and Lilly would often walk along the pathways between those little buildings when they stayed at the Park overnight."[12]

Both before and after opening, Martin worked on projects that never saw the light of day. "I wanted to put in a camera obscura[13] in the highest tower of the Castle, so that people could see the whole park from that vantage point. We got Eustace Lycett, the head of the Studio Camera Department, to go down to Santa Monica Park to see the camera obscura they had down there. He came back and said we couldn't do it because there wasn't enough light for the forty-foot throw, so the tower became just a tower.

"We were working for all kinds of things to be interesting, and one was the shoe," Martin adds, discussing a Frontierland attraction that was essentially a lookout tower designed to look as if it were the giant hob-nail boot of legendary woodsman Paul Bunyan. Guests would have climbed through the inside of the shoe to a viewing platform high atop the monster footwear. A giant double-blade axe and other oversize props would be sited nearby. "I designed a shoe there—it never caught on. We never built it. Walt was interested in it for a while, but we had other things to do."

Another project that was proposed in two different configurations was an "International District." One version was located behind Main Street's east side, between Main Street and Tomorrowland.[14] "I worked on that," Martin said. "You go down the street—the houses are all designed to look at the street, and you'd turn around and it was a different street on the way back. Same houses, but the juxtaposition of it and the designing, they were different types of international cities." Another version was an additional "International Land" located on the northeast "spoke" off the hub (between Fantasyland and Tomorrowland, at the current site of Matterhorn Bobsleds and its surroundings). "We had the water circulation system in place, and London Bridge would have crossed the flow to an island surrounded by a lake on the other side," Martin explained. Water wheels and barges would have plied the "Thames," and visitors would also have found a taxicab ride through the streets of Paris, an Italian/Mediterranean area with a gondola ride, and a Bavarian/German compound with a fountain, shops, and a museum. "This was all dream stuff, you know, and none of this really happened. We were short of money in those days, but we never threw anything away, and a lot of these ideas ended up in other places years later.

"In 1958, I did all the plans that routed the Submarine, Monorail, and the Tomorrowland and Fantasyland Autopias, all in one complex area. We were running out of room and had to pile things on top of each other. There was no Fantasyland Autopia before this, and when the cars come down off those slopes, they're coming off the roof of the Submarine ride [show] building. That was our first construction job after the Park opened, and I oversaw

12 These buildings can still be seen adjacent to the vehicle loading platform of Big Thunder Mountain Railroad in Disneyland.

13 *Camera obscura* is Latin for "dark room," which describes this entertainment's simplest form, a darkened room into which light is admitted through a small opening in a wall or window. An inverted image of the outside scene appears, and can be aimed, magnified, or reflected by mirrors against the wall or screen.

14 Liberty Street was proposed and announced as was Edison Square. The Liberty Street concepts became Liberty Square in Magic Kingdom Park in Walt Disney World, Edison Square evolved into the General Electric (later Walt Disney's) Carousel of Progress.

RIGHT: Roger Broggie, Jr., Marc Davis, Al Bertino, and Bill Martin at a meeting about the "Bear Band" concept for Mineral King, 1966.

both the Submarine ride and the monorail at the same time. I wove those Autopia tracks together so they overlapped each other and they had to miss the Motorboats and the Submarine, which were underneath, and the monorail, which was above everything. Walt saw all of this and later he gave me an indirect compliment. He said, 'I think you should do this new job I've got in West Palm Beach,[15] because you're good at these complicated layouts for railroads, these jigsaw puzzles.'"

Martin was also a key planner in Walt's plans for an "Old New Orleans" area, a concept that dated back to the days right after the Park opening, but begun in earnest in 1962. It included a Pirate Wax Museum as its centerpiece attraction; accessed through the first floor, and into the basement of the main building. "Originally that was supposed to be a walk-through. We dug this big hole in the ground and we were going to put New Orleans Square on top of it, which we finally did anyway." Work on the New York World's Fair caused a delay to the New Orleans Square project, and by the time attention returned to it, things had changed. "As the thing progressed, the operations people didn't think you could get enough capacity of just a walk-through." Two innovations from the Fair helped bring the project forward. One was Audio-Animatronics—fully-animated figures now replaced the original idea of a wax museum—and a pedestrian scheme was supplanted by the water flume system that had transported passengers of "it's a small world." "So we went to the boats, the canals, the waterways, through there. That solved a lot of questions," Martin said.

Walt was always the driving force behind Martin's efforts, and that of his fellow Imagineers. Martin recalled with particular fondness a Saturday ritual that went on for years. "We would meet Walt in Joe Fowler's office, downstairs in City Hall, at about nine o'clock in the morning. There would usually be Walt, Joe Fowler, John Hench, Dick Irvine, Tommy Walker,[16] Truman Woodworth (who was in charge of construction), and me. Marty Sklar would be along sometimes with a cameraman. Marty was working for the Publicity Department, and wrote a lot of Disneyland copy at that time. Later he wrote a lot of Walt's speeches. They would be shooting pictures of Walt and the rest of us, and of things we saw and talked about. We'd walk through each land before the Park opened, and each area manager of operations would be there. Walt was looking for ways to make the Park better, mainly ways to augment the Park. Of course, Walt would have a few ideas in mind before we started walking around, and that's how we'd find out about them," Martin mused. "He was getting the status from us, and finding out how we felt about the projects at that point. It would often be a creative thing, and he was looking for new ideas. Some idea would come up during the walk and he'd say, 'Hey! We ought to do this. This would be fun to do!'"

As Walt began to assemble his team for his ambitious Florida Project, Martin was among the first to be called. His place-making

15 Dick Irvine recalled an early possible location for EPCOT. "We did some preliminaries for another deal in Florida with . . . RCA and a fellow named McCarthy, an insurance man. He had some property at West Palm Beach. At that time, [Walt] knew he could do that."

16 Thomas Luttgen Walker (1922–1986) was director of entertainment at Disneyland during its first twelve years of operation, and later produced spectacular events at celebrations including three Olympic Games and the centennial of the Statue of Liberty.

skills would be required for a whole new Magic Kingdom, and Walt needed reliable colleagues on the job, since he needed their experience and instincts to guide the Magic Kingdom while planning to supervise a whole separate team on his EPCOT vision.

"I was working on the Florida Magic Kingdom when Walt passed away," Martin recalled. "I heard about it indirectly from someone, and it was a shock, that's for sure. You know, Walt used to come into our office there, coughing like mad. Then, all of a sudden, he was gone. Of course, Walt 'greased the wheels' for a lot of things we were doing after he passed away, but he had always worked that way." Martin and his colleagues strode on, completing New Orleans Square, Pirates of the Caribbean, and The Haunted Mansion[1] in Disneyland while moving tentatively forward on plans for Walt Disney World in Florida. In 1971, Bill became vice president of Design at WED Enterprises. His projects included Main Street, U.S.A.; Cinderella Castle; the "Utilidors"[2] beneath Magic Kingdom Park; and the canal systems for the entire 27,000-acre property.

As he had with Sleeping Beauty Castle in Disneyland, Martin collaborated with Herb Ryman on a new, and far grander, castle for Florida. "The one in Disneyland was 82 feet tall, and the one

we did in Florida is 182 feet tall.[3] We couldn't do the same thing again twice. And of course, they did it again in Japan. They took the same drawings and reproduced it in Japan, the one [from] Disney World."

Lessons learned from Disneyland were applied to the planning of Walt Disney World, another strong reason that Walt trusted his team to bring their best game to the Florida Project. "I laid it all out with the idea of supplying the background of what we had in Disneyland—or what we didn't have," Martin told author Steve Mannheim in 1998. "In other words, we had to close the Park two days a week, you know, in order to service the different stores and shops and the restaurants and so forth, because we didn't want that going through the public when the Park was open—except after dark or after hours. So we started that underground passage business when I did New Orleans Square in Disneyland, but it only fed New Orleans Square. We did another one over in Tomorrowland with some of the restaurants over there, but it was very inadequate.

1 Bill's "tombstone" in The Haunted Mansion graveyard reads: "Here lies a man named Martin/The lights went out on this old Spartan."

2 "UTILity corrIDOR"

3 Sleeping Beauty Castle is actually 77 feet tall, Cinderella Castle tops out at 189 feet.

OPPOSITE: The Haunted Mansion nears completion in Disneyland in 1963—but the attraction wouldn't actually open for six more years.

BELOW AND BOTTOM: Few Walt Disney World Magic Kingdom Park visitors realize that merchandise, services, food, and Cast Members are being transported out of their sight—and beneath their feet—in a network of corridors that run beneath the Park.

"So when we built the Park [in Florida], we were going to do a real job. We had one 'main' [Utilidor tunnel] that ran from Fantasyland straight down to Main Street, then the rest of them branched off and went around the Park, completely circled it, and had branches to all the different restaurants, so they could supply food to the restaurants and merchandise to the shops without anyone knowing it. They came in from the back of Fantasyland. Of course we ran into problems because the water table down there was only about three feet deep. So these were just like a bathtub, you know, and we still had to pump water out of the area there to dry it up so they wouldn't float. They still have to do that.

"We never used the Utilidors for transporting people.[4] Strictly for servicing and utilities, because in these Utilidors, we run all of our hot and cold water lines, electrical lines, sewage, and so forth. That's all strung up on the wall over there on racks. It goes all the way through the whole thing. So we didn't have to dig up any holes. We had the 'ditch' already there. And the wardrobe department was down there, as well as a cafeteria, computer rooms, storage rooms, electrical, and workshops. We did everything underground there because you never knew when it was going to rain. It rains every afternoon at two o'clock, all summer long." Martin was also responsible for the design of various watercrafts in Walt Disney World, including the *Admiral Joe Fowler* and *Richard F. Irvine* riverboats, steam launches, and side-wheel steamboats.

He retired from the company in 1977; however, he returned to WDI as a consultant on EPCOT Center and Tokyo Disneyland. Martin lives in Malibu, California, with his wife, Marty. His hobbies include painting, horticulture, and astronomy—and he still holds many fond memories of working with Walt, and the innovative and collaborative nature that he still finds noteworthy. "He was always a few steps ahead, and he wouldn't give up. He was very conscious of how things would play with his audience, and of the Disney image. He was very much in control, I'll say that.

"He was a visionary. That's why he brought in so many people who had their finger on a certain aspect he didn't know anything about. He had to take their word for it and let them prove themselves."

4 Although not "transported," Cast Members did use the Utilidors to walk from wardrobe, lockers, shops, etc., to their "Land."

"I'm never sure myself what will please the public. With the story men, I think it's easier to give 'em plenty of rope. Let 'em alone and let 'em go. When they get in a hole, they'll yell for help. There's a time to argue and a time to find an excuse to get the hell out."

—Walt Disney

The Story Department

Walt Disney knew from his filmmaking experience that story was everything to an audience. But he also knew that "story" was a deceptive term, and related not just to a script or the description and execution of a series of events. Story is a combination of details, including character, situation, setting, lighting, color, and other media. In conceiving Disneyland, his concept was to immerse the visitor in living storytelling scenarios. He knew, however, that audiences experience stories differently, and so his challenge was to deliver enough detail to communicate clearly, while adding a further level of detail to enhance a sense of exploration and discovery. And again, he assembled a mix of talents whose diversity—and often, conflict—achieved and exceeded his goals.

Marc Davis: The Story Man

"I've rarely felt confined to the animation medium," said Disney veteran Marc Davis upon his retirement in 1978. "I've worked as an 'idea man' and love creating characters, whether they be through animation, or any other media."

During his forty-three-year association with The Walt Disney Company, Davis was responsible for designing and bringing life to such classic characters as Bambi, Cinderella, Alice (of Wonderland), Tinker Bell, Aurora and Maleficent (from *Sleeping Beauty*), and Cruella De Vil. Davis, one of Disney Animation's legendary "Nine Old Men," was regarded as one of the top talents ever to work in the animation medium and is revered as one of Disney's all-time greatest Imagineers. He went on to play a key role in the creative planning for Disneyland. Although he did not join the WED team until six years after the Park opened, Davis left a significant legacy there, creating story and character concepts for half a dozen of the most memorable Disney attractions.

The only son of Harry and Mildred Davis, Marc was born in Bakersfield, California, where his father was engaged in oil-field developments. The Davis family lived in San Francisco; Reno, Nevada; a Nevada mining town called Tonopah; Comanche, Seminole, and Tulsa, Oklahoma; Little River (now a part of Miami), Florida; Kansas City, Missouri; Smackover, Arkansas; Galveston Texas; Klamath Falls, Oregon; and Los Angeles, Sacramento, and Marysville, California. "Harry was just a restless man," Davis recalled. "Had to have a lot of action." Wherever a new oil boom developed, or wherever his fancy took him, footloose Harry moved the Davis family, and Marc received his early education in more than twenty different schools across the country.

It may be surmised that many of the characteristics that made Davis such an exceptional artist were encouraged by the nomadic nature of his youth. Forever the new kid in town, Davis was confronted by a perpetual parade of fresh characters and frequently strange situations, and developed remarkable skills of observation. Everywhere he went, he had to develop new friendships, and often a clever drawing created an introduction—or saved him from a bully's black eye. "In a new town where I wasn't acquainted with anyone," Davis told John Canemaker, "I would amuse myself by drawing." After high school graduation, he enrolled at the Kansas City Art Institute for his first formal art training, after which he attended the California School of Fine Arts in San Francisco and the Otis Art Institute of Los Angeles. Later, he toured Europe for seven months as a student artist.

Davis was enraptured by two particular Disney short cartoons of the 1930s: the Silly Symphonies *Three Little Pigs* and *Who Killed Cock Robin?* Davis approached the Studio, but was, at first, a victim of the sexist nature of the animation profession in the 1930s. He had sent a letter requesting an interview, and signed it "M. Fraser Davis," and was informed: "At the present time, we are not hiring any women artists."[1]

Davis overcame his initial frustration at the confused response, directed a revised missive to the Studio, and in December of 1935, he went to work for Disney. "Everyone who joined the Studio at that time," he said, "was an apprentice animator. We continually attended art classes and worked our way up by doing in-betweens." He was promoted to assistant animator when *Snow White and the Seven Dwarfs* went into production, working with the legendary Grim Natwick (who had developed Betty Boop for Max Fleischer) on the animation of the title character. Joe Grant saw Davis's work and was anxious for the young artist to join his Character Model department. This area worked with artists to develop and approve the way characters looked, but also developed story material and generally functioned as a Disney "think tank."

Davis was more intrigued about *Bambi*, entranced by its poetic story, and captured

1 Marc's first screen credit, on *Bambi*, reads "Fraser Davis."

by its naturalism and focus on anatomical credibility in its animation. "They're not animal but they're not human," Davis explained to author Bob Thomas. "They're somewhere in between. But they're also not a person in an animal suit. They're something unique all to themselves."

He spent three years doing character design and storyboards for the feature, and Walt was impressed by the drawings. Davis was promoted to animator and he spent the next three years, working closely with Milt Kahl and Frank Thomas as his "tutors," in that role. "That's how I became an animator," Davis said humbly. He is credited with developing the characters of young Bambi and Thumper, and his skills with personality animation provided a breakthrough on that film, which played a key role in making it a success.

Because of his versatility, Marc was often involved in character and story development as well as animation, working on most of Disney's animated features and many short subjects. He was involved with the Goofy cartoon *African Diary* and the Donald Duck short *Duck Pimples*; and the special shorts *Adventures in Music: Melody* and its Academy Award–winning sequel *Toot, Whistle, Plunk and Boom*. He also worked on such features as *Song of the South, Fun and Fancy Free, So Dear to My Heart, Cinderella, Alice in Wonderland, Sleeping Beauty,* and *One Hundred and One Dalmatians*.

"Marc was a true Renaissance man and an amazing talent who helped to define the art of animation and raise it to incredible new heights," Roy E. Disney says. "His abilities as a draftsman were second to none, and, as a result, he often took on the most complicated assignments."

"Because of my expertise in the development of characters and figure drawing," said Davis, "Walt had me create characters such as Tinker Bell, Sleeping Beauty, Maleficent, and Cinderella." He earned a reputation for being Disney's "ladies' man" because of his memorable female character creations. His reputation as a "ladies' man" extended to Davis's animated social life. The artist had developed into what John Canemaker termed "a sophisticated bon vivant." His taste for pretty girls was so celebrated that even Walt was known to tease Davis about his wolfish reputation. At the start of World War II, Davis married an attractive woman named Marion, who later worked for bandleader Bob Crosby, but the marriage only lasted three years. "We just grew apart," Davis said, "and that was that."

Beginning in 1947, Davis taught advanced classes in drawing at Chouinard Art Institute one night a week, a responsibility he relished and continued for more than seventeen years. It was there that he met Alice Estes, a fashion and costume design major and artist. "He had quite a harem," Alice admitted. Her charms, beauty, intelligence, and talent captivated her professor. They remained friends, and were married nine years after their meeting—remaining so for forty-four years.

After the completion of *One Hundred and One Dalmatians* in 1961, Davis had no imminent assignments at the Studio. In fact, there was serious discussion of closing the Animation Department. "They contended that it was too expensive, took too long, and so on, and said that Walt should discontinue cartoons and animated features," Davis told *The E Ticket* in 1989. "When Walt was going to discontinue cartoons, he knew my drawings, so he wanted me to work on something for Disneyland. One of them was Nature's Wonderland. Then he wanted me to look at other things, including a 'pirate show.'"

It might seem that an artist at the top of his form in the animation medium might consider this idea of a reassignment a demotion, an insult, or a vote of no confidence. But Davis was canny in his understanding of what was actually being communicated by Walt about his trust in the artist, and Davis was excited by the unique opportunity. "I guess it was working with Walt himself. There was something about him as a personality. When he liked what you were doing, you felt good. You bet on him," Davis said.

Davis was sent to Disneyland to give a critical review to Mine Train through Nature's Wonderland. This was a train ride through the American Southwest wilderness and the Painted Desert, with a large cast of somewhat crude, pre-Audio-Animatronics mechanical animals—more than two hundred of them.[2] The first thing Davis noted was that the passenger cars

2 It is said that Walt was so dissatisfied with the show quality of the attraction that he had even taken the show drawings home and had a crack at redesigning them himself.

did not provide the best view of the animal tableaux, and he suggested that the seating be rearranged. As far as the animals themselves, Davis found that they were simply on display, without storytelling relationships to their surroundings or each other. "They had no gags in it, no story at all," Davis said. He soon restaged and reimagined several of the show scenes to Walt's abundant satisfaction. "He was buying everything I'd done," Davis said, "and was quite intrigued with it." The attraction remained a favorite until it was closed for the construction of Big Thunder Mountain Railroad in 1977. Davis had found a perfect application of one of his key talents. Imagineer Tom Morris explains: "This guy knew how to stage a scene, or any kind of business, and make it a quick, if not classic, 'read.'"

Davis also soon became immersed in Walt's new passion for Audio-Animatronics. Walt explained to Fletcher Markle in a 1963 interview: "You see, our whole forty-some-odd years here has been in the world of making things move, inanimate things move." The idea of dimensional animation was at the core of the Disneyland idea, but the idea for the ambitious aviary show in Adventureland came from an animated mechanical bird Walt had picked up at an antique store in New Orleans. Why couldn't he use the latest electronics technology to create life-size birds that could put on a show at the Park? Walt Disney's Enchanted Tiki Room got its lengthy name from the fact that there was already a Tiki Room Restaurant in Pennsylvania, and the Disney show was originally designed as a dinner theater. Guests would be seated in a large dining room and served Polynesian fare while the amazing Audio-Animatronics show went on all around and above them. Financial and operational impracticalities removed the dinner show, but the attraction was quite unlike any other that audiences of the time had ever seen. Davis contributed dozens and dozens of sketches, character, action, and story ideas for the birds, flowers, and Polynesian accoutrement of the attraction. "I have long had an interest in oceanic art, so I knew what I was looking for," Davis recalled. "I designed those 'talking totem poles' and the walls, and all of those things that came to life there."

Davis was off and running at WED; everything he contributed to each successive attraction seemed to create a greater reaction from the boss, and generate more enthusiasm for the shows from the creative teams. Davis soon found himself immersed in all four of the Disney shows for the 1964–1965 New York World's Fair. Marc continued to bring his manifold talents in story, character situation, and humor to works, and contributed to the Ford Magic Skyway, the General Electric Carousel of Progress, and Great Moments with Mr. Lincoln. "It was rough," Davis recalled of the Fair activities that consumed the Disney organization, "and the most terrible thing was that Walt wanted to do these [Audio-] Animatronics figures and they had to be pretty sophisticated."

"Walt told me he wanted to build Abraham Lincoln," Davis said. "He knew I knew a lot about anatomy and things, so I went ahead and put these drawings together." Davis's drawing sequence shows Lincoln standing up, and going through the different movements that Lincoln would need to go through in his performance. He leans forward and begins to rise, maintaining his center of gravity. The breakthrough for credibility with the Lincoln figure came when the design team divorced their thinking from both the historical human being on which it was based and the technology by which they were executing their replica. "We weren't building a mechanical man," Davis stated, "we were building an illusion. An illusion of a man. That took a while to soak into me, and into everybody else."

On "it's a small world," Davis brought characters into form from Mary Blair's colorful and graphic styling and Rolly Crump's oversize toys. Again he brought charm and humor to animated character tableaux for countries around the world through the most basic suggestions of staging and movement. Dutch children recline atop giant tulips, clicking their wooden shoes together; an Indian girl and boy dance with a happy tiger; and a kilt-clad Scottish boy plays bagpipes while a Scottish girl dances a Highland fling.

Enervated by the smashing success of his complex presentations in New York, Walt returned from the Fair with more ambition than ever for the opportunities that existed for this new kind of storytelling within Disneyland. Certainly the Fair attractions would find permanent homes in the Park, but the lessons learned in story, show technology, and ride systems could be applied to creating exciting, all-new attractions.

Well, not exactly all-new—two show concepts that had existed for many years were actually re-invented based upon the lessons of the Fair: the "pirate show" and a long-standing plan, dating back to a 1951 Harper Goff drawing, for a "haunted house."

The idea of a "pirate show" in its earliest form had been planned as a "museum of piracy" and a wax museum, meant to showcase both historic artifacts and tableaux with static figures of famous pirates such as Blackbeard, Henry Morgan, and Jean Laffite. "So I designed a walk-through pirate ride, all the way through,"

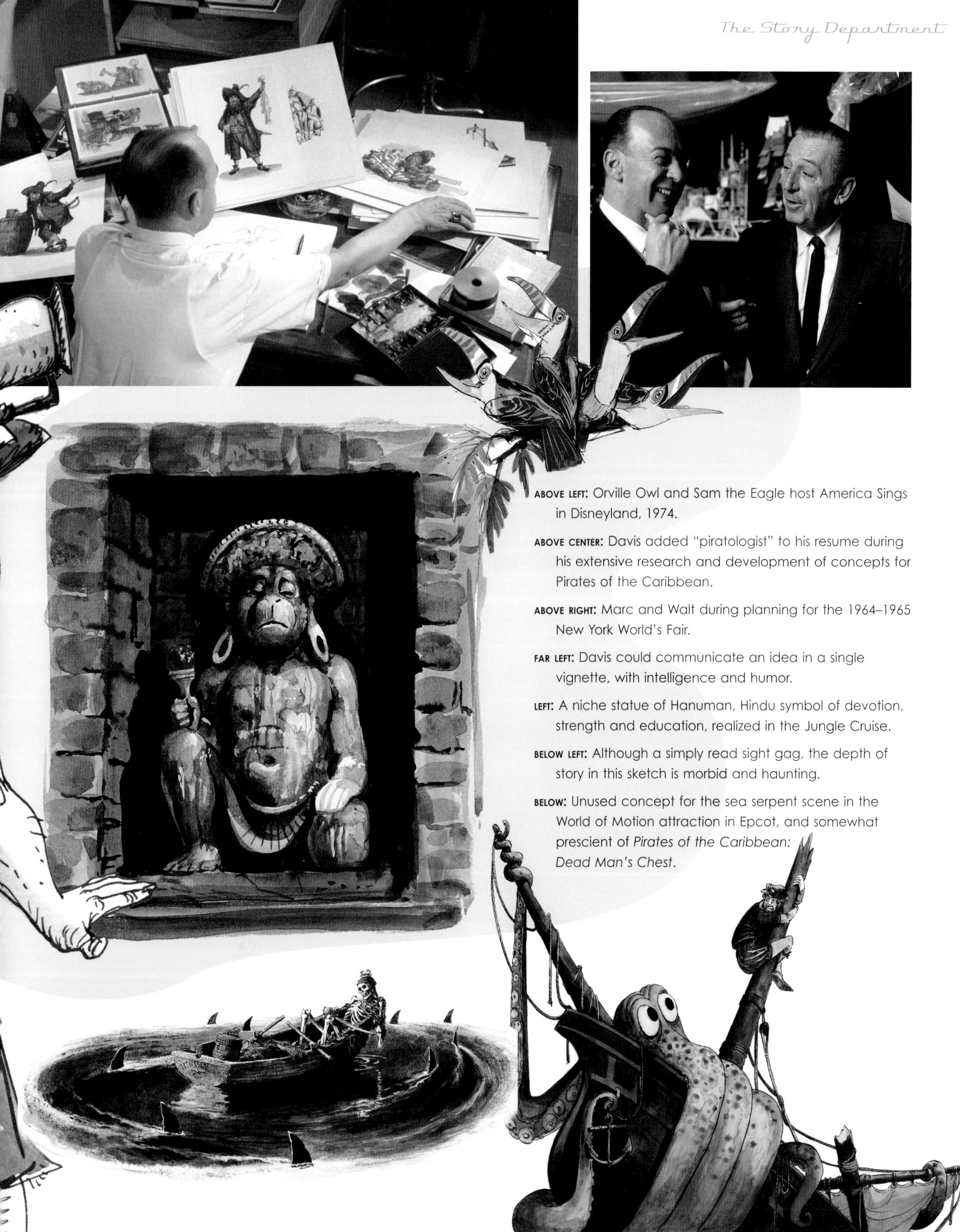

ABOVE LEFT: Orville Owl and Sam the Eagle host America Sings in Disneyland, 1974.

ABOVE CENTER: Davis added "piratologist" to his resume during his extensive research and development of concepts for Pirates of the Caribbean.

ABOVE RIGHT: Marc and Walt during planning for the 1964–1965 New York World's Fair.

FAR LEFT: Davis could communicate an idea in a single vignette, with intelligence and humor.

LEFT: A niche statue of Hanuman, Hindu symbol of devotion, strength and education, realized in the Jungle Cruise.

BELOW LEFT: Although a simply read sight gag, the depth of story in this sketch is morbid and haunting.

BELOW: Unused concept for the sea serpent scene in the World of Motion attraction in Epcot, and somewhat prescient of *Pirates of the Caribbean: Dead Man's Chest*.

Davis said. "It was done so it would be behind glass, and each section that you would come to would be a scene, and it would light up as we told the story of each particular sequence." Now that the Audio-Animatronics process had survived its baptism by fire, and the boat flume of "it's a small world" had proven operationally successful, Walt scrapped the pirate museum and decided to reconceive the entire show. Davis would play a central role in developing this ambitious new attraction called Pirates of the Caribbean.

It is interesting to note, given Walt's proclivity for team-building, the composition of the Pirates of the Caribbean show production. He certainly must have recognized that Davis's swift ascent in the realm of theme park design had created a certain tension within the ranks of the Imagineering staff that had preceded him in the medium. Yet he put Davis, with his strong sense of character, staging, and easily communicated "gags" in a leading project role. Alongside Davis, Walt put Claude Coats, who had been at WED since 1955. Coats and Davis had something of a creative rivalry, since Coats was as skilled at storytelling through creating a sense of place as Davis was at doing so through character. Walt quite probably knew that together they would drive the new pirate show to greater experiential heights than anything before. Today, Pirates of the Caribbean remains a touchstone of dimensional environmental experience. Davis felt the show owed much of its success to its reliance on strong story and characterization: "If you see the 'Pirate' ride or something of that sort in Disneyland, the one common denominator between that and film animation will be story—a storytelling situation."

While Pirates of the Caribbean was entering construction, Walt came to Davis with the idea of creating some of his specialized show scenes beside the Disneyland Railroad route, acting as a sort of "marquee" for the key attraction of each of the Park's lands the train was entering. "I did a whole flock of them," Davis said, "and one I did was this 'trapped safari' with the rhinoceros and all those guys up the post, and Walt just loved the thing. He said, 'Marc, that's too goddamn good to use out there. Let's put that in the ride.'" Several of Davis's humorous new scenes were incorporated into the Jungle Cruise during the early 1960s. "Well, you know I missed the first five years in Disneyland," Davis said, "I came down and kind of looked at things critically, and said to myself, 'I think I can help this stuff.' Humor and amusement—I think people want that. You know, it's easy to do the heavy aspects, but it's hard to do the funny stuff."

The Haunted Mansion was similar to Pirates of the Caribbean in that it had been in concept development for ages, and Walt called for a complete reconception after the New York World's Fair. In fact, Marc Davis began putting his first concepts together in July of 1964.

It was also similar in the demands it made on the Imagineers who created it, and the same creative tensions were at play—mood and humor, place and character. Phantoms of the dead and piracy were similarly grim subjects, and a balance would have to be struck. However, one critical team member was missing when the attraction reached its final design phases—Walt himself. The end result for The Haunted Mansion was an anecdotal feeling. The entry area establishes a mood of foreboding and eeriness, followed by haunted portraits in an elevator that reveal their punch lines as the room stretches. An entry corridor once again establishes a setting of decay and a mood of dread, but decorating this haunted hallway are humorous portraits by Marc Davis. The endless hallway and attic featured setting and mood, while the ballroom and graveyard spotlighted character and humor.

After Walt's death, there was no "last word" to make the final decisions about which elements of the story took priority, or how the elements might function together to create a greater whole. "They put practically everyone that was at WED at the time on the thing, eventually," Davis said. "A lot of my stuff ended up in there because I was the one producing entertainment. If I had a complaint about how The Haunted Mansion project was organized, I would say that there were too many men of about equal standing working on different parts of the ride at the same time. I think I supplied most of the ideas, but it was done in a kind of group decision process."

Davis's last two significant attractions saw the artist taking over the project lead, and creating two memorable shows that were all about character and performance, with little or no attention at all to setting and environment. Country Bear Jamboree was born out of Walt's suggestion to Marc that the artist take a crack at "something with bears" for a Disney project called Mineral King, a planned resort development in the Sierra Nevada mountains of California. Working with animator and story man Al Bertino, Marc created a simple, multiproscenium auditorium with rotating turntable stages, featuring a hillbilly bear band and a country collection of animal performers. Although the Mineral King project was abandoned (the property became part of Sequoia National Park), the show was revived for the Frontierland area of Magic Kingdom Park in Walt Disney World in 1971.

America Sings was Davis's final, most personal, and favorite of all his Disney works. Again teamed with Al Bertino, the project was created to replace the Carousel of Progress in Disneyland, while still using the unique rotating carousel theater. The pair came up with a whirlwind tour of two centuries of American musical history told in a twenty-four-minute show. Davis designed the 114 new Audio-Animatronics cast members for the revue, which featured thirty-nine musical selections in a six-act show representing what the men had identified as the four major

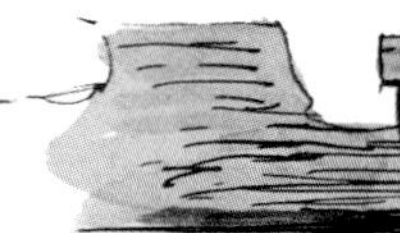

LEFT: This sketch of a trapped safari led to an infusion of humor in the Jungle Cruise, 1964.

ABOVE: Walt and Marc Davis "confer" with one of the Audio-Animatronics performers for the Ford Magic Skyway attraction at the New York World's Fair, 1964.

BELOW: Rabbit and Fox flee the oncoming "Fireball Mail" in a scene from the America Sings attraction, 1974.

cultural and geographic styles of American music. The hosts were an avuncular Audio-Animatronics eagle named Sam, voiced by Burl Ives, and his avian sidekick, Ollie Owl.[3] With hundreds of music cues, moving scenery, and the revolving auditorium, the show presented more programming, timing, and technical challenges than any other attraction to that date.

The result was undiluted and absolute Marc Davis. The artist considered this attraction exemplary of his finest work, and it was the purest representation of his unique amalgam of anatomy, caricature, animation, staging, and humor. The attraction opened in 1974, and was a cornerstone of Disneyland's celebration of the American Bicentennial in 1976. Many of the Imagineers, however, were always uncomfortable with the cartoon fantasy of America Sings in the heart of Tomorrowland, and the attraction was closed in 1988.[4] Marc Davis was angry ever after about the cavalier way his theme park magnum opus was more or less thrown away from Disneyland.

Davis remained at Walt Disney Imagineering until his retirement in 1978. He returned to Imagineering as a consultant on World of Motion for Epcot, and numerous attractions for Tokyo Disneyland.

Late in his life, Davis was honored with many distinctions and awards. In 1989, he was honored at the Annecy Film Festival. In 1992, the Academy of Motion Picture Arts and Sciences paid tribute to his career, and the Academy has conducted an annual "Marc Davis Lecture on Animation" since 1994. The International Animation Society, ASIFA, also presented him with their top honor, the Winsor McCay Award.

"Marc Davis was also a very versatile artist and had an incredible sense of line," Tom Morris says. "Staging, of course, everybody knows that, but I also think he had an amazing command of color and form, and is not given enough credit for that." His impressive artworks included such diverse subjects as bulls and bullfighters, dancers and harlequins as well as the warriors and jungle life of New Guinea. Davis collected artifacts from New Guinea, and his evocative New Guinea paintings have been collected for a forthcoming book, *The Bite of the Crocodile*. "The people and country are fascinating—it's the last great primitive culture the world will ever see," he said. "I'm trying to document it for posterity." He had also completed an unpublished book on the anatomy of motion. Marc Davis passed away January 12, 2000, following a short illness. He was eighty-six years old.

Davis remained fairly unsentimental about his association with Disney, instead tending to focus on the techniques, methods, styles, and personalities involved in the artistic processes there. He was also disinclined to great sentiment about his boss of forty-four years. "I didn't seem to have much trouble with him," Davis said frankly, "and during those last years, I think I became closer with him than at any time in my career. Roger Broggie once said that the wonderful thing about Walt was that he was such a 'quick study.' You only showed him how to do something once, and he knew it from then on. This also made him a very difficult man to work with at times. At one point he said to me, 'Well, that wasn't what you said to me three years ago!' That could be a desperate situation to work in, because it was incredible how he could stay ahead of you."

3 A decade later, in somewhat altered and streamlined form, Sam became Sam the Olympic Eagle, the cartoon mascot of the 1984 Summer Olympics in Los Angeles.

4 Nearly a hundred of the various animal figures were relocated from America Sings to be adapted into new characters for Splash Mountain.

Claude Coats: A Gentle Giant

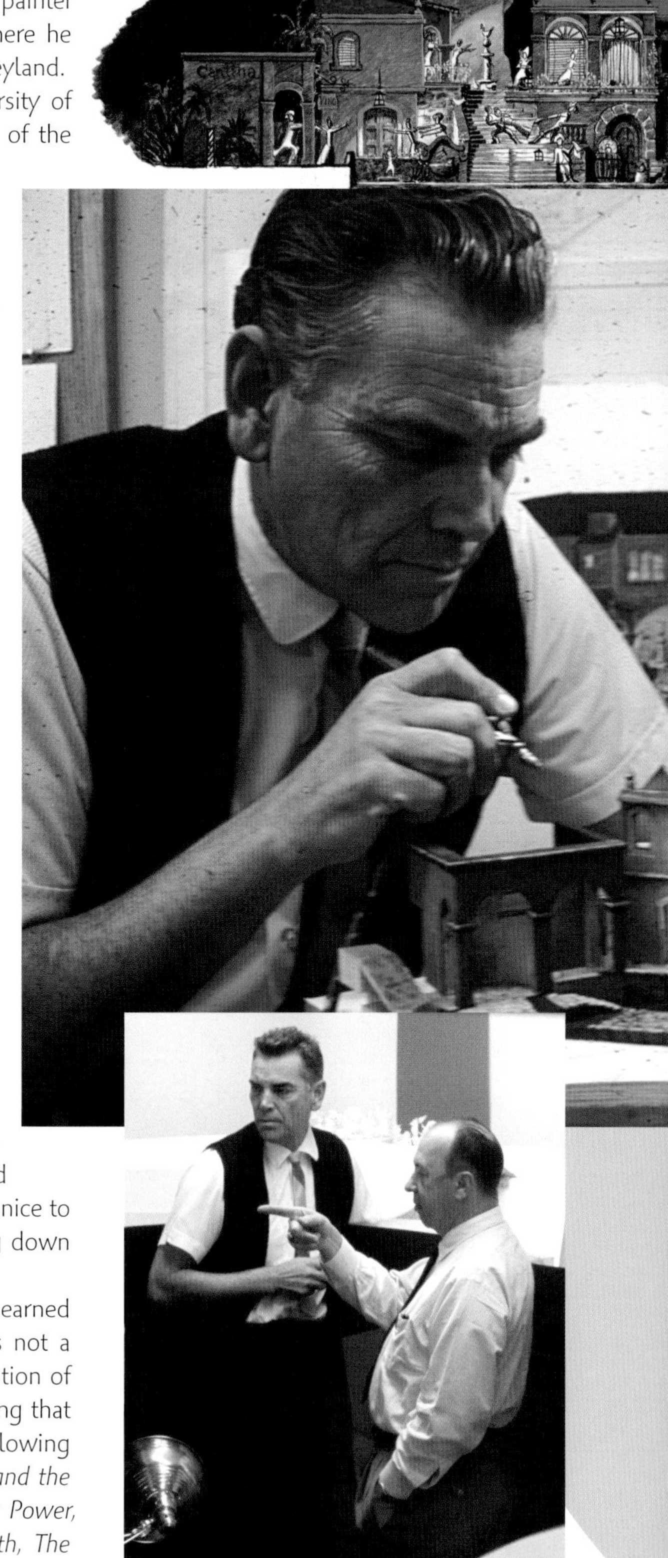

The gold ring on his left hand had the image of Mickey Mouse and the date, 1935. That wasn't a birth date, it was the year that Claude Coats went to work at the Walt Disney Studios. He stayed with Disney for fifty-four years, beginning as a background painter and color stylist in Animation. In 1955, he transferred to WED Enterprises, where he contributed to the evolution of Disneyland, Walt Disney World, and Tokyo Disneyland.

Coats was born in San Francisco in 1913, and graduated from the University of Southern California in 1934 with a BA in architecture and fine arts. A member of the California Watercolor Society, he studied watercolor painting with Paul Sample and Dan Lutz. After his graduation, he began exhibiting with the California Watercolor Society. He was active as a watercolor artist for the next decade.

At the suggestion of his friend Phil Dike (one of the leading California Style watercolor artists beginning in the early 1930s, and a color consultant, designer, and instructor for Walt Disney Studios), who had seen Coats's work at a watercolor gallery show, Coats went for an interview at Disney's Hyperion Avenue Studio in 1935. Ever a pragmatist, Coats prepared by painting several examples of what he considered to be appropriate backgrounds based on the Disney cartoons he had seen.

Coats was hired as a "background apprentice" during a time of enormous change and growth at the Studio. The worldwide success of Mickey Mouse and the Silly Symphony short subjects charged the organization with excitement, and the anticipation of the creative breakthroughs in the latest project, *Snow White and the Seven Dwarfs*, meant an increase in new staff and daily innovations in the animated art form. Walt even gave his employees art lessons in order to improve the work that bore his name.

Even as Coats began in background painting, the nature of that art was being changed. Ken Anderson created vivid new colors and detail in the background designs for *Ferdinand the Bull*, and *The Old Mill* redefined the appearance of the Disney cartoon through its realism and depth through the use of the Multiplane Camera. Coats quickly became a master in backgrounds, stepping up to each new challenge with ingenuity and skill.

During early preproduction of *Snow White*, Coats met a pretty young "Ink & Paint Girl" (the employees who applied the ink and paint to animation cels were exclusively female) and began courting her. In 1937, Claude Coats and Evelyn Henry were married, and built a house in Burbank, not far from the location of the new Studio, where they would raise two sons, Alan and Lee.

Quiet, humble, and self-effacing, Coats stood in contrast to many of his rather boisterous and self-motivated colleagues at Disney in those days. His soft-spoken manner and gentle nature earned him a reputation as a thoughtful and reasoned gentleman, to the point where even Walt took notice. "Walt was always nice to Claude," Evie Coats says. "He knew that Claude was sensitive. Instead of putting down something Claude was doing, he'd suggest an alternative."

The high standards of quality in his work and his collaborative spirit earned Coats a reputation as an abundantly talented and generous colleague. He was not a "showboater"; his focus was on the end result of a collaboration, not the glorification of his own art. "I believe from working in Backgrounds that the animation is the thing that really tells the story, and the background has to support all of that." Over the following twenty years, his credits in background and color styling included *Snow White and the Seven Dwarfs, Pinocchio, Dumbo, Fantasia, Saludos Amigos, Victory Through Air Power, The Three Caballeros, Make Mine Music, Fun and Fancy Free, Song of the South, The Adventures of Ichabod and Mr. Toad, Melody Time, Cinderella, Alice in Wonderland,*

Peter Pan, and *Lady and the Tramp*. Even though he had had a hand in every significant animated project in the first two decades of Walt Disney Feature Animation, in 1989 Coats remarked, "I didn't realize it at the time, but a lot of this was pretty boring work compared to show design at Imagineering."

As the opening of Disneyland drew closer, Walt began to pull more and more of his Studio staff into the fray in order to be ready for opening day. "And so I guess I had a break in my background work where I wasn't busy, so I got to do the model for the Mr. Toad attraction," Coats said of his first step toward Imagineering. "When I had finished the model, Walt took a look at it and okayed it."

"Claude paved the way in turning sketches and paintings into three-dimensional adventures," says Marty Sklar. Coats had seen how much further design concepts went with Walt if the boss could see them. Sculptures of key characters had long been a part of the animation process, and models of the clocks from *Pinocchio* and Ken O'Connor's detailed dimensional model of Cinderella's pumpkin coach had quickly solidified the team's thinking on these ideas. Coats could now take his experience with animation settings and likewise bring it into dimensional reality and a true spatial interaction with the characters. "I greatly admired his style and his versatility," Imagineering show producer Tom Morris says. "He was one of the pioneers in spatial problem solving for our rides, especially considering constraints of space and money."

Coats recalled that Ken Anderson's storyboards had shown that the Peter Pan and Snow White attractions could be told in a way that communicated a sense of the story, and gave the visitors a feeling that they were experiencing perhaps more than they actually were. Part of this success had to do with an exceptional utilization of a very confined building footprint. "Those dark rides were crammed into little garage spaces, and the fact that they work as well as they do is another example of creative resourcefulness," Morris says. "The Walt Disney World and Tokyo Disneyland versions are larger—but not better."

"There really has never been, and there still isn't anybody his equal in laying out a ride. This ability to understand how things were going to work dimensionally helped him as a leader, to hold the overall concept of a project," Marty Sklar adds.

It was at this time that Coats began to create his work in three dimensions, a talent that enthralled his colleagues. Of course, like all acts of genius, this only makes common sense, since he was moving from a two-dimensional medium to a three-dimensional one. "Some of his paintings for *Pinocchio* are fabulous, and I was astounded because he really didn't do much painting at Imagineering," Sklar says. "Walt saw how Claude could translate his talents into three dimensions, and not everybody could do that."

"'Stay hands on,' he used to say," Tony Baxter adds. "'Don't kid yourself with a rendering.' He was aware that you can exaggerate in a painting, but he worked almost exclusively in models in order to make sure that whatever he was conceiving was really going to be practical."

Again, the looming deadlines of Disneyland's opening helped push Coats toward the exit of animation, and the entrance to a new career. The scenic design studio that had been hired to paint the "dark rides" in Disneyland realized that they could not handle the whole job, and Ken Anderson and Coats were recruited as de facto scenic painters for Mr. Toad's Wild Ride. "So, having painted cel-sized backgrounds for twenty years. I went from a foot-high format to sets that were eighteen feet high!" Coats said. Roger Broggie laid the ride track down in the corner of a soundstage at the Studio, and Coats and Anderson got to work on Mr. Toad. "So we got our feet wet in a big hurry," Coats recalled. "We had the mock-up, and brought it down and installed it in Disneyland, and we were ready for opening."

Coats was also working in the relatively new medium of fluorescent paint under black light. Long before the groovy posters of the 1960s and 1970s made black light common, Coats and his contemporaries were experimenting with applications and techniques to add show value to the rides in Disneyland. The interior sets for these rides were originally made of two-dimensional images painted on theatrical flats and cutouts, which hearkened to their origins as animated cartoons. Coats's use of black-light paint techniques helped increase the illusion of dimensionality. "The rides wouldn't be nearly as good if they were under incandescent, regular light, because they're not large enough," Coats explained.

Something else that should be noted about Coats was his stature, not as an artist, but as a man. At six feet, six and one-eighth inches tall, Coats tended to tower over his colleagues. Imagineer Blaine Gibson recalled: "He was a heck of a tall guy, and whenever we went for a walk down in the Park, I had to take two steps to his one." Coats himself remembered when the Disneyland Stagecoach was

TOP: This scenic elevation by Coats for Pirates of the Caribbean incorporates settings, color, and lighting.

ABOVE: Coats translating the scenic elevation into a three-dimensional model.

LEFT: Claude Coats and Marc Davis, 1966.

ABOVE: All signs point to a successful project, no matter what the science says.

ABOVE LEFT: Walt and Coats discuss scene staging with the elaborate model of Pirates of the Caribbean, 1966.

FAR LEFT: The Grand Canyon, including wild turkeys.

LEFT: The construction of the Submarine Voyage in Disneyland, 1958.

BELOW: A storm brews over the Grand Canyon in a mural painting based on Coats's magnificent concept illustration, 1958.

completed at the Studio, and Walt and a driver were giving rides around the lot. "He wouldn't let me get in," Coats said with a laugh. "He said I spoiled the scale."

In 1956, Coats and effects wizard Yale Gracey responded to Walt's enthusiasm for the promise of fluorescent dyes that could be added to water. They proposed an idea to expand the Mine Train to incorporate a trip inside Rainbow Caverns, where the water pools and waterfalls would flow in brilliant fluorescent color. "I had one waterfall planned for the finale that had all six primary colors falling side by side in one big, wide waterfall," Coats explained. "The water was in separate troughs, but as they hit the bottom, we wanted them as close together as we could, so they were separated by a very few inches."

At the time, Ward Kimball was at work on the *Man in Space* TV series at the Studio, and rocket scientist Heinz Haber looked at Coats's fluorescent water scheme. Haber told Coats that his "rainbow" would turn gray in a week, that keeping the water colors apart was statistically unfeasible. When Coats told Walt that no less authority than Heinz Haber had told him that their new project was impossible. Walt shrugged his shoulders and responded, "Well, it's kind of fun to do the impossible." Coats and Gracey created a series of bevels, grid work, and baffles, with the glowing water flowing through a rubberized hog's hair material that eliminated the splash and overflow. These Imagineers did the impossible, and for twenty years the fluorescent rainbow falls glowed in Frontierland. "That was a good example of what Walt meant by 'imagineering,'" Coats said. "It means that some imagination all by itself doesn't get anywhere, and engineering all by itself isn't very entertaining."

Coats worked with Studio matte painting expert Peter Ellenshaw on a Tomorrowland attraction called Space Station X-1, which involved a huge view of the United States from a "space platform." Much like Ellenshaw's original painting of Disneyland, created for the debut of the TV show in 1954, this image changed from a "daylight" view to a "nighttime" view through the use of fluorescent paint under black light.

Walt was always looking for ways to add interest to existing attractions in Disneyland. Long before the landscape elements and development around the perimeter of the Park were built up, he was concerned that there wasn't much to see on the Disneyland Railroad. His solution was one of the world's largest dioramas, presenting a 300-foot-wide pictorial view of the scenery, animals, flora, and foliage of the American Grand Canyon. Real (taxidermied) animals, including a mountain lion, porcupines, skunks, a golden eagle, and mountain sheep, populate the realistic settings that are dotted with preserved aspens and pine trees. The environments change through snow, a cloudburst complete with rainbow, a sunset, and a parched desert. The diorama backdrop is painted on a 306-foot-long, 34-foot-high seamless handwoven canvas, and reportedly required 4,800 man hours to complete, using 300 gallons of paint in fourteen colors. ("That was a great, big background," Coats said.) The diorama is scored by "On the Trail" and other strains from Ferde Grofe's Grand Canyon Suite.

Walt asked Coats to visit Arizona to do research for the diorama, and the artist dutifully returned with hundreds of photographs, sketches, and assorted research materials. The team created storyboards, as was usually the case with any idea presented to the boss. "Walt went along with pretty much everything I had in there," Coats recalled, "until he got to the turkeys." Coats had put a scene of mountain sheep with wild turkeys roosting in a foreground tree trunk. Walt insisted that there were no turkeys in the Grand Canyon. Coats assured Walt that he had seen the turkeys in the museum there, Walt just frowned and muttered, "I didn't know that." A few days later, Walt was showing the Grand Canyon storyboards to some visitors, when Coats suddenly heard Walt shout: "ARE YOU SURE ABOUT THESE TURKEYS?" Luckily, Coats had called the park ranger after Walt's first inquisition, and was able to assure him that not only were there turkeys in the Grand Canyon, but their flocks were on the increase.

For the 1958 Alice in Wonderland attraction, Coats was the show designer for the entire project—the concepts, story, track layout, backgrounds, and even the ride vehicles. Coats had originally designed a vehicle made of playing cards like those in service to the Queen of Hearts, but Walt didn't like it. Walt said, "Do a caterpillar," so Coats did, sketching a design that Blaine Gibson sculpted. "Later the Legal people came around and they had a patent application for it," Coats recalled. "And I said, 'Well, I didn't do it. It's Walt's idea.' Nevertheless, Coats had done the record drawing, and received United States Patent Number 187,036 in his name. "I think they gave me ten dollars to sign the patent over to the Studio," Coats laughed.

Coats also did concept drawings, storyboards, and models for the Submarine Voyage, which surfaced in Tomorrowland in 1959, helping develop the underwater scenes and environments—and again applying his finesse with fluorescent paints.

When Walt created show pavilions for the 1964–1965 New York World's Fair, Coats was right in the midst of the design teams for the Ford Wonder Rotunda featuring the Magic Skyway, General Electric Progressland featuring the Carousel of Progress, and "it's a small world." Of course, the next big project represented something of a career pinnacle for everyone involved in it, Coats included. He remembered coming back from the Fair and hearing that the "pirate museum" walk-through was now going to be a water flume ride like "it's a small world." Coats's experience fitting ten pounds of attraction into a five-pound bag in the Fantasyland dark rides was immediately put to use. "I started getting information on track radiuses and so forth, and we tried to fit everything into that little model. One morning I came into work and Walt was standing by my little quarter-inch model." Walt saw the challenge Coats was facing, and immediately realized that the wealth of good ideas for Pirates of the Caribbean would never fit in the existing basement. "We should start all over again," Walt conceded. "We'll just make a grotto out of this part in the front." With a tunnel leading out of the grotto and into a show building constructed outside of Disneyland's protective berm, the Imagineers had a blank parchment for their pirate adventure.

Coats worked as an art director and designer, creating the swashbuckling environments and settings for character tableaux that were by and large created by Marc Davis. Coats's set designs were both inventive and evocative, as was his particular emphasis on dramatic lighting. "Light is the thing that always focuses attention," Coats said. "In backgrounds, it is done with shadows and lighting, and it's a way of giving a feeling of space around an animated character."

Coats understood the design balance of creating a memorable setting that still allowed its players to be the center of attention. Pirates of the Caribbean contains an exceptional and complex overall set design. "Luckily, I had studied architecture at USC," Coats said in a 1982 interview, "and I had a degree in fine arts, but I was really more interested in the art end than the engineering part of it. For the twenty years I spent at the Studio doing backgrounds, I thought in terms of mood and color and the way you tell that part of the story, with the colors and shapes and emphasis on where you wanted people to watch, and what you wanted them to see, and that's really the same thing in the rides."

"Claude was superb at creating environments, Marc was superb with the characters," Imagineer Tony Baxter says. "When Walt was there, he made them work together and they created Pirates of the Caribbean, which has unbelievably great characters and a fabulous environment."

Adventure Thru Inner Space, which also opened in 1967, was a Claude Coats tour de force, just as America Sings was for Marc Davis. It was an ambitious attraction with a difficult task—to make the complexities of molecular science understandable and interesting to a broad public. The premise of the attraction was to send Omnimover[5] cars and their passengers into the Mighty Microscope, shrinking them into the molecular makeup of a snowflake. The success of the show depended upon selling the ideas through interesting and effective environments so the attraction scenes communicated setting, scale, and mood, since the featured "characters" were actually the ride passengers who needed to believe that they were truly being reduced in size.

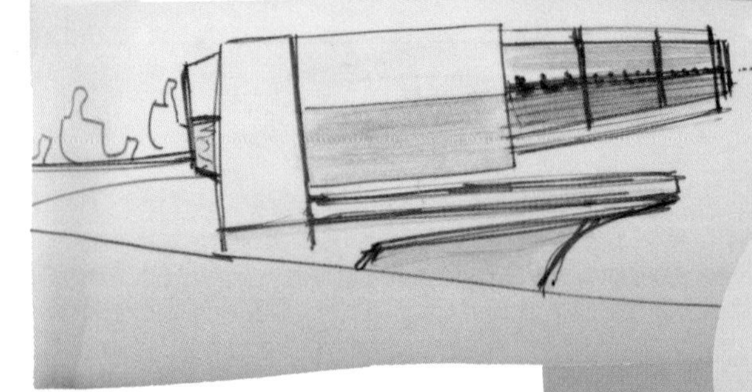

Coats's next project, The Haunted Mansion, presented many difficulties in design and execution, most importantly the loss of its "director," Walt, before it was completed. As has been noted, the resulting show sways back and forth from mood and setting to character and comedy, without the feeling of an overall story with a beginning, middle, and end.

"Marc Davis had made a whole lot of interesting drawings, so many that we weren't able to use them all. The best ones seemed to drift to the top, and everyone seemed to be satisfied with the final selections," Coats graciously recalled. "Marc would work up drawings and I'd find space to put his ideas into the show." The gentlemanly détente between Davis and Coats has been alluded to for decades, the inference that they got along, but somehow resented each other. Davis's comments about Coats are somewhat more clinical. "He was a background man, and he studied architecture at USC," Davis said of Coats, "His work was very commendable. He would do the settings for things, the environment within the attraction. I guess he did the framing, and I did the dancers within the frame. He was a nice fellow."

Blaine Gibson remembers: "I used to admire Claude's painting, over at the Studio, and I always thought his facility in a rather broad range of art techniques was just amazing. He would carry an idea through enough steps so others could visualize what the concept was. I think Claude was a very receptive guy, and yet he had strong ideas in his head and eventually they would always come out right. He was an easy guy to work with, and had a wonderful disposition. He could make room for others' ideas, but he never lost sight of the overall plan on a project."

"After Walt died, everybody kind of worked on their own," Tony Baxter says. "So Claude did rides that were environments but without any characters, like Adventure Thru Inner Space and If You Had Wings; and Marc did things like Country Bear Jamboree and America Sings, which had a lot of characters but a very thin environment. I found it interesting to see that when Walt was alive he was able to pull everyone together, and I think that was his great talent: to be able to get everyone to work together in harmony."

---

5 The Omnimover ride system was created by Roger Broggie and Bert Brundage to give passengers a motion picture-type experience in which the line of sight of the rider is controlled. The term was coined by Imagineer Bob Gurr and is a portmanteau of OmniRange and PeopleMover.

After Walt's death, Coats worked on the Mickey Mouse Revue and numerous attractions for Magic Kingdom Park in Walt Disney World, many of them reiterations of Disneyland attractions he had worked on before.[6] For Epcot, Coats worked on the Universe of Energy, Horizons, and World of Motion; while at Tokyo Disneyland, he contributed to Meet the World and the Cinderella Castle Mystery Tour.

Coats also liked to talk about what he called his "Never Never Land" projects, because they were rides, shows, and attractions that were "never, never" built. A few of them are the Dorothy of Oz Birthday Party, Candy Mountain, Fantasia Mountain, Uranium Hunt (complete with Geiger Counter and low-grade Uranium), World of Science, Garden of the Gods, Arabian Nights, and World Showcase pavilions for the Philippines, Venezuela, Brazil, and Russia.

More importantly, during this time, Coats began to pass on his expertise in the arts of Imagineering to a new generation of artists and designers. Part of his daily routine was to amble the corridors of Imagineering, a foam coffee cup cradled in his giant hand, and "make the rounds" discussing projects, art, current events, or personal problems with the younger Imagineers.

"I don't think there was anybody at the Disney organization, especially at Imagineering, who was more of a mentor than Claude was," Marty Sklar agrees. "He just helped everybody. Young people gravitated to him, and he would show them what the Imagineering business was all about."

"I appreciated Marc Davis who is a great animator," Tony Baxter says, "but Marc was very much in control of his designs. He knew what he wanted and he did every bit of it himself—the color, the painting, the styling. Claude, however, was much more open to young people. He was in his sixties when I was just out of school, and he would say, 'Well, what do you think about this? What do you think if we did this or did that?' He would say: 'Why don't you take that back to your desk and work on it, and then I will come and see how you are doing.' He would let you do your own design and he would say, 'Oh, that looks good, let's use that.' I thought, 'Wow! My idea is actually going to be used! My scene in Snow White, my spiderweb, my scene with the dwarf mine, or whatever it was, in a Disney attraction.' Claude was my mentor, but he never acted like my boss," Baxter says.

After fifty-four years with Disney, Coats retired from Walt Disney Imagineering on November 30, 1989. An avid traveler, his first journey after retirement was "a few weeks in Antarctica" in February 1990. Coats died of cancer on January 9, 1992, at the age of seventy-eight.

Claude Coats's uncanny ability to visualize ideas with clarity, skill, and beauty made him a good fit with Walt Disney. "Working with Walt was really easy," Coats recalled. "If you could show him exactly what he wanted to see," he added with a wry smile.

TOP: The hilltop castle of Cinderella's Prince Charming was visualized by Coats for the 1950 film, and became part of the Storybook Land attraction in 1956.

LEFT: An early concept sketch of the Mighty Microscope (top) and the final product in action in Disneyland (bottom).

RIGHT: Walt, the story man, during construction of Storybook Land in 1956.

6 Mickey Mouse Revue was relocated to Tokyo Disneyland in 1983.

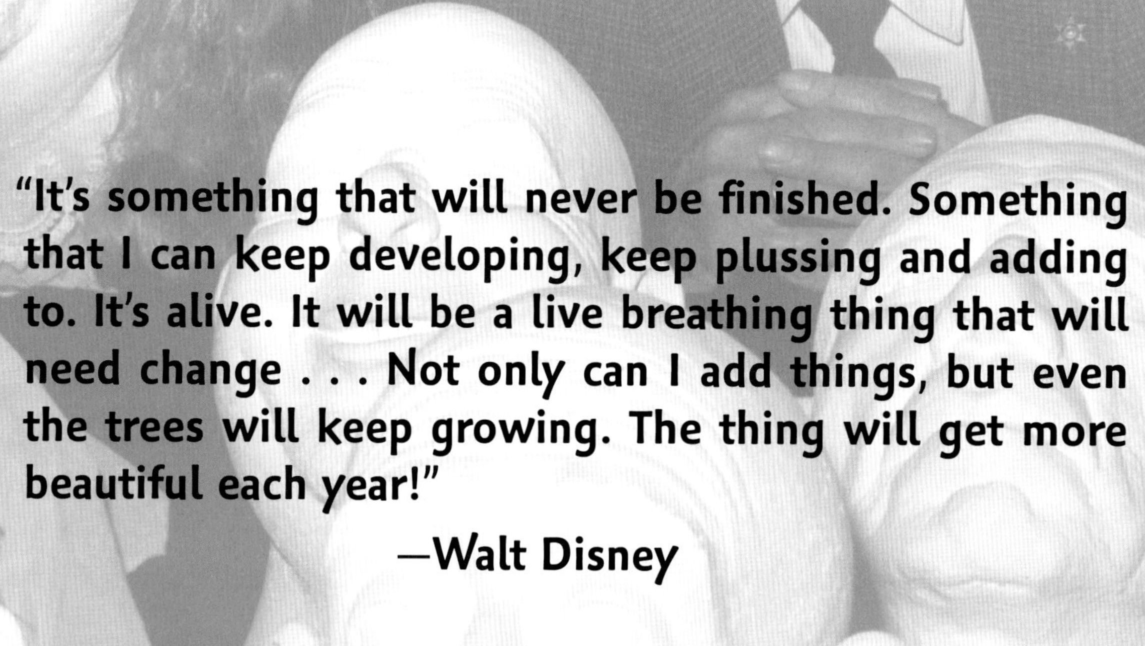

"It's something that will never be finished. Something that I can keep developing, keep plussing and adding to. It's alive. It will be a live breathing thing that will need change . . . Not only can I add things, but even the trees will keep growing. The thing will get more beautiful each year!"

—Walt Disney

Walt knew that the details were what made any of his projects work as a whole. In animation, it was not just the draftsmanship skills of an artist that made a film work, but also the designs of a stylist, the color palette, the backgrounds, the music, the voice casting, and any number of talents and crafts. In creating Disneyland, Walt approached his story in the same manner, but in animation he had never really needed a landscape designer, a dimensional illusion expert, or a kinetic artist. But it was his ability to seek out (and in many cases, to discover or encourage) this talent that brought the extra level of design sophistication and attention to detail that immediately set Disneyland apart from any other amusement enterprise in the world.

Morgan "Bill" Evans: The Living Palette Artist

In 1952, third-generation horticulturist Morgan "Bill" Evans was called upon to landscape the grounds of Walt Disney's Holmby Hills home, including the gardens that surrounded his backyard railroad, the Carolwood Pacific. Little did he know at the time, however, Walt had another "little" task percolating in the back of his mind, and in 1954, Walt asked Bill and his brother, Jack, "How about you fellows landscape Disneyland for me?"

Within a year, Bill helped transform eighty acres of Anaheim orange groves into lush theme park attractions. "We landscaped all of Disneyland in less than a year with a maximum of arm waving and a minimum of drawings," Evans said of the project.

His forthright approach and innate understanding of how landscaping fit into the art of place-making was a talent that must have not only pleased Walt aesthetically, but was a godsend to his evolving design and construction of Disneyland. Evans quite simply knew how to use his medium for storytelling. He was as much an artist with living plants as Marc Davis was with pen and ink or Blaine Gibson is with clay. Evans knew how to use his palette to inform and add to the overall story being told without his work taking center stage. His grasp of creating storytelling environment first evidenced itself to Walt in Holmby Hills, and continued for nearly half a century thereafter.

Born June 10, 1910, in Santa Monica, California, Bill's first botanical classroom was his father's three-acre garden, which was filled with exotic plants, including 150 varieties of hibiscus collected by his father. In 1928, Bill joined the Merchant Marine, and while he traveled the world aboard the SS *President Harrison*, he gathered exotic seeds for his father's garden from distant lands including the West Indies, South Africa, and Australia.

Upon return from duty, Bill studied at Pasadena City College, followed by Stanford, where he majored in geology. His education was cut short by the Great Depression, and in 1931 he helped transform his father's garden into a nursery business—Evans and Reeves Landscaping.

TOP: Bill Evans in 2001.

ABOVE: Bill (right) describes to Disneyland Pony Farm manager Owen Pope how he plans to transform orange groves into a convincing jungle in time for the opening of Disneyland, 1955.

Their inventory of rare and exotic plants soon caught the attention of Hollywood's elite. Among their celebrity clientele were Greta Garbo, Clark Gable, Elizabeth Taylor, and, ultimately, Walt Disney. Evans was eager to import, and was an enthusiastic propagator of, numerous subtropical species of trees, shrubs, vines, and bamboos. The Evans and Reeves nursery in West Los Angeles became a weekend destination for avid Angelino gardeners. Indeed, Evans's love affair with plants changed the landscape of Los Angeles. One of the several examples are the hundreds of South African Flowering Coral Trees that grace San Vincente Boulevard through Brentwood. The three islands off Long Beach, California, where swaying palms and tropical landscaping camouflage the presence of oil derricks, is another of Evans's designs.

This last project relates to one of the key storytelling ideas contained in Disneyland. Often it is not only the story that is being told that is important to the experience, it is the function of the storyteller to exclude distractions from the key narrative. Thus, Walt and Evans created the "berm," which is simply a twenty-foot-high mound of earth completely surrounding the Park. The separation was further effected by dense plantings of trees and shrubs on top. Today, this berm forms a created horizon for many of the vistas from inside Disneyland.

BELOW: Evans on the Walt Disney World property with Richard Irvine, Card Walker, and John Hench, 1967.

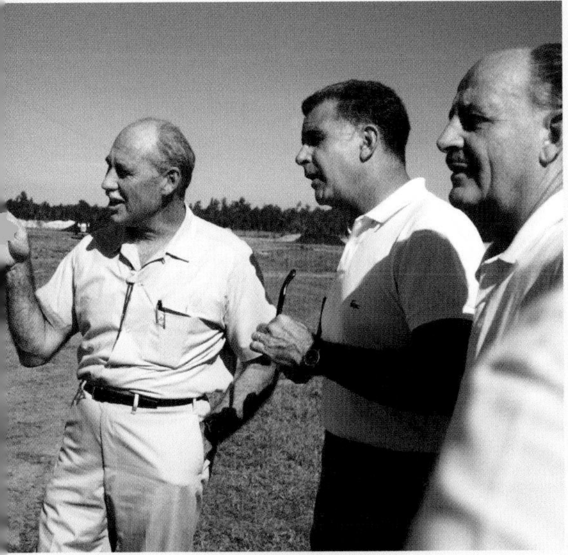

Landscaping in Disneyland followed in the wake of the bulldozers that reshaped the flat "tabletop" of former orange and walnut groves into rivers, canals, hills, and valleys. "First came the big trees," Evans wrote, "their roots packaged in heavy boxes. Some weighed as much as twenty-two tons. Then came the smaller trees, shrubs, vines, and the irrigation systems to supply the rainfall for these plants from faraway lands. At the last minute came the flowers (already in full bloom from the greenhouses) and the grass, which was unrolled, carpetlike, as fully established lawns."

The trees that Evans used in Disneyland could not, of course, be limited to the orange and walnut trees he found there. Shade trees of appropriate size and variety were needed, and Disneyland's needs soon exhausted the available supply of mature trees from local commercial nurseries. However, just as the expansion of the Southern California freeways promised easier access to Walt's new amusement enterprise, they also left something in their wake: thousands of unwanted trees. Evans and his crews worked in advance of many of the freeway construction routes, and handily removed a wide variety of mature specimens from the jaws of the bulldozers.

In Disneyland, nothing presents Evans's calling card more succinctly than the Jungle Cruise. "What we endeavored to do was to create what the armchair traveler might envision as a 'jungle experience,'" Evans said. "We picked out material from Brazil, material from Africa, material from India and Asia and Malaysia, and pushed it together. It's all quite compatible in the sense that it all has that lush, that vigorous growth, really strong growth." In complete accord with Walt's thinking was Evans's attitude toward what might have been a quite showy botanical exhibit. "What we attempted to do in planting this jungle was to make it look as if we had nothing to do with it."

In this project, Evans not only brought plants back to the United States from locations around the world in order to get just the right effect; he also used plants in unusual ways. As former Imagineer Terry Palmer explains, "In the Jungle Cruise, there's a group of orange trees that most people would never recognize, because Bill planted them upside down. He decided the gnarled roots of the orange trees looked like suitably exotic jungle branches." With its canopy of bamboo, ficus, and palms (that today towers seven stories overhead), the two-acre man-made jungle was described by Evans as "the best darn jungle this side of Costa Rica."

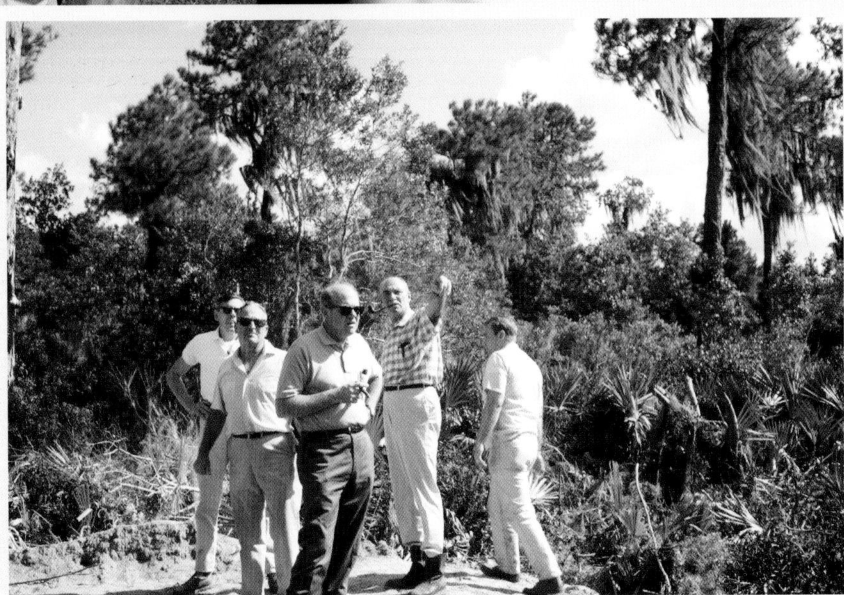

ABOVE: From swamp, Scrub Pine, Spanish Moss, and a freakishly high Florida water table, Evans created Disney magic.

"I accosted that orange grove in Anaheim and planted a eucalyptus tree when it was about the size of my little finger in caliper," Evans said in a 1980 interview, "and now that tree is fifty feet high or better, with a massive trunk. A really handsome tree. I mean, it has dignity, this is a beautiful tree. This is something that wasn't in Anaheim thirty years ago, and look at this tree now. I literally wrapped my arms around the trunk of that tree. I love that tree. It's a beautiful tree. It has embraceable bark, I should point out."

Evans once said, "I certainly feel that trees are living, breathing individuals. They're alive and respond to the elements. A building doesn't yield to the breeze. I can see the life in the trees by the way they move. We have some giant bamboo in the jungle that grow to a height of thirty or forty feet, and in the breeze, you get an effect like a ballet dancer."

Evans also created a new twist on an ancient horticultural art at Walt's urging. "Topiary goes back about three thousand years," Evans recalled in 1983. "It's an ancient art. Well, it takes about fifteen years to get those trees into any kind of recognizable shape. That wouldn't do for Walt, so he asked us if we could speed up the process a little bit." Evans created new methods of bending, tying, training, and shearing ordinary specimens such as olive trees and eugenia into recognizable shapes. Evans shortened the topiary timetable to a few years instead of a few decades, and the sculpted character shrubbery has become a standard component of every Disney park around the world.

Former Walt Disney Imagineering director of landscape design Paul Comstock (whose father, also in the landscape business, knew Bill for forty years) asserts that the landscape of the continental United States would not be the same without Bill Evans. "In Hawaii, he took a cutting of a tree and started a plant at the place he stayed when he was there. He talked the gardener there into taking care of it until he returned the following year. When it was big enough, Bill just smuggled it back to California on the plane. In fact, there are at least thirty to fifty plant species now common in the trade that wouldn't be here if Bill and his brother Jack hadn't smuggled them in from Central and South America."

After Disneyland opened in 1955, Bill stayed on as a consultant, drawing landscape plans, installing plant materials, and supervising maintenance of the Park's flora. In 1956, he was named director of landscape architecture, working on Disneyland additions as well as the master plans for Walt Disney World and especially Epcot. "Bill Evans defined Disney theme park landscaping, and trained just about everyone who has created theme park stories in living environments," says Marty Sklar.

In 1975, Bill retired from Disney, but was summoned back to consult on the landscape design of Tokyo Disneyland. Additionally, he consulted on the schematic designs of Disney's Polynesian Resort, Discovery Island, Typhoon Lagoon, and Disney Studios, among other elements of the Florida resort. He was also fundamental in selecting plant material for Disneyland Paris, Disney's Animal Kingdom Park in Florida, and in planning the landscape palette for Hong Kong Disneyland, which opened in 2005.[1]

PLEASE
DO NOT FEED
ANIMALS

In Hong Kong, the landscaping is a culmination of the effort and experience of Evans and all of his several protégées. A number of the trees are flowering varieties never before seen in the area. And for the first time, Disney's landscape designers have used species known primarily for their fragrance. Because Hong Kong residents traditionally have a strong interest in horticulture, Disney designers made a great effort to appeal to this love of growing things. Many of the plants are natives of southern China (such as the Chinese banyan tree), while others come from Africa, India, Australia, and New Zealand.

The storytelling through horticulture in Hong Kong Disneyland is perhaps more multilayered and sophisticated than any nascent Disney park. Among other treasured trees are pohutukawa trees used by the Maori in New Zealand as a place to lay the ashes of a departed loved one. Maori believe the deceased one's soul rises through the bright red blossom to the afterlife. A pohutukawa is planted in front of Sleeping Beauty Castle.

In her book *The Making of Disney's Animal Kingdom Theme Park*, Melody Malmberg recounts the three-part philosophy of this master landscaper and acknowledged leader in the field. "The first consideration was guest comfort—shade and shelter. The second was screening visual intrusions—creating

1 Bill even landscaped the entry area of the Walt Disney Imagineering headquarters in Glendale, California.

ABOVE: Square trees at Le Château de la Belle au Bois Dormant in Disneyland Paris.

LEFT, CLOCKWISE FROM TOP LEFT: A long view to the Alpine foothills in Disneyland, Florida flora in Walt Disney World, topiary animals growing backstage in Walt Disney World, Jungle Cruise in Tokyo Disneyland, Evans and disciple Paul Comstock.

CENTER: Evans in Epcot in 1989.

BELOW: Bill ponders and plans the landscape of the future, 1965.

a berm, a ring of earth and vegetation surrounding the park to hide the real world; or using strategic planting that camouflaged a building or electronics or lighting. The third principle was telling a story through landscaping—creating the right look for the setting, from the mixed broadleaf forest of Tom Sawyer's Mississippi River banks to the serene gardens of Japan."

Evans was the author of the 1965 book *Disneyland: World of Flowers*, devoted to the Park's famed flora, and he wrote many articles on horticulture and landscaping for horticultural publications. He was a fellow of the American Society of Landscape Architects and served on the board of trustees for the Los Angeles Arboretum. For more than twenty-five years, he was a member of the Garden Advisory Board for *Sunset* magazine.

In 1996, Evans was honored by the Landscape Architecture Foundation with a Special Tribute award. According to Comstock, "Bill garnered an entire roomful of awards—probably every award the ASLA gives. Bill has also received awards from the American Horticulture Society and almost every other international horticultural, botanical, and arboreta organization.

"Bill defined 'Imagineer,'" continues Comstock. "He also defined 'gentleman.' And by his humble example—a simple comment or a single glance—he taught us what is right and what is wrong. Bill's vast living professional contribution is truly legendary along with his compassion toward people, plants and animals." Paul Comstock learned much of his craft under Bill's tutelage. "On a tour of the botanical garden on Kauai, Bill would quietly tell me things the tour guide didn't know," Paul recalls. "As people overheard him, they gradually started asking him questions—even the tour guide, who asked him more than anyone else. He had the entire group hanging on his every word."

Other colleagues encountered Evans's worldwide fame and reputation in unusual ways. When Tony Baxter was in Holland on a fact-finding trip, he tried to visit the gardens of Keukenhof only to discover that they had closed for the season. He explained that he was from Disney, but to no avail. Finally, Tony said, "Bill Evans sent me," and the groundskeeper let him right in and gave him a grand tour of the entire gardens.

"He has a gentle quality and he'll listen to you," former Imagineer Joe Parinella said in 1989. "He can gently redirect your thoughts in a better direction and push you into doing more. Bill made me realize that even when a project is done, it's not finished. You can always go back and add more; you can always go one better."

Until the time of his death at the age of ninety-two in 2002, Bill still walked through the tangled vines of the Jungle Cruise, checking out the flora, and offering the benefit of his extraordinary experience to a new generation of "Horticultural Imagineers."

Says Marty Sklar, "A walk through a Disney park with Bill Evans was a lesson in plant history, landscape storytelling, and Walt Disney do's and don'ts from one of the very few who could truly say, 'Walt told me . . . ' He taught generations of landscape architects how to do their jobs with passion, skill, and tender loving care," Sklar adds.

Sir Francis Bacon wrote: "God Almighty first planted a garden, and indeed it is the purest of human pleasures, without which edifices are but gross handiworks. And we shall ever see that as ages grow to civility and elegance, man comes to build stately sooner than to garden finely, as though gardening were the greater perfection."

"This was Bill's favorite quote," Paul Comstock says. "He made me memorize it."

Roland "Rolly" Crump: The Evolution of a Designer

"I think any description of me at Disney should be called 'the evolution of a designer,'" said Rolly Crump. "I was trained by Walt to try anything that he asked me to do."

Before his retirement from Walt Disney Imagineering in 1998, Rolly Crump enjoyed a career at The Walt Disney Company that spanned more than forty years. It began with Feature Animation and led up to a role as an executive designer, supervising such projects as the refurbishment of The Land pavilion in Epcot in 1994. Crump's varied career was a serendipitous combination of his own eagerness to stretch his artistic boundaries and Walt Disney's refusal to classify or pigeonhole the talents of his staff. "We all did a little of everything, because we weren't categorized," Crump recalls. "Walt never allowed us to be categorized. He always just said, 'My guys can do that,' and because of that, we all chipped in."

Crump's own philosophy about his life and art fit Walt's like a glove. He often expresses the wonder and delight that design and art inspire in him by saying that he got "turned on." Another Crump motto is "change is good," and expresses his genuine desire to grow as an artist. Not simply a casual belief to justify a change of scene, it truly defines Crump's career, and illustrates the fact that his Disney work is separated into three distinct periods. Each period was divided by several years, while he went out into the world to collect more experience, knowledge, skill, and insight, "like a worker bee whose queen is Design," says former Imagineer Danielle Burd.

Born February 27, 1930, in Alhambra, California, Rolly took a pay cut to join Walt Disney Studios in 1952. "At that time I was a head dipper at a ceramic factory, dipping plaster pieces into the glaze. But I always wanted to work for Disney because I liked to draw when I was a little guy. My mother said, 'Well, why don't you apply for a job?' So I did. I applied for a job as an in-betweener at the Disney Studios and they called me back and said, 'Yes, we'd love to hire you.' 'Fine,' I said, 'Okay, good.' And they said, 'Your starting salary is thirty dollars a week.'" This would have been wonderful if not for the fact that Crump was already making seventy-eight dollars a week as the head dipper—and his wife was pregnant with their first child. As is often the case, mother gave the sage advice. She said, "Honey, you always wanted to work for the company."

Crump took the job, but like many of his colleagues in the animation field who didn't make much money, he got a second job. On weekends, Crump worked with a friend building sewer manholes. "I mixed the mud and lowered the bricks and the mud to him so that I could continue working at Disney," Crump says. "Of course, it all paid off, because what I learned from the Company was absolutely unbelievable," he adds. "I only had a high school education and all of the sudden I was put into rooms with guys that were graduates of Art Center, Chouinard, all different art schools and colleges. And here Rolly is, you know?"

Crump was the last in-betweener hired on *Peter Pan*, and was promoted to assistant animator for *Lady and the Tramp*, *Sleeping Beauty*, and *One Hundred and One Dalmatians*. He worked alongside animator Wathel Rogers, who had a pushpin on his desk with a little propeller turning on it. "Every time I would go to have my scene checked, I would look at this little propeller," Crump says. "I was really intrigued with kinetic sculpture." After teasing Crump relentlessly for weeks about how the propeller worked, Rogers finally sold his kinetic wonder to Crump for a penny, and showed him how to make them.

Soon, Crump's entire room was filled with propellers. "After about six months I was making propellers all day long, and once in a while, I'd do a drawing," Crump says. Ward

Kimball saw Crump's propellers and told Walt, "You gotta see this guy's propellers." Walt came down one evening and saw the propellers and said, "You know, we oughtta get that kid to come work with us on the Disneyland project."

In 1959, Crump joined WED Enterprises. "I didn't have a clue what I was going to do, but I couldn't do propellers for the rest of my life," Crump recalls. "The nice thing about Walt was that he really believed in you." Crump's first project was working with Claude Coats on the Emerald City of Oz attraction (also known as Dorothy's Birthday Party in Oz) then in development. For many years, Walt owned the rights to all of L. Frank Baum's Oz books subsequent to the original *Wonderful Wizard of Oz*, and he tried to develop a feature film, television property, or Park attraction based on the books.[2]

When the Oz project was shelved, Crump joined illusion specialist Yale Gracey in developing early concepts for what would become The Haunted Mansion. "Yale Gracey and I were asked to design all of the illusions for The Haunted Mansion, and so we had this big room and we blacked out all of the windows. This was still in the Animation Building. We had skulls and skeletons and stuff all around the room. One of the things that we had was a great big monster that we painted with all kinds of things on it and a weird head. We'd take this gun and shoot the monster and the monster would blow up, the lid would come off, and there was some black stuff underneath and the head would come off and swing around the room. My wife made a China silk ghost that you'd put over a small caged fan and when you turned it on, the ghost would fill up and start shaking and everything. We were just playing around and didn't know how we were going to use it."

One day, Crump and Gracey got a stern call from the personnel department. Unnerved by the work going on in The Haunted Mansion room, the janitors had requested that they leave a light on. Gracey and Crump agreed. They left a light on—but they also rigged the room.

"Right in the middle of the room we had an infrared beam, and when you came in, the lights were kinda low, but they were on. When you broke the beam, the black lights came on, the real lights went off, the monster blew up, and up comes the ghost! We came to work the next day, and the ghost had been going all night long, and the head was hanging in the center of the room, and right in the middle of the floor was a broom."

Another harsh call from the personnel department followed. Gracey and Crump would be stuck emptying their own wastebaskets and cleaning their room. The janitor had sworn never to go back. "So this was it," Crump says with a grin. "No matter what you were doing, there was this little craziness that kind of stayed with you when you were doing stuff."

This freewheeling creative culture only evolved beginning in 1960, when WED relocated to nearby Glendale. In a small building on Sonora Avenue, free from the social structures and business formalities of the Studio, WED became a creative conclave so enjoyable that Walt soon began calling WED his "laughing place" (a reference to the 1946 feature film *Song of the South*).

"We had handstand-walking contests in the middle of the model shop. When I was in Animation, that was the rage, to be able to walk down the hall on your hands. I thought it was pretty cool, I could do that. Our lawyer came in and I said, 'We're having

2 The only public result was an unfilmed script titled *Rainbow Road to Oz*, which was part of The Fourth Anniversary Show broadcast on the *Disneyland* TV series on September 11, 1957; along with a series of popular Disneyland Records albums.

LEFT: Rolly Crump and Walt proudly display the kinetic Tower of the Four Winds, which marked the entry to "it's a small world" and became an icon of the 1964–1965 New York World's Fair.

a handstand-walking contest.' 'Well, can I enter?' He took his jacket off—I didn't realize that he had been a gymnast in high school, All-City. He jumps into a handstand and just goes all over the room. And that was our lawyer. We had some fun with that.

"We played Frisbee," Crump adds. "I want you to know that Blaine Gibson, who was our head sculptor, was the finest Frisbee player that we had. We had yo-yo contests at break times. I gave magic shows at break time. We just had a marvelous, marvelous time."

One of Crump's most memorable stunts is still talked about. "I had this motorcycle and I had been riding it at lunchtime. I came back in and I was getting ready to park it, when one of the secretaries said, 'You know, I've never ridden a motorcycle before.' So I said, 'Get on the back and I'll take you.' So I went through the building, right up to her desk and dropped her off. Dick Irvine, the lead art director, opens up the door, looks out, and says, 'Oh, it's just Rolly,' and shuts the door."

Crump soon found himself responsible for his first solo assignment as a designer, supervising the refurbishment and expansion of the Adventureland Bazaar retail shop in Disneyland. He was provided a team of five carpenters, five painters, and a budget of $38,000. He also had access to Disneyland's "boneyard," a salvage collection of objects, architectural embellishments, and other castoffs from other refurbishments or demolitions. Much of the haphazard, improvised interior design that made the Bazaar feel as if it was located on the edge of nowhere was achieved through the cost-saving use of these castoffs. (Today, Disneyland visitors can still see turned Victorian posts from the long-demolished Swift Chicken Plantation restaurant at the corners of the back cash wrap of the Bazaar.) Crump did most of the design and drawings in a somewhat "seat-of-the-pants" fashion, right on site. "I worked for seven days a week for six weeks, driving back and forth to Disneyland in a little Volkswagen," Crump remembers. The night the Adventureland Bazaar reopened, the rumpled and unshaven Crump was greeted by none other than Walt Disney and his wife, Lillian. Ignoring the fact that Crump looked like something that had crawled out of the jungle river across the road, Walt proceeded to show off the young Imagineer's work. "Walt was really sweet, as he walked through the new Bazaar and pointed things out to Lilly," Crump recalls fondly. "It was very spontaneous and fun."

Crump's next major project was Walt Disney's Enchanted Tiki Room. "I remember—and these are the things

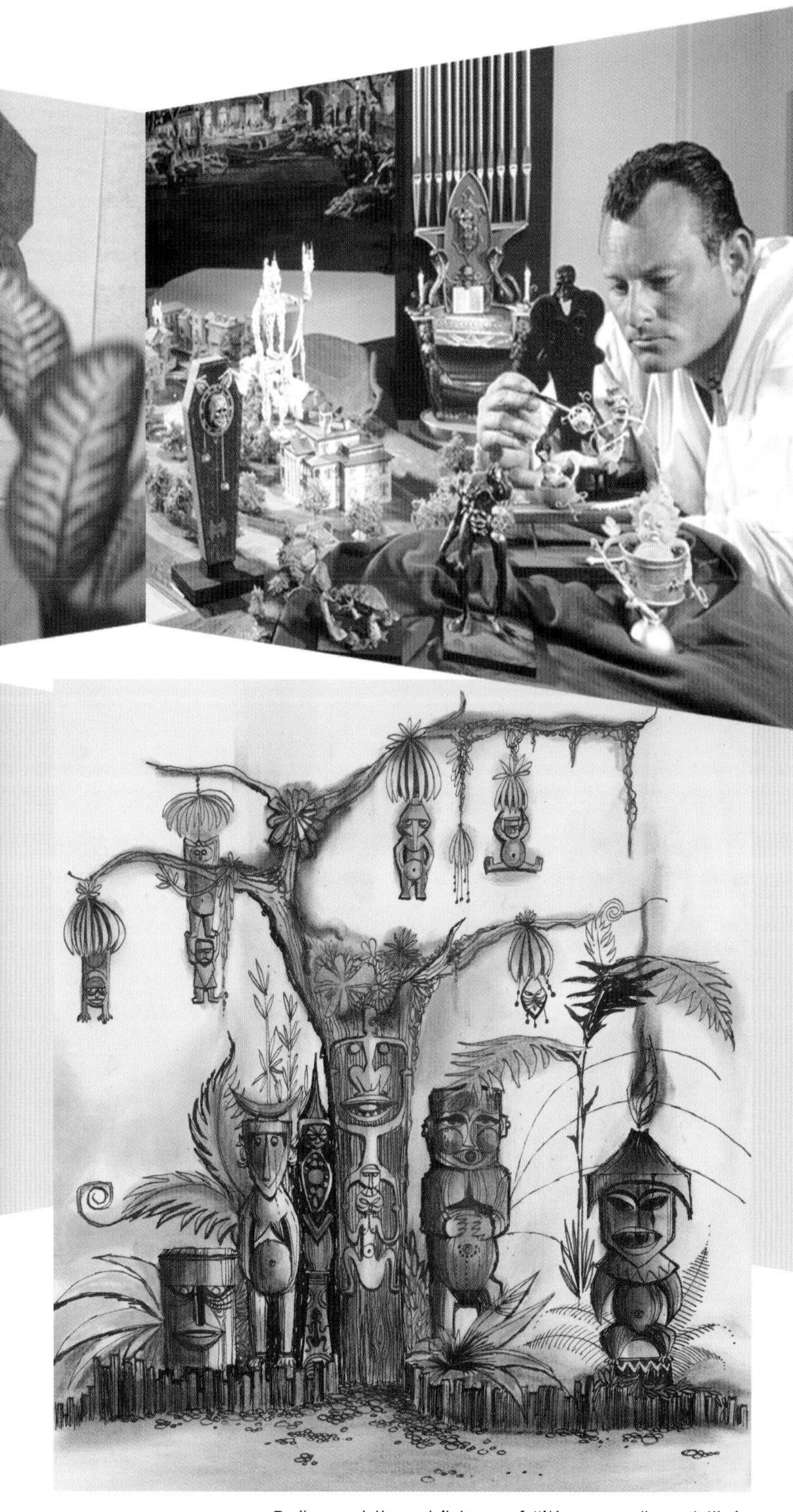

TOP, LEFT TO RIGHT: Rolly and the children of "it's a small world"; in 1980 developing The Land for Epcot; and in 1966 designing the Museum of the Weird (never realized) for The Haunted Mansion.

LEFT: Marc Davis and Rolly review concepts for "it's a small world."

ABOVE: Rolly's concept sketch for the Garden of the Gods pre-show at Walt Disney's Enchanted Tiki Room.

that I remember that are so special—our sitting in a room with Walt when he would come up with an idea. And then all of a sudden it was one of the attractions in Disneyland," Crump says. "Being there when the idea was first kicked off was very special."

"Walt said, "I want to do a little Tiki Room. I just want a little Tiki-Tiki Room for over in Adventureland. We're redoing Adventureland.'" John Hench was asked to do a rendering of what the Tiki Room would look like, a beautiful painting of birds in cages and the restaurant interior. Crump remembers, "Walt took one look at it and said, 'John, you've got birds in there.' Hench said, 'Yeah,' and Walt said, 'Well, you can't have birds in there, they're going to poop in the food!' Yeah, he really said that."

Hench explained that they were not real birds, but stuffed birds, but Walt immediately replied, "Disney does not stuff birds." Hench replied, "No, no, no. They're little mechanical birds that cheep." Walt said, "Well, maybe they can cheep and cavort with each other."

"And that's how we started the Tiki Room," Crump says. "Then all of a sudden we started to develop the works of these little guys and the sounds and everything," Crump says. "So all of a sudden that was in production." This is one of Crump's fondest memories of how Imagineering worked under Walt. A spontaneous idea led to action, not discussion.

Walt assigned Crump to design Tiki sculptures for the pre-show in the restaurant's outdoor waiting area. Crump began drawing sketches, and researched the gods and goddesses of the islands of the Pacific. "In the Orient, they have these fountains where they drip water into a little piece of bamboo and when it fills, it dumps," Crump says. "And when it comes back, it hits a log and scares the rabbits and the deer away. I thought, 'Yeah, I'll do that.'

"I'm showing all these pictures to Walt," Crump recalls. "He looks at them and says, 'Are these all authentic, Rolly?' I said, 'Yes, sir, they are.' 'What's that the god of?' He pointed right to the one with the bamboo—and I didn't know what to say. Luckily, John Hench was standing next to me and said, 'That's the god that tells the time.' When the meeting was over, John said, 'You'd better go find out who the god is that tells the time!' which I did. It's Maui."

Maui and the other Tiki Garden sculptures designed by Crump were just quick sketches, which the boss approved. "Build 'em," Walt said. Crump took his designs to lead sculptor Blaine Gibson, who said, "Rolly, I'm too busy. I don't have time for that." Crump asked, "Well, who's going to sculpt them?" Gibson replied, "You are." Crump had never sculpted before, but Gibson explained how to build armatures, and how to put the plasticine clay onto that structure, what the best tools were—and Crump added "sculptor" to his resume.

When the sculptures were completed, Crump sent them to Disneyland where they were molded and rendered in fiberglass. The Disneyland shop returned them, and Crump painted them himself. "Then I took them to Disneyland, and I actually took a wrench and installed them. If you were to have that done today, you'd probably have about fifty people. There would have to be renderings done and engineering done. In those days, and that's why I call them my naïve days, we just did it. We did whatever it took to do it. In those days, again, there were only thirty of us and that included the janitors and the people who worked in the accounting department and everything. It was marvelous."

Crump was a key designer on all the Disney attractions at the 1964–1965 New York World's Fair, including "it's a small world," for which he created oversize toys and props, and helped translate Mary Blair's art style into dimensional reality. "Walt called us in one day and said, 'We have one piece of real estate left over at the World's Fair, and I've got a little idea for a boat ride.' A little boat ride? What was this all about? We had done Mr. Lincoln. We had done Carousel of Progress. We had done all of this high technology, and he wants to do a 'little boat ride.'"

Nine months to the day later, the Imagineers installed "it's a small world" at the Fair. "Nothing has ever been done in that time frame, that quickly," Crump says, "And that was because we had Walt. If you were asked to do something by Walt, everybody stepped away—management stepped away. It was between you and him to get this thing done. So, we did. We got it done."

"We actually had it constructed in Los Angeles," Crump says. "We had all of the [Audio-] Animatronics figures made at the machine shop at the Studios. And then we built the sets, lit them, and put in the sound system. Then we set it up dry in one of the soundstages at the Studios and we pushed Walt through in a boat on wheels at the right speed so he could look at it like he was really on the ride. And once he bought off on it, off to the Fair it went. We all got shipped off to help install it, which was an exciting time."

The WED culture survived its transcontinental voyage completely intact. "One morning we came in, and they had put soapsuds into the trough and we had foam going through the whole ride," Crump says. "So we had to spend the whole day to clean the foam out. Two days later, we came in and the trough was filled with koi. In the middle of the night, someone had gone next door to the Kodak pavilion and stolen the koi and brought them over and stuck them in the ride trough."

Although Crump continued to grow as an artist and expand his repertoire of skills, Walt called on his interest in kinetic sculpture to create one of the most memorable icons of the 1964–1965 New York World's Fair—the Tower of the Four Winds. The elaborate and colorful twelve-story, 200,000-pound structure featured dozens of propellers and revolving mobiles, many of which were shaped like animals from around the world such as lions, llamas, birds, and turtles. "The mobile represents the boundless energy of youth," Walt said.

When "it's a small world" was relocated to Disneyland in 1965, Crump supervised not only the renovation and reestablishment of the attraction into a more generously proportioned building, he also translated Mary Blair's whimsical new facade design into a working model.

After the Fair, Crump returned to WED and continued as a designer. He worked for some time on continuing concepts for The Haunted Mansion, such as the Museum of the Weird, "a place where strange and unusual artifacts that had been collected around the world were kept." It would serve as a spillover area for people waiting to enter The Haunted Mansion itself. The idea came from Walt's review of several of Crump's more surreal drawings, including a kinetic Gypsy cart, a coffin-shaped grandfather clock, a chair that would rise and speak to visitors, and a burning and melting "candle man." After Walt's death, the Museum of the Weird concept was shelved.

Crump also worked on the 1967 Tomorrowland, and served as Disneyland's Chief Designer, working at the Park itself to improve its overall design appeal and exterior lighting, and serve as a liaison between WED and Disneyland. "There was kind of an 'Iron Curtain' between the two organizations, and Park requests were not getting priority at WED," Crump says. He worked with the department directors in Disneyland and created a design order system. Their needs for renovation, rehab, or lighting were

formally submitted as work requests. "Then I would hand carry it to Dick Irvine, answer questions about the project, and then 'mother hen' it to completion." Crump was later involved in the initial design for Magic Kingdom Park in Walt Disney World in Florida. He also developed the story content and set design for the 1970 season of the "Disney on Parade" traveling arena show. "At that point, they brought me back to do 'it's a small world' for Walt Disney World," Crump says.

Crump left Disney in 1970 to consult on a number of projects, including attractions for Astroworld (Texas), Busch Gardens (Florida and California), Ringling Brothers Barnum & Bailey Circus World (Florida), Knott's Berry Farm (California), and the ABC Wildlife Preserve (Maryland).

With Epcot development under way, Crump returned to Imagineering in 1976 as the project designer for The Land, and later, Wonders of Life. He also participated in master planning for the expansion of Disneyland.

In 1981, Crump again took leave of Imagineering to pursue a number of outside interests, including leading a design team on a proposed Cousteau Ocean Center in Norfolk, Virginia, and a term as president of his own design firm, the Mariposa Design Group (which he bought from Warner Communications). With Mariposa, he was involved with projects ranging from mall entertainment in Alberta, Canada, and Sherman Oaks, California, to an international celebration for the country of Oman, to a Portuguese theme park.

He continued to design and direct an impressive list of restaurants, shopping malls, and numerous theme parks and outdoor entertainment projects around the world until his 1992 return to Imagineering where his son, Chris, was an Imagineering show designer—and a chip off the old block.

Crump now lives in northern San Diego County, where he enjoys growing flowers and avocados in his free time. He feels great good fortune to have worked with such an array of talent, and particularly the man who brought them together.

"I think the secret to Disneyland is that there were so many different designers that it became this wonderful melting pot of styles. If you really look at that group within WED, and in Disneyland, you'll see an incredible team. Walt seemed to know how to get the correct group of people together, and it worked. He was like the coach of a team. He spoke to us each individually and never played favorites. After we lost Walt, as time went on, the team evolved and became something different. Walt was in charge and knew what he wanted. He knew how to get it done."

Rolly's team spirit and lack of ego has garnered enormous respect from his colleagues. Former Imagineering show writer Jim Steinmeyer says, "The idea is king with Rolly. It doesn't have to be his vision, as long as it works."

For himself, Crump found Imagineering to be the greatest of academic endeavors. "I was trained by Walt to try anything that he asked me to do. I hadn't done any of the things that I did at WED, but neither had Walt when he built Disneyland. It was a constant educational program, and one thing that Walt taught me was never to be afraid when you're handed a project. Just take it and go with it."

TOP: Crump and Walt share a laugh while discussing the clock tower designed for the permanent home of "it's a small world" in Disneyland.

BOTTOM: Crump presents a series of concepts for an early version of the Life and Health pavilion in Epcot, 1984.

Yale Gracey: The Illusioneer

It is odd but appropriate that the acknowledged master of illusion at Imagineering also seems to be the most mysterious. Not because Yale Gracey and his life are deeply inexplicable, but because of all the essential Imagineers, Gracey has had the least written about him and the least serious analysis of his art and expertise. Always interested in devising gadgets and building models, animation artist Gracey's office at The Walt Disney Studios in Burbank was always cluttered with some of his lunch-hour experiments.

The son of an American consul, Gracey was born in Shanghai, China, in 1910. He attended an English boarding school and after graduation moved to the United States. Like so many children of transient residence, Gracey was compelled to look to himself for amusement and activity, as friendships were most often brief. He faithfully read *Popular Mechanics* magazine whenever he could and he was the proud owner of a set of the popular *Boy Mechanic*[3] books originally published in the mid- to late teens. Another hobby was magic. Gracey attended art school in San Francisco and at the Art Center School of Design in Los Angeles.

In 1939, Gracey joined Disney as a layout artist working on the animated classic *Pinocchio*, after which he was an art director on *Fantasia* and a layout artist on *The Three Caballeros*. During this period he also acquired further art training at the Art Institute of Chicago, the University of Southern California, and Chouinard Art Institute. He also contributed to the layouts and backgrounds of more than fifty animated shorts between 1944 and 1956, most featuring Donald Duck.

Rolly Crump describes Gracey as something of a "Geppetto," always at work tinkering with little gadgets, miniature objects and models, illusions and effects. He would often construct set pieces for no particular reason other than to satisfy his own curiosity and to see whether he could get things to work.

One Saturday afternoon, as Walt made his rounds through deserted offices to see what his staff was working on during the week, he came across one of Yale's gadget mockups, featuring an illusion of falling snow. Walt was impressed, and since Gracey enjoyed miniature making, Walt's own special hobby, a special bond was formed.

Walt removed Gracey from the Animation Department and gave him a pair of large rooms in the building solely for tinkering with gadgets, effects, and mechanics. Gracey had no pressure of meeting deadlines or performing specific tasks; this was Walt's own version of a research and development lab for Disneyland attractions. Yale was simply encouraged to think things up. Bob Gurr recalls, "He would literally sit in his room and fiddle with this stuff, and occasionally invent something, and Walt was totally happy with that."

"Everything he did, well, he just kind of screwed around with the stuff," Rolly Crump remembers. "I started working with Yale in 1959." One of the first projects the pair tackled was that year's rehab of the Fantasyland dark rides in Disneyland. With Opening Day looming, the original rides had been constructed quickly, with no eye for durability. By 1959, many of the mechanical effects were broken, much of the original art had been crudely repainted, and several of the character cutouts were unrecognizable as the animated characters they were meant to represent. Crump handled most of the art-

3 "700 Things for Boys to Do: How to construct wireless outfits, boats, camp equipment, aerial gliders, kites, self-propelled vehicles, engines, motors, electrical apparatus, cameras and hundreds of other things which delight every boy!"

related problems, returning to the original model sheets of the animated films for reference, and repainting or replacing characters as needed.

Gracey improved the barrel gags in Mr. Toad's Wild Ride, created the endless stream of tea pouring from the Mad Hatter's pot into Alice's cup, and added volcano and campfire effects to Never Land in Peter Pan's Flight. Gracey had Crump design kinetic mobiles of sinister eyes to hang in the scary forest of Snow White's Adventures, adding eerie spectators of malevolence floating in the dark tree branches.

After completing their Fantasyland efforts, Walt asked the pair to work on ideas for a long-planned Haunted House attraction. "All we did was read ghost stories and see ghost movies," Crump says. "In fact, we took Walt along with us one time to see a movie called *13 Ghosts*. Yale and I just played around and we had a great time, and out of that, of course, came all the illusions of The Haunted Mansion. Yale was a genius; all I did was just sort of build the boxes for him and help him build the illusions."

"He'd build physical demonstrations of stuff that came out of his head," Bob Gurr says. "Then somebody on a project would find a way to weave Yale's gag into their show story. He would often have things on the shelf that we could use later." Rolly Crump remembers one such occasion. "I was actually there the day he came up with the head in the ball, which was incredible! He got a film projector to play Hans Conried's face as the Magic Mirror from one of the television shows. He took this projector and played it around the room and was showing it on everything. I left for lunch, and when I came back he had lined it up with a bust of Beethoven. Nothing was in sync, but the little face looked like it was alive, and the result was incredible. Of course, Walt fell in love with it, and it became Madame Leota in the crystal ball."

"Whenever we needed a special effect," John Hench recalled, "we went to Yale. Sometimes it took a while to get what we were asking for, however, along the way he'd develop other marvelous effects we could use. I remember one time we asked him to create a particular illusion and in the process of experimenting he developed a gopher bomb, which we all used in our yards. It worked very well!"

"He was a thinker," Gurr agrees. "He had a broad background on how things worked, and a general idea of the physics of things. He would walk around, puffing on his pipe, and a few days later he'd have some apparatus set up on a bench, running."

In 1961, Yale began the second and most profound stage of his Disney career, as his tinkering became an official role as a "special effects and lighting artist" at WED Enterprises. Now officially an Imagineer, many of his colleagues playfully dubbed Gracey the "gadgeteer" or the "illusioneer."[4] With no special-effects training other than his own hands-on experimentation, Gracey continued creating illusions, such as the "999 grim grinning ghosts" featured in The Haunted Mansion. This attraction repeatedly uses a simple Victorian theatrical illusion called "Pepper's Ghost" to stunning effect.[5] Gracey also rigged the "pop-up" ghosts that appear in the attic scene using a dummy head and a blast of compressed air, an illusion of a ghostly sea captain perpetually caught in a cloudburst over his head, and a ghost whose head disappears from his shoulders and reappears in a hatbox in his hand.[6]

From cloudy skies to misty grottos, Gracey added his art to the atmosphere and special effects of Pirates of the Caribbean with a variety of illusions and mechanical gags, including a cold fire effect for the burning city scene. Gracey developed a method where imitation flames were created with Mylar sheeting, fans, and lighting effects—but the effect was almost too real for some. Arrow Development's Karl Bacon recalls walking through the set with Anaheim's fire department chief. "I remember the head of the fire department coming through the lower doors way down there, and he looked up there and saw it and said, 'You can't have fire in here!' As he got closer, he saw that it was done with colored plastic. He was going to shut them down." Even though the chief regained his composure, he insisted that a "kill switch" be installed to shut down the entire fire effect should a real fire break out, and nixed visual smoke illusions and smoldering smell effects.

ABOVE: Yale working his magic with every trick of the trade.

4 As a tribute to Yale Gracey, the ghostly family that haunts The Haunted Mansion in the 2003 feature film is named Gracey—and the house itself is Gracey Manor.

5 The Pepper's Ghost effect invented in 1858 by Henry Dircks, and refined by "Professor" Henry Pepper in 1862, was developed to create the illusion of a "ghost" interacting with actors on a stage.

6 The cloudburst effect was never used, however the hatbox ghost did appear briefly in The Haunted Mansion at Disneyland when the attraction first opened in 1969. It was removed shortly after when the effect didn't work as well as anticipated.

Gracey also contributed to the 1964–1965 New York World's Fair attractions, including the Carousel of Progress, for which he developed a pixie dust projector that blocks out everything on the stage (during scene changes) via the illusion of glimmering pixie dust, the only light source in a darkened theater. The technology is also used in Space Mountain to block out the surrounding roller coaster structure.

After thirty-six years with the company, Gracey retired on October 4, 1975. He continued to consult on special effects and lighting for attractions in Magic Kingdom Park and Epcot in Walt Disney World in Florida.

It is purely conjecture, but it may be that Gracey's legend of mystery has grown because of the tragic and senseless circumstances of his passing. On September 5, 1983, at the age of seventy-three, Gracey and his wife were in a cabana at the Bel Air Bay Club on the beach in Pacific Palisades, California, when a transient broke in and shot the sleeping Gracey and his wife. Gracey was pronounced dead at the scene, and the circumstances of the murder were never really resolved. It was a heartbreaking and random end for a gentle and genuinely gifted man.

"Yale had an unusual personality," Crump remembers, "and you had to know him well to see it. When he talked of his childhood, he described a shy, little guy who studied magic and concentrated on his hobbies and looked within himself. He was quiet, with a dry sense of humor, and he used to say the damndest things. He was an introvert, but he could be abrupt and opinionated. There was no strong image that came from Yale until you got to know him. He just wanted to tinker and create, and that was his life."

Blaine Gibson: The Skills of The Sculptor

Visitors to the Illinois Pavilion at the 1964–1965 New York World's Fair were greeted by an all-new entertainment medium, the culmination of a long research and development process completed solely through the passion and persistence of Walt Disney. Narrator Paul Frees earnestly introduced this groundbreaking presentation of Audio-Animatronics not with a celebration of its technological innovation or explanation of its electronic marvels, but rather by an acknowledgment that "the skills of the sculptor and the talents of the artist will let us relive Great Moments with Mr. Lincoln." The sculptor was Blaine Gibson, for whom dimensional design had simply been a hobby. Under the guidance of Walt Disney, this hobby was nurtured into an artistic career that Gibson had never imagined.

The artist was born on February 11, 1918 in Rocky Ford, Colorado, where his father was a farmer. He attended Colorado University, but left there to join The Walt Disney Studio. "All of the young artists had the same objective," Gibson told *The E Ticket* in 1995, "and that was to become an animator. I was about twenty-one, and that was my goal."

Starting with Disney in 1939, Blaine worked as an in-betweener on *Pinocchio, Fantasia,* and *Bambi*. After that, there were no opportunities for young Gibson except on short cartoons. He moved to effects animation for the animated shorts *Lucky Number* and *Bee on Guard* (1951), *Donald Applecore, Two Chips and a Miss, Let's Stick Together,* and *Pluto's Party* (1952), *For Whom the Bulls Toil* and *How to Dance* (1953), *Casey Bats Again* (1954), and the features *Song of the South, Alice in Wonderland*, and *Peter Pan*.

Finally, Gibson heard of an opening in character animation. "It's not that I disliked effects—it was fascinating," Gibson says, "but after a while I realized that what I was interested in were faces and expressions and action—drawing things that were alive. Luckily, Gibson wound up as an assistant animator to the great Frank Thomas. "I felt Frank Thomas was absolutely the peak," Gibson says. "Some of the things he had done at the time, the life he was able to project into his animation, made me think I might not be able to do as well but I sure wanted to try."

While an animator, Gibson also took evening classes in sculpture at Pasadena City College and studied with a private instructor. "I started out using sculpture more as an illustrator would,

BELOW: Blaine with a gallery of great Americans: Will Rogers, Ben Franklin, and Mark Twain, 1981.

BOTTOM: Gibson and a good friend.

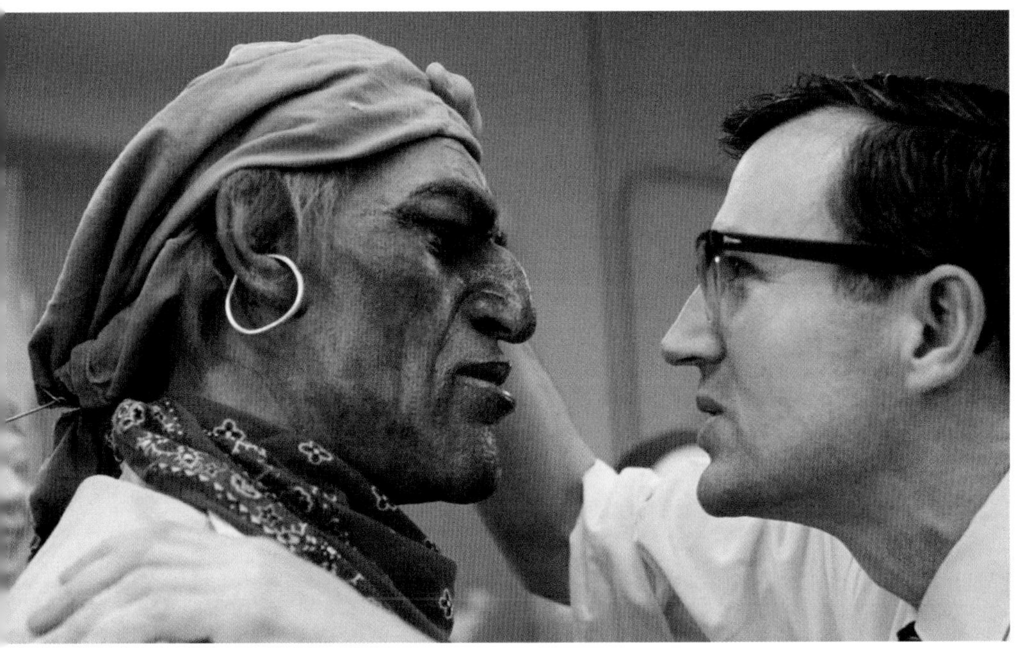

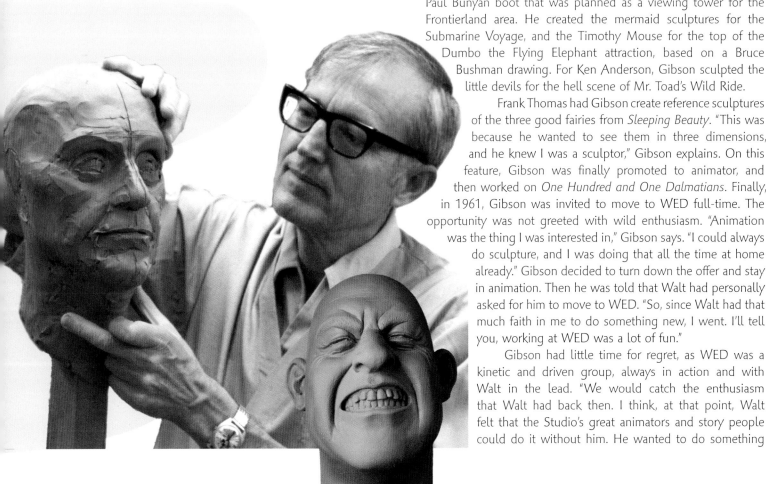

finding out how you would approach different character types. Back then I would read a novel, and the author would describe a character, and I would sculpt a little head that would fit that." In the late 1940s, Gibson exhibited some of his hobby sculptures at a Studio art show, including those miniature human heads and a stylized full-figure gorilla. "I learned later that Walt and Herb Ryman were thinking of using that gorilla for a giant entrance to the Los Angeles Zoo."

Finding out about Blaine's hobby, Walt Disney recruited him in 1954 to sculpt an Indian head for the Indian Village in Disneyland. "I was still with Frank Thomas at the time, working on *Lady and the Tramp*," Gibson recalls. He did the sculpture at home, and brought it in for Walt to see. "He came in and looked at it, and those were really my first personal dealings with Walt Disney," Gibson says. Gibson continued to create special sculptures for the development of Disneyland, even as he continued to work as an assistant animator. "Frank Thomas would come up to me and say, 'When are you going to get through with this?' I was still hoping to work with Frank, you know, and advance as an animator."

ABOVE: Blaine faces down one of his pirate creations.

BELOW: The artist at work.

Gibson created sculptures of characters based on drawings by Joe Rinaldi for the often-discussed Oz projects, and a giant Paul Bunyan boot that was planned as a viewing tower for the Frontierland area. He created the mermaid sculptures for the Submarine Voyage, and the Timothy Mouse for the top of the Dumbo the Flying Elephant attraction, based on a Bruce Bushman drawing. For Ken Anderson, Gibson sculpted the little devils for the hell scene of Mr. Toad's Wild Ride.

Frank Thomas had Gibson create reference sculptures of the three good fairies from *Sleeping Beauty*. "This was because he wanted to see them in three dimensions, and he knew I was a sculptor," Gibson explains. On this feature, Gibson was finally promoted to animator, and then worked on *One Hundred and One Dalmatians*. Finally, in 1961, Gibson was invited to move to WED full-time. The opportunity was not greeted with wild enthusiasm. "Animation was the thing I was interested in," Gibson says. "I could always do sculpture, and I was doing that all the time at home already." Gibson decided to turn down the offer and stay in animation. Then he was told that Walt had personally asked for him to move to WED. "So, since Walt had that much faith in me to do something new, I went. I'll tell you, working at WED was a lot of fun."

Gibson had little time for regret, as WED was a kinetic and driven group, always in action and with Walt in the lead. "We would catch the enthusiasm that Walt had back then. I think, at that point, Walt felt that the Studio's great animators and story people could do it without him. He wanted to do something new. Disneyland and WED were all his, and I think for him it was a rekindling of the excitement and involvement he felt working on *Snow White* back in the 1930s," Gibson says.

As director of sculpture at WED, Gibson supervised the entire dimensional design and execution area. "Jack Ferges and I were the entire department at the time. We had to do the sculpting and the painting, and Jack was such a wonderful model builder we didn't need anyone else."

Their first major project was the creation of new animals and scenes for the Jungle Cruise, which had remained unchanged since 1955. "They were rather crudely done," Gibson says. "I don't mean to put anybody down, but they weren't all that they could be." It was at this point that Marc Davis added several scenes to the attraction, which Gibson and Ferges executed. "Walt came in and saw our model," Gibson says, "and I remember he said, 'You know, we need an elephant climbing out on the bank, maybe reaching up for some of the branches, like in our nature pictures.' Then he pushed his pants down a little bit, so he could get that 'elephant look,' and he used his hand for a trunk, and he got up on a chair, you know. And I actually went ahead and modeled him as that elephant. It was Walt's acting that made me visualize that elephant like that. The others are from Marc's drawings, but Walt was the inspiration for that one. And I know Walt liked it later, when he saw it."

The four Disney pavilions for the New York World's Fair resulted in the creation of scores of new sculptures including dinosaurs and cavemen for the Ford Wonder Rotunda, a globe full of children for "it's a small world," an entire extended multigenerational family for the General Electric Carousel of Progress, and perhaps his most famous, Mr. Lincoln.

"I actually did the Lincoln head before, while I was still animating. I was approached by Walt with the idea of doing a whole bunch of heads for Hall of the Presidents, and being taken off animation altogether. Walt was already thinking about a Hall of the Presidents back in the late fifties."

Perhaps the most interesting thing about the combination of sculpture and space-age electronics was the fact that all the mechanics to operate the animation (other than the power source) had to be housed within the framework of the sculpted head. "That's a lot of equipment for one human-size head," declared Roger Broggie, Jr., who was working in the machine shop with his father at this time.

All of the solenoids and their related hardware turned out to be more than the Lincoln head could hold. "That first Lincoln head we did, we couldn't get all of the machinery in it," remembered Gibson. "Wathel Rogers called me in one day and said, 'Blaine, we can't get all the actuators in his head. We're going to have to add to his head!' I told him we can't do it, because his head was based on human proportions. He said, 'Well, we have to do something.' We came up with this idea—I sculpted part of his hair on his head, so I raised his head up a half an inch, and then the wig went over that. The only problem we had was sometimes the makeup men in New York wouldn't get the wig on right, so the bump would show."

Along with Ken O'Brien, Gibson sculpted characters for Pirates of the Caribbean, creating the illusion of dozens of individual pirates by sculpting several basic head designs that were then individually made up with different skin tones, wigs, and facial hair to

differentiate their characters.[7] Gibson also created ghosts for The Haunted Mansion, and continued to revise and update sculptural elements throughout Disneyland, such as the animals alongside the Rivers of America.

Gibson continued to move forward with the many projects then on the drawing board at WED, but suddenly found he and his colleagues without their benefactor. "When Walt died, we felt that we'd lost the drive that we had always had before. We didn't have anybody around with the vision that Walt had. I felt so strongly about it that I even explored the possibility of working in some other area."

With the strong support of the Imagineering leaders, including Walt's brother Roy O. Disney, much of Walt's work continued, the massive Walt Disney World project among them. Gibson finally sculpted figures for the long-delayed Hall of Presidents, as well as the Country Bear Jamboree, America Sings, and later, the Future World pavilions in Epcot.

Gibson retired from the Company in 1983 to Sedona, Arizona, then moved to the Santa Barbara, California, area after the death of his wife, Coral. He returns occasionally for special projects, of which his most recent works are the "Partners" sculpture of Walt Disney and Mickey Mouse, unveiled in Disneyland in the fall of 1993, and sculptures of Presidents Bill Clinton and George W. Bush for The Hall of Presidents in Walt Disney World.

Gibson still expresses gratitude for the encouragement and support he received as an artist from Walt. "He made it possible for me to have a career that was absolutely something I wouldn't have dreamed of as a farm boy," he says.

He is also humble about his role, giving recognition where he feels it is due, always crediting his colleagues and inspirations when discussing his body of work. "I remember when Walt asked me to do the Lincoln head. I thought at the time we'd be fooling with something that the American people considered almost sacred. I just couldn't see us doing it in an acceptable way. Then, much later, I was sitting in front of somebody at the actual Lincoln show in Disneyland and I heard them crying. I thought, 'Well, how wrong can you be, Blaine? And how right can Walt be?' It was clear who had the vision around there."

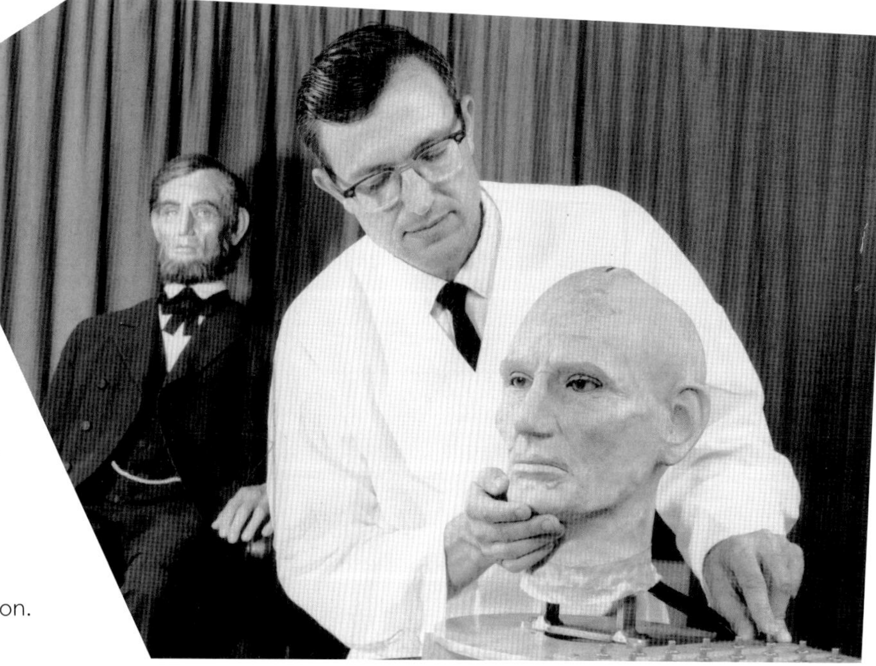

TOP LEFT: Blaine continues to keep The Hall of Presidents current—here he is sculpting George W. Bush.

TOP RIGHT: The Partners Statue in Disneyland.

MIDDLE: Walt and Blaine review a dramtically posed sculpture for Pirates of the Caribbean.

LEFT: Blaine and a pair of geese.

RIGHT: Blaine sculpts Lincoln as Lincoln looks on.

7 For example, the mayor being dunked in the well and the fife player nearby are actually the same sculpture head.

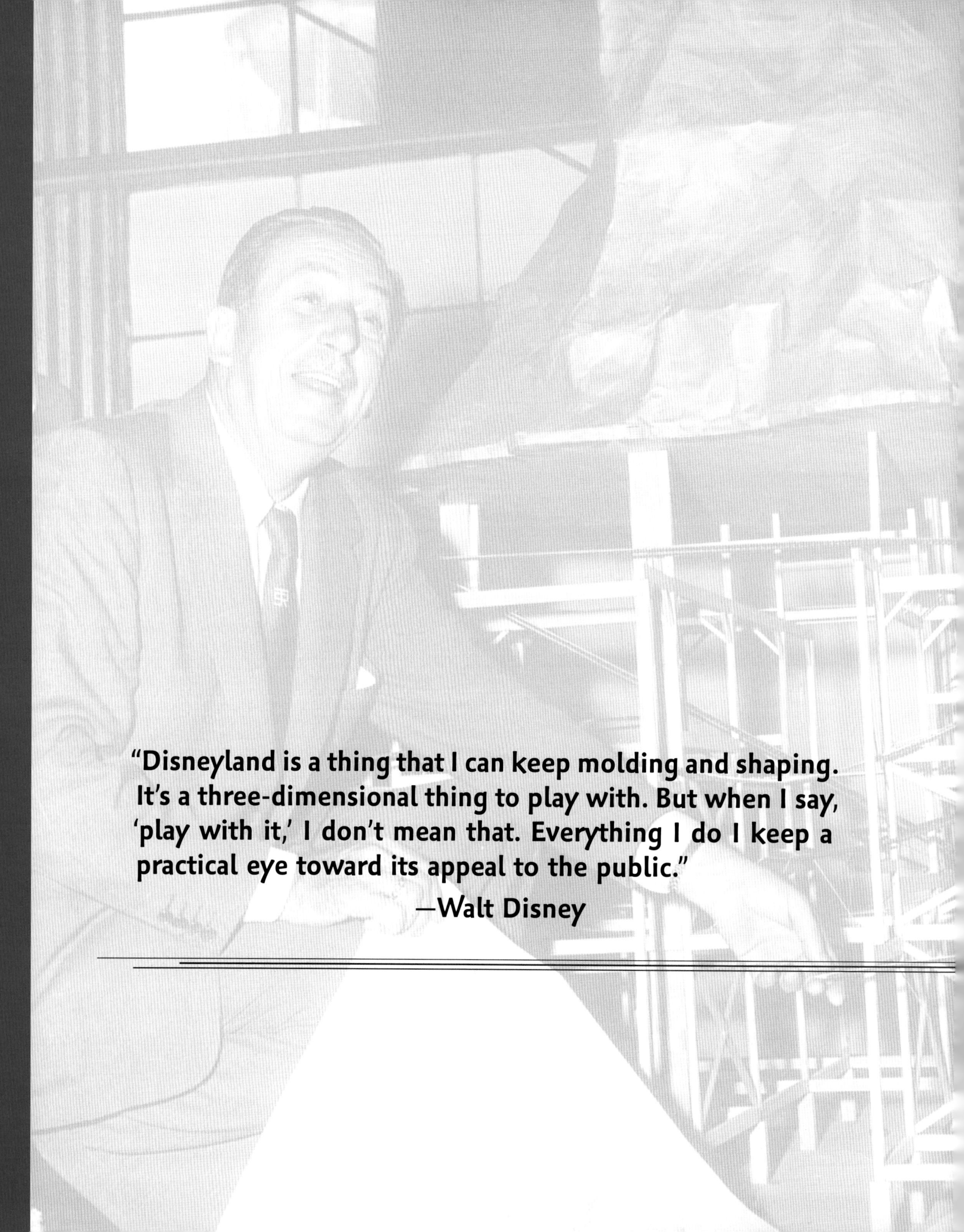

"Disneyland is a thing that I can keep molding and shaping. It's a three-dimensional thing to play with. But when I say, 'play with it,' I don't mean that. Everything I do I keep a practical eye toward its appeal to the public."

—Walt Disney

The Model Shop

Walt liked to see things in an optimal reality. He knew from long experience at creating the "illusion of life" in animation that a painting or drawing could "fool" the viewer. He was more clearly able to see the possible problems, and potential enrichment, of a particular project by seeing it brought to life in three dimensions. So when he began developing Disneyland, he founded the WED Model Shop. Walt is quoted as saying, "A model may cost $5,000, but it's sure less expensive than $50,000 to fix the real thing."

Fred Joerger: Three-D Designer

"The remarkable thing about Fred was that he could do large-scale constructions just as beautifully as tiny miniatures," longtime Model Shop colleague Harriet Burns mused. "Whether he was building a 1/64-scale model for the Germany Pavilion in Epcot, or supervising the full-size concrete construction and painting the interior sets for the Pirates of the Caribbean attraction in Disneyland, no job was too small or too large for Fred."

ABOVE: Joerger prepares paint and palette in his Studio workshop.

OPPOSITE: Joerger keeps busy as Walt reviews the construction of Storybook Land in 1956. Wathel Rogers works in the background.

As Fred recalled, "I was given artists' drawings of an interior set or a building and interpreted them into models. It's very easy to make something like The Haunted Mansion look good on paper, but if you don't get it into three dimensions first, you may have a disaster. My job was to create the model to avert disaster, which was fun, but a challenge."

Born in Pekin, Illinois, on December 21, 1913, Joerger graduated from the University of Illinois with a fine arts degree in 1937. Moving to Los Angeles, he joined the art department at Warner Bros. Studios, building models of movie sets. "My first job was freelance, building a model of an apartment house for Tucson," Joerger told Don Peri in 2004. "Then I went to Warner's because a friend of mine had a job as the head of the department there, so that made it simple!" Joerger worked on dozens of Warner Bros. films during that studio's golden era.

In 1953, Walt Disney recruited Joerger to craft the scenics and decorative backgrounds for the Project Little Man vaudeville stage and for the barbershop quartet. When Joerger arrived, all the mechanics for Project Little Man were completed. A cabinet beneath the miniature stage concealed the puzzle of drums, wires, and cams that ran the tiny figure, He and the other Model Shop staff called it "the telephone booth." Joerger fondly remembered the disproportionate scale of effort to result, backstage to onstage, "All the 'to do' over that little guy!" This animated figure was, of course, the first step toward creating Audio-Animatronics technology.

"The sculptor Cristadora had carved him, and Harper Goff's wife [Flossie] made the costume for him," Harriet Burns said. "I know she did the barbershop quartet, too. Walt made the stage, and Fred did the drapery. The articulated limbs were wired together by Wathel [Rogers]. We worked on whatever Walt wanted, it was his hobby. I called it 'the oddball department' because we did all sorts of oddball things that the animators didn't do."

His work on the Little Man complete, Joerger's talents were not allowed to lay fallow. He built miniature sets and props for *20,000 Leagues Under the Sea* (released 1954), including the intricate models of the submarine *Nautilus*. Soon after *20,000 Leagues Under the Sea*, Joerger was assigned to create models of the planned attractions for Disneyland. In 1954, there wasn't an established model shop at the Walt Disney Studios. Joerger took space in the decidedly unusual machinists' workroom, which was actually a converted railroad boxcar on the Buena Vista Street parking lot, near the main gate of the Studios. He was given a work space as far away from the noise and dust of the lathes and drills as one could get in a boxcar. Alongside him, a pretty young woman was busy creating sets and props for *The Mickey Mouse Club*, under the direction of Bruce Bushman. Harriet Burns would become his lifelong friend. "Fred would help me paint props," Burns recalled, "and then if Fred was in a bind, I would help him on the models."

The first model that Joerger recalled building in the Model Shop was the *Mark*

Twain riverboat. Joerger's calm exterior concealed a zealous perfectionist lurking just below the surface. Although often engaged in building several miniatures at once, he devoted painstaking attention to detail to every one. His knowledge of architecture, combined with his skills in model construction, frequently enabled him to abandon the blueprints and come up with a finished model by way of an impeccably accurate eye. For the model of the King Arthur Carrousel, Joerger hand-carved all of the horses. His exactitude and work ethic was exactly what Walt Disney wanted (and expected) from his employees—qualities that Walt demanded in himself.

Walt would often join the model makers in their ramshackle boxcar, sitting beside Fred and crafting elements for his elaborate Granny's Cabin miniature. "He sort of hung out," Burns remembers. "He seemed to like to relax back there. He would just be one of us and kick the stuff around." Walt was also no doubt put at ease by the amiable nature and calm pleasantness of both Burns and Joerger. Bob Gurr recalled: "I think anybody that you talk to will say that Fred was one of the very few persons who never yelled, never raised his voice, and no matter what critical situation he was in, he was unflappable. He was always smiling, always pleasant. That's the kind of person you want to work with."

Although he spent his time behind the scenes and knew the origin and development of every detail of Disneyland, Joerger was not above being dazzled by Disney magic. He recalled being sent by Walt down to the Park to help prepare for opening day. Joerger blanched when he saw the Tomorrowland entry plaza. "The Park was pretty well finished, but Tomorrowland, the plaza was just a pile of junk. They apparently used it as a disposal for everything. It was a disaster. There was no way they could do anything with that. I went out there about seven-thirty the next morning, and there's a beautiful garden. All the flowers are in bloom, and shrubbery in it. Big trees and everything! All overnight!"

In addition to his skills with models that helped define projects in concept development, Joerger established the standards for field art direction. He was responsible for assuring that shows and attractions achieved the creative goals designed by WED designers and art directors. Fred Joerger was the master of the Model Shop, Rolly Crump recalled, "Fred could build anything. He was probably one of the most versatile guys who worked at WED. He was just absolutely marvelous."

On a fact-finding visit to Disneyland in preparation for the "walk-through" attraction inside Sleeping Beauty Castle,

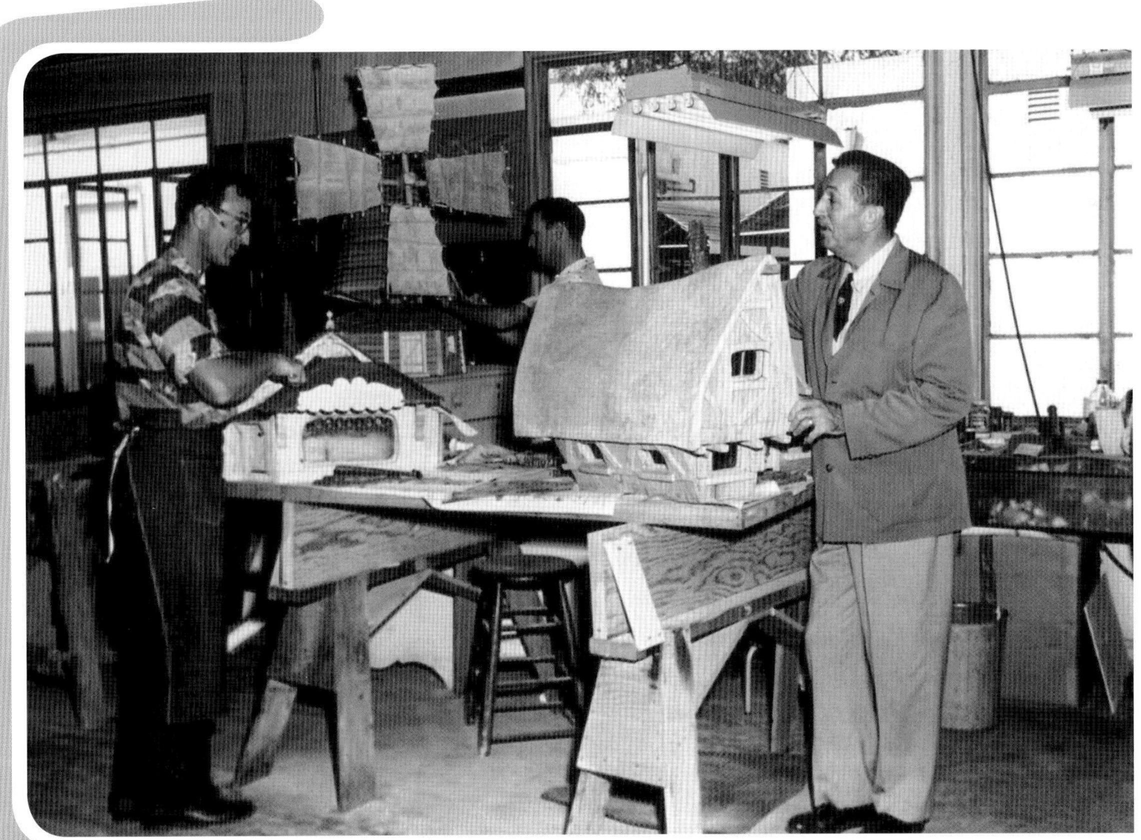

Joerger found far more than a creative challenge. Along with Ken Anderson and Emile Kuri,[1] Joerger discovered that the unfinished interior of the castle had been infested by dozens upon dozens of feral cats. "I had on khaki pants. When I looked down, it looked like I had on brown pants!" Joerger recalled. His legs were covered from the ground up with thousands of swarming fleas, courtesy of the castle's feline court. "It blended up to the knees. Kenny got some on him, but not many. And Emile was so fastidious; a flea wouldn't dare get near him. But we got out on the balcony over the courtyard and I took my pants off and we beat them on the parapet." Joerger finally had to scurry, trouser-free, across the Park to the Disneyland Wardrobe Department, where he was properly dressed to go home.

ABOVE: Fred (in blue hard hat) consults with Claude Coats, standing aboard the pirate ship *Wicked Wench* during the construction of Pirates of the Caribbean in Disneyland.

ABOVE RIGHT: Fred checks on how the new Matterhorn caverns measure up.

OPPOSITE: The Big Thunder Mountain "splashdown" in Disneyland surrounded by rockwork.

The Pirates of the Caribbean attraction was a particularly challenging experience for Joerger, who supervised the elaborate preconstruction miniature models, did all the rockwork sets (many of the rock grottoes are, in fact, made of insulation paper normally used in home construction, crumpled to resemble a rock surface, then sprayed and flecked with paint to give it the texture and color of rock), in addition to overseeing the set painting, and the interaction of the sets with the air-conditioning vents and lighting. In the interest of efficiency, during the interior construction of Pirates of the Caribbean, Walt Disney had Joerger flown to Disneyland every day for several months. Joerger would drive to Burbank Airport in the morning, then the Disney plane would fly to Orange County, where Fred would be picked up and taken to the Park.

Joerger was hesitant to tell Walt that his generous act and attempt at efficiency was actually creating the opposite result. "Instead of being down in Disneyland at seven thirty, I'd get there about ten thirty. In fact, one day we didn't get there until after lunch because of the fog." The commuter service finally ended, the legend goes, when

1 Eight-time nominee and winner of two Academy Awards, set decorator Emile Kuri (1907–2000) served as set designer on *20,000 Leagues Under the Sea* (1954), *The Absent-Minded Professor* (1961), *The Parent Trap* (1961), *Mary Poppins* (1964), *The Love Bug* (1969), and *Bedknobs and Broomsticks* (1971), among many others. Kuri eventually served as head of the decorating department for the Studio, overseeing all TV and film set decoration, as well as contributing to the design of the Park.

Walt encountered Joerger at the Park especially early one morning. When Walt asked him what occasioned this dawn arrival, Joerger forthrightly explained to Walt that he was early because he had driven instead of flying.

Fred's unusual knack for creating gorgeous rockwork out of plaster led to his reputation as Imagineering's "resident rock expert." Among his rocky mountain highlights are the caverns in Submarine Voyage, the caves and rocks on Tom Sawyer Island, and the rock cliffs and ruined temples of Jungle Cruise.

After Walt's passing, Joerger continued to work in Disneyland, but expanded his role—and "hands-on" creative approach—on the creation of Walt Disney World. Joerger enjoyed getting his hands dirty, and was frequently found on-site, continuing the field art direction (and providing on-the-job training) that he loved.

"I remember how he was in the Model Shop in 1955 with Harriet Burns and Wathel Rogers," Bob Gurr recalled, "where it's nice and quiet, and you're doing nice clean work. Later I saw him in the middle of a construction zone where it's hot and you have construction subcontractors, which are miserable conditions in summer in Orlando. He was totally unflappable, never raised his voice, as dozens of people shoveled concrete and moved stuff around. All this was because he had drawings and he had built a model. In his mind, he knew how it was supposed to be when you blew it up to full size. He would walk around all day long and say, 'Move this over here,' and, 'Do this there,' and, 'I'll show you how to do concrete here,' and 'I'll help you sculpt this thing over there.' He would just go up to anybody and show him or her how to do it. He was going to do the job, but he wasn't going to be like a bombastic order giver. He was a Disney guy, a designer and a model maker at heart, who just interfaced with people no matter who they were. Maybe he was a shy model builder, but when you got him out into the field, you had this big guy of about six feet tall who'd take off his shirt and look like a construction worker. He'd get everybody to get their trowels and work on the stucco and concrete with him—no yelling—and people respected that."

Joerger designed and constructed most all of the rockwork at the Florida theme park for its 1971 opening, including the breathtaking atrium waterfall featured in Disney's Polynesian Resort. "The hotel was all built except for the foyer, and of course, odds and ends," Joerger said. "It was due to open. Some architect designed the foyer, but it ended up that we had to build it—and we had to build it practically overnight. In fact, they gave the fellows guest rooms to stay overnight."

Joerger retired from WED in 1979, after completing work on Big Thunder Mountain Railroad. But after only two years he was back at work, because they needed his help on the development of Epcot and Tokyo Disneyland.

Fred Joerger entered the Motion Picture Country Home in Woodland Hills, California, in 1998. He was later diagnosed with Alzheimer's disease, and passed away on August 26, 2005, at the age of ninety-one.

Unlike some of his colleagues, Joerger wasn't adept at, or interested in, promoting his own achievements, except to those fortunate souls he worked closely with. Unfortunately, the result is that his particular genius and incomparable contributions to Disney are often understated, or entirely overlooked.

Rolly Crump agreed. "He was such an unassuming, quiet gentleman that you didn't realize his importance until you kind of dug into it a little bit."

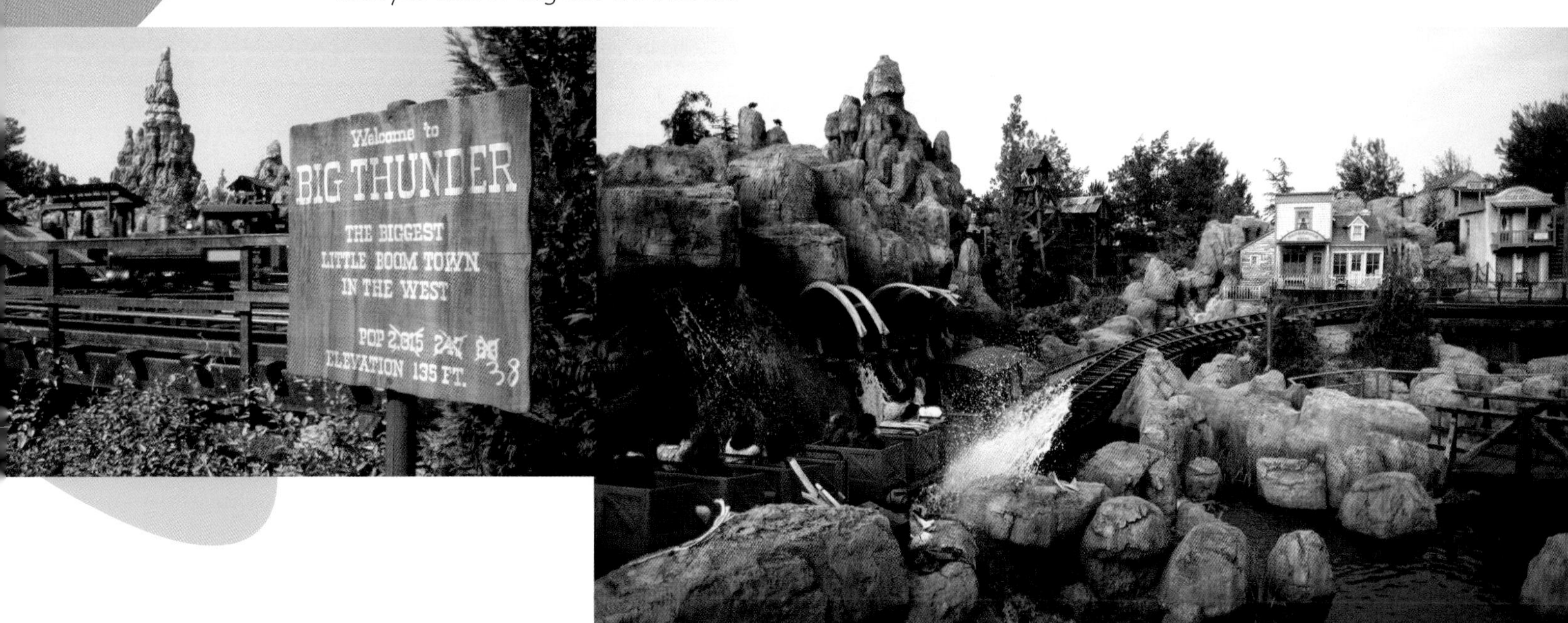

Harriet Burns: The Lady Imagineer

As the first woman ever hired by WED in a creative rather than an office capacity, Harriet Burns helped design and build prototypes for theme park attractions, as well as final products featured in Disneyland and the 1964–1965 New York World's Fair. And while she worked padded-shoulder-to-shoulder with men in the model shop, wielding saws, lathes, and sanders, she was still the best-dressed employee in the department.

"It was the 1950s," she explained. "I wore color-coordinated dresses, high heels, and gloves to work. Girls didn't wear slacks back then, although I carried a pair in a little sack, just in case I had to climb into high places."

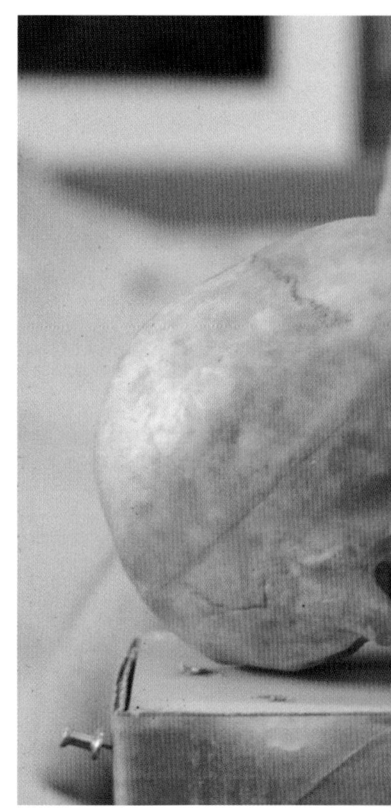

Born on August 20, 1928, in San Antonio, Texas, Harriet received her bachelor's degree in art from Southern Methodist University in Dallas, and went on to study advanced design for another year at the University of New Mexico in Albuquerque. "I got a scholarship in music as well, but I didn't take it, because I didn't want to teach music and I didn't want to be a concert pianist. I thought that's not very practical, so I switched entirely then to art."

In 1953, she moved to Los Angeles with her husband and small daughter. There, she accepted a part-time position at DICE (Display Industries Cooperative Exchange), where she helped design and produce props for television's *Colgate Comedy Hour*, and interiors and sets for Las Vegas Hotels, including the Dunes.[2] She also spearheaded the creation of the fanciful Southern California tourist destination Santa's Village,[3] located near Lake Arrowhead.

When DICE went out of business in 1955, a colleague who had once worked at Disney told Burns that the Studio was hiring for a new television program and invited Harriet to come along to apply. Burns got the job and soon she was painting sets and props for *The Mickey Mouse Club*. Burns soon began coordinating the show's color styling, a peculiar role since the program was only broadcast in black-and-white. "Yes, done in color—thankfully," Burns told Don Peri in 2003, "because we used wild colors, you know—pinks and yellows; I mean, things that really vibrated. It was much more fun. If you had to do it in shades of gray, you wouldn't have been nearly as creative. Think how farsighted Walt was in saying, 'Shoot it in color,' in that day. Think of that! It's amazing. And he wasn't a space man, you know what I mean. Coming from Marceline and the whole thing—you just can't imagine him being that much of a genius."

Burns also contributed, along with art director Bruce Bushman and concept designer Roy Williams, to the decidedly modern, graphic styling of the show. At the same time as Walt Disney's art designs were beginning to be classified in the eyes of the intellectuals as traditional and homogenized, Disney's designers continued to experiment with bold new stylistic initiatives. "Well, [Walt] wanted a variety. We did wild things for that period; we had various props and backgrounds that were fun and lighthearted. We often used a Steinberg[4] art style. And he dug that. It seemed really amazing because he had a lot of 'Victorian' and 'Main Street' in his background."

2 The Dunes Hotel opened on May 23, 1955. The site is now Steve Wynn's Treasure Island and Bellagio Casino/Resorts.

3 H. Glenn Holland, a Southern California developer, opened Santa's Village in 1955, in San Bernardino County. He opened two more, in California and Illinois, but sadly, all these Christmas-themed parks are now gone.

4 Saul Steinberg (1914–1999) was a Romanian-born U.S. cartoonist and illustrator. His works were often surrealistic or whimsical and frequently employed odd versions of pop-culture icons.

Burns shared a makeshift space in the Machine Shop "boxcar" workshop. "The whole thing was just a little space. Fred Joerger had been hired to do the models, and they had said, 'Well, you can work out there in the machine shop.' So they stuck Fred out there in this little thing. He brought his own tools—a band saw, a table saw, a lathe, and other stuff. We used them for like ten years or more."

Burns saw all the odds and ends of projects that would ultimately evolve into Disneyland, including Project Little Man, the barbershop quartet, and the various dioramas that constituted Walt's early vision of "Disneylandia." "There were panoramas and these little vignettes that Walt had constructed three-dimensionally in a model. Then he would cut holes in the walls, put these boxes behind them. From each one you could see across the street to the barbershop or to the garden or whatever was down the way. That was Walt's complete play toy. And he did all of that; virtually all, I think."

It was a time of enormous growth and diversification for a studio that had only recently been almost exclusively a "cartoon factory." Those artists and employees who had the proper skills, initiative, attitude, and smarts quickly found themselves likewise growing and diversifying. Soon, Burns was part of the WED group working on Disneyland, helping create models for Sleeping Beauty Castle among other Opening Day attractions. She helped construct Storybook Land, which features model-size locales inspired by such Disney animated movies as *The Three Little Pigs, Pinocchio, Cinderella,* and *Alice in Wonderland*. These handmade models are like jewels, featuring hours of personal care and effort. Burns recalled soldering copper gutters, hammering lead for hinges, and handcrafting dozens of seemingly minor details for the tiny houses, streets, and settings.

The Storybook Land builders were stumped when it came time to thatch some roofs in their miniature world. "So I said, 'Well, let's just use brooms.' So we ordered all these brooms and cut them up. Then we set the houses down in Disneyland—and birds came down to get the thatch off the roofs to make their nests! We'd have to rethatch every now and then."

Ingenuity was complemented by resource, as Walt was never hesitant in providing his Imagineers with the tools that would aid them in making their work more efficient, more accurate, and of better quality. "He didn't hesitate to get us anything we needed that would help. Any books. Rare books. He'd just say, 'Tell the library to get them.' Any tools we needed. At first we were very conservative, because we didn't know what would work. But if we said we needed something, he'd get it."

Sometimes, the boss himself would become the Model Shop procurement agent. "He would bring little miniatures to us, that he collected when he went on his trips. Beautiful little porcelain jugs and washbasins, and tiny things. When he went to Paris, he went to a milliner's shop, where he bought a cheap, cardboard, dime-store suitcase. Then he packed it full of these wonderful little miniatures and all sorts of things that you could use down the line for any number of projects. Things like that were just amazing to me—that he would have the interest and concern for the rest of us."

OPPOSITE: Burns is part of the playful spirit of WED. Even in the looming threat of a Stone Age attacker, Harriet always looks her best.

ABOVE: When you're cool, the sun is always shining. Burns engages in Model Shop skulduggery, circa 1967.

After the opening of Disneyland, Burns joined the ever-increasing staff of WED Enterprises, moving off the Studio lot into facilities about three miles away in Glendale. Although they missed being on the lot, they were often visited by Walt. "We kind of knew when he was coming over—most of the time. I had dubbed him 'Yellow Shoes,' because once he had worn golf shoes that were sort of a mustard color and I said, 'I guess he's trying to imitate Mickey Mouse.' So I'd say, 'Yellow Shoes is coming today.' This was adopted as sort of a nickname, so when [the switchboard operator] would call over the loudspeaker and say, 'Yellow Shoes alert,' it meant [Walt] had just parked in the parking lot—so we could shape things up a bit."

Burns added the special talent of "Figure Finishing" to her artistic repertoire. This entailed the application of fur, feathers, skin, makeup, and just about any other material that would take a figure from raw construction to show-quality appearance. Burns was instrumental in the elaborate plumage of the Walt Disney's Enchanted Tiki Room avian actors, and like so many of her WED counterparts, threw every talent she had to offer, and a lot of new ones, into the creation of the attractions featured at the 1964–1965 New York World's Fair. Burns was especially proud of the depth of detail in each attraction, and particularly in "it's a small world," given how quickly the project went from concept to completion. "Walt said, 'The first time they go through, they'll just get the gist of it. Then the second time they go through, they'll start looking at the finer points. Then the third time they'll see the little frogs and the lily pads and all the little things they didn't ever see before.' And that was exactly what Walt wanted, all the little 'plus' things."

On occasion, Burns would appear on segments of *Walt Disney Presents* and *Walt Disney's Wonderful World of Color* when Walt would introduce new theme park attractions to television audiences. Walt's approach was to remain as loose, unrehearsed, and unscripted as possible. "He had this very wise idea of [having] no scripts. You'd be honest and human. He might say, 'What is that glass doing over there?' and then he'd want you to talk about it. Then they would cut, and if he didn't like what you said, they would shoot it again until it came out right. And maybe it wasn't a hundred percent what he had in mind, but he went with it, because it was spontaneous."

As the Fair and other projects such as *Mary Poppins* that Burns worked on reached completion, she was immediately occupied with Pirates of the Caribbean. Without a doubt, this show featured the most elaborate interior miniature concept model ever created by the WED Model Shop. "Walt wanted the [model] because we could make additions or corrections on anything without having to do it on the final set. The model itself was forty feet long and one-inch scale. We put it up on sawhorses at Walt's eye height, so that you could walk through this room filled with sections of the model. It really was an interesting thing. Some people said they thought it was better than the live one, because of the miniaturization!"

LEFT: Eye makeup for a cast member of the Mickey Mouse Revue, 1971.

BELOW: Feathered frills for a Tropical Serenade headliner, 1971.

OPPOSITE RIGHT: Burns and the boss review some of Harriet's handiwork.

OPPOSITE, FAR RIGHT: Walt and Disneyland Ambassador Julie Reihm oversee the exterior design for the Plaza Inn Restaurant as Harriet Burns looks on, 1965.

In addition, Burns worked on all of the human and animal figure finishing. After the realistic humans of Great Moments with Mr. Lincoln and Carousel of Progress, she was happy to engage in the caricatured style of Marc Davis's pirate crew. "They didn't have to look like anything but characters; we could make them any which way. I did the Auctioneer blonde, brunette, and red-haired, with a beard and with a mustache, and other different effects."

It was during this project that Walt died. "It was just so shocking. Bill Cottrell was at my desk and got a phone call. He said, 'I'll be right there,' and he turned to me and he said, 'Walt Disney just died.' He used the name 'Disney.' He didn't say Walt. He said, 'Walt Disney just died.' I said, 'That's impossible. He can't be.' I was just in disbelief, and he said, 'Don't tell anyone.' So I was horrified, you know, I had tears in my eyes and I lowered my head. Then everybody's radios were announcing it. The whole world was shocked, just shocked. And then everything was in disarray. [Switchboard operator] Pat Morganelli said that people called from all over the world. Finally they had her tape something that said, 'The Studio is now closed because of Walt Disney's death,' and finally Dick Irvine came around and said, 'We're going to close WED now.'

"I just didn't realize how affected I was. Walt was a father figure, but he was more

. . . he had been a part of our lives for so long, and such a major part. He had been such a wonderful influence and enthusiastic spark to everybody, you know? He was just something else."

Burns remained at WED and continued to bring her artistic flair to every project that came her way, as well as teaching a new generation of Imagineers. In 1986, after thirty-one years with Disney, Burns turned in her smock. She is an active member of the art and music community in Santa Barbara, California, where she now lives.

As for being a woman in a business monopolized by men? "I really didn't think that much about it," Burns admits. "I mean, you know you're going to be kidded, they're going to kid you about something. And they had to be good sports facing a woman, too, so everybody had to be a good sport. You just didn't think that much about it." In her previous experience at DICE, Burns had become adept at using all manner of power tools and machines—saws, drill presses, lathes—and had become an expert at soldering. "I had used the heavy equipment. I was the only female that was insured on the back lot! So when guys would come down on their lunch hours wanting to cut something for their kitchen cabinet or something, I had to do it, because they weren't allowed to, being uninsured. If they cut a finger off, well then the Studio would be responsible." Burns's colleagues were supportive and protective. "Fred was a wonderful person and Wathel, too. They were both just great. Everybody accepted it, so I just didn't think a thing about it. It was a man's world."

One place that wasn't a man's world, however, was the ladies' room. "When we were still at the Studio, the men had a restroom but the women didn't. The women, meaning me. And so I had to run over to the warehouse. So finally they said, 'We're going to build you a restroom, Harriet,' and they built this lovely lavender restroom. Just about ribbon-cutting time—they moved us over to Glendale!"

Her memories of Walt Disney reveal myriad feelings and reflections. "I think people think of him in many different respects, but he's remembered everywhere. Almost everybody says, 'Think of the pleasure he brought to the entire world. Think of the joy, the smiles on so many people's faces.' Burns says that curiosity and persistence led the way for Walt. "He would ask all these questions. He was just so eager to learn and he did. He was such a quick study. Just phenomenal. And with us, he was just a delight to work with, because like I said, it was nothing cut-and-dried. It was always a new innovation or something, and he would be pleased. And he would never be bubbly, you know, he was not that type. 'That's what I had in mind; that's what I wanted.' And he'd smile, you know, he'd look back and be very pleased. But for him to be pleased, yes, it was great to think that he finally got what he wanted out of the thing.

Harriet Burns experienced—and contributed—an enormous amount in what she actually always considered a temporary job. "I never planned to stay. I'd tell my daughter, 'Well, next year when I quit, then we'll do so-and-so.' Even at the beginning, I told my husband, 'This is great to work on, but who's going to drive that far to a play park?' No one had the foresight that [Walt] did. It was amazing how he had an ability to judge the public. He also had a phenomenal outlook in that if it didn't work, we could just go back to movies. He was always optimistic. He never was discouraged about anything."

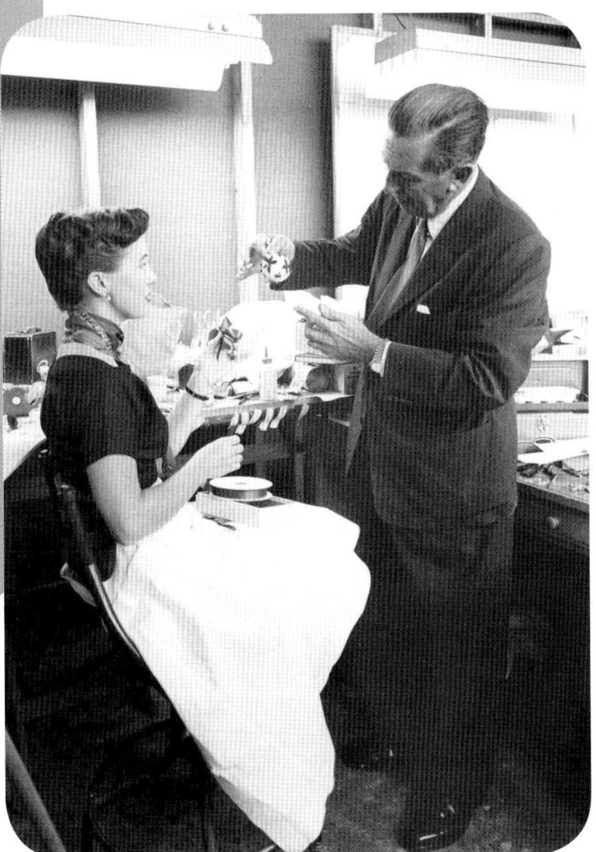

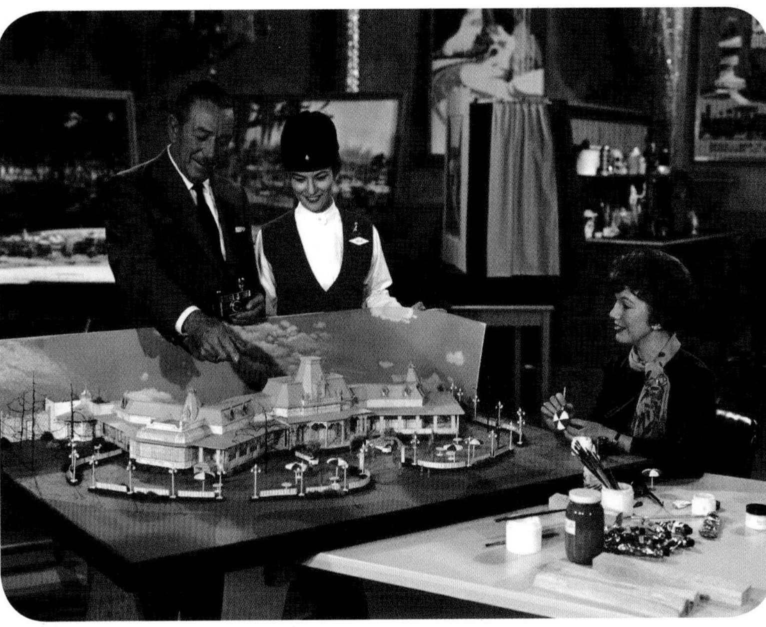

Wathel Rogers: A Man on The Move

Roy E. Disney remarked, "It's often said that attending our Parks is a magical experience, like walking through a three-dimensional movie. Well, all magic needs magicians, and Wathel was one of those; he was one of the head magicians behind Disney magic."

Wathel Rogers was the man to call whenever inanimate objects needed to come to life in grand Disney fashion. Wathel breathed life into Audio-Animatronics figures featured in such theme park attractions as Walt Disney's Enchanted Tiki Room in Disneyland and The Hall of Presidents in Walt Disney World. John Hench recalled, "Wathel was always making everything come to life. If it was stationary and we wanted it to move, all we had to do was call Wathel and in his quiet, calm way, he'd make it work."

Born and raised in Stratton, Colorado, his unique artistic ability became evident when Rogers was a boy, making one-of-a-kind toys out of household junk, and odds and ends. As a teenager, he created mechanical toys from used radio parts and other scrap material. Following his high school graduation in 1937, he applied for a job at the Hyperion Studio. "They liked my work," Rogers told Imagineer Betsy Richman in a 1987 interview, "but suggested that I go to art school for some formal training." Rogers subsequently enrolled at Chouinard Art Institute where he studied life drawing, animation, and composition.

"When I left Chouinard in 1939, I went right back to Disney," said Rogers. The application form requested the would-be animator to draw, among other characters, a fat man digging a ditch. Rogers joined the Traffic Department[1] soon after. "I was making sixteen dollars a week, and I bought a fifteen-dollar watch with my first paycheck—how can you deliver things on time if you don't have a watch?" Rogers was rarely without a Mickey Mouse watch from that day on. He finally joined the Animation department, becoming an in-betweener on *Pinocchio* and *Bambi*, along with a number of Donald Duck cartoons. World War II briefly interrupted his career in 1943, when he enlisted in the U.S. Marine Corps and served as a staff sergeant in the photographic section. After the war, he returned to Disney's Animation Department, where he soon became an assistant animator, working on *Cinderella, Alice in Wonderland, Lady and the Tramp, Sleeping Beauty*, and various short subjects.

Rogers sculpted figures on his own time, and when he'd built up a sizable collection, he showed it to the head of the Sculpture Department, who liked his work and hired him. "Three days before I was scheduled to start, the Sculpture Department[2] was phased out," said Rogers. "I decided to give the Background Department a try—and then they had a lay-off."

In his spare time, Rogers continued to sculpt and build toys, including model railroads, which caught Walt Disney's attention. "It kind of started with Walt, and this little mechanical bird in a cage that he had. One of those that you could wind up and it would whistle. It was a collector's item and I don't know how much it was

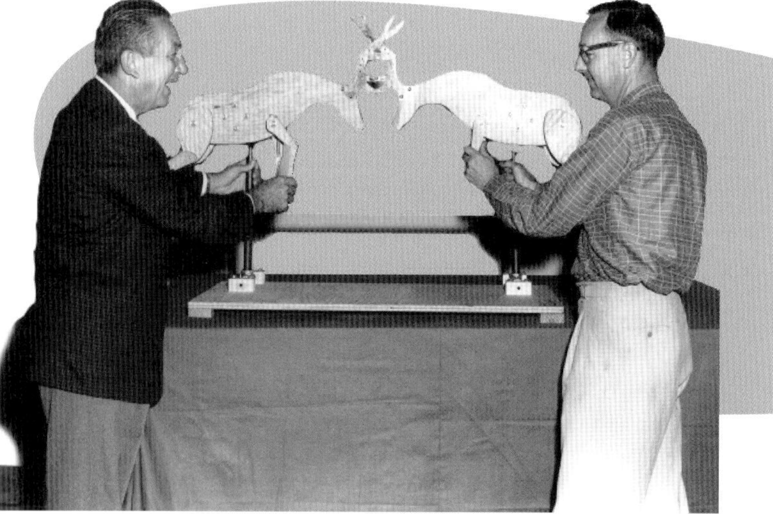

LEFT: This was the only way to butt heads with Walt and keep your job. Bighorn Sheep for Mine Train Through Nature's Wonderland, 1960.

OPPOSITE, TOP: Rogers works with an early version of the Lincoln figure, 1962. It was a particular challenge to put all the necessary machinery into a human-sized head.

OPPOSITE, RIGHT: With high-tech gadgets like a stopwatch and clipboard, Rogers monitors the show timing at an audio-control console.

1 Traffic was essentially the on-lot messenger, delivery, and mail service. Most employees without prior work experience served a stint in Traffic to become familiar with the layout of the Studio and the function and location of employees and departments.

2 Rogers may be referring to the Character Model department, disbanded in 1949.

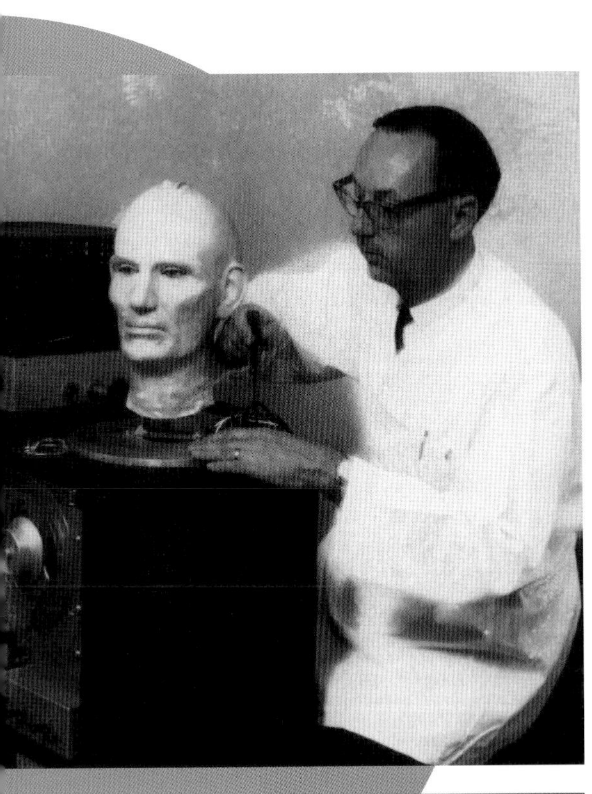

worth. Walt gave it to me and asked me to look inside it. I was supposed to take it apart and it was like taking apart a piece of jewelry. When I laid everything out, I found a little bellows made of canvas, and some little cams and other parts."

As work on Disneyland and other projects progressed, the workload in the Model Shop increased. Harriet Burns recalled, "Walt asked Fred [Joerger] to build a model of the Los Angeles Orthopedic Hospital, and Fred said, 'Well, Walt, I'm working nights and weekends on Disneyland, what is your priority? Walt said, 'I didn't realize that! Well, I'll bring another fellow down from the animation building.' And that was a big advantage—that Walt knew his people so well. He knew what they did inside and outside of work. He said, 'I'll have Wathel Rogers come down for a couple of weeks to help.' So, Wathel came down to help Fred for a couple of weeks, and of course, he never left!" Rogers was brought in for additional manpower, but also for his mechanical and electronics aptitudes. Walt pulled Rogers on to Project Little Man. "Walt wanted me on the Project Little Man research and development team because of my interest in mechanics," Rogers said. "We created a nine-inch-tall figure that was wired through the feet and hands to cams underneath the figure."

Rogers became an ace Imagineer, and assisted in construction of architectural models during the Park's design and development phase. "The first model I did for Disneyland was a little mock-up for the Jungle River ride," Rogers told *The E Ticket* in 1996. "I did the Main Street buildings, too, and these were the models you see Walt demonstrating in the first television programs about Disneyland. All that came about because of the little railroad models that I had in my office at the Studio, during the years just before Disneyland opened."

"I did other things too, in the motion picture side of things. I made some scale models for Ward Kimball's Man in Space programs. I modeled the Moon Rockets themselves—the ones with the big round tanks, which were demonstrated on television. Wernher von Braun and Willey Ley were around the shop a lot, checking the models to their designs and drawings. The rocket model with the tanks was mechanical, and I had to design it so the fuel tanks would break away for the filming, in stop motion. I did models for all of the shows in that series."

He was often asked to contribute his sculpting talents to Studio projects, too, creating props and miniatures for *Darby O'Gill and the Little People* and *The Absent-Minded Professor*, as well as television shows including *The Mickey Mouse Club* and *Zorro*. "It was a lot of fun working on the films, because they'd come rushing around saying, 'Hey, we have a problem here. Wathel, can you help us out?' I worked on the original storybook, with the jewels on it, for the opening scene in *Sleeping Beauty*. It ended up, after the movie, in the Sleeping Beauty Castle exhibit, and I think it's in the Disney Archives now."

In the early 1960s, Rogers also continued to investigate new technology. Project Little Man had paved the way for Walt Disney's real interest, which was to develop an electronically powered, full-size figure. "The next step was to install electromagnetic coils powered by a sound track into a small head we created," Rogers recalled, "so we could synch the movements of the mouth with the sound track itself." The team created a Chinese mask head, a Confucius[3] character that would be the central figure in a Chinese dinner theater setting. "That was our first talking head," said Rogers. "We miked it for sound, and we learned how to create an 'interactive' character." The Enchanted Tiki Room opened in 1963 in Disneyland, featuring animated birds that were distant relatives of the talking head.

3 The Chinese teacher and philosopher Confucius (551–479 B.C.) was the founder of a humanistic school of philosophy known as the Ju, which taught the concepts of benevolence, ritual, and propriety. His Analects contain a collection of his sayings and dialogues compiled by disciples after his death.

The sixteenth President of the United States was Rogers's next big project. He had been working on an animated head of Abraham Lincoln in the early 1960s, for a "Hall of Presidents", an evolution of the talking-Confucius-head project. When the president of the 1964–1965 New York World's Fair asked Walt to showcase this new technology, Wathel and a team at the Studio Machine Shop began to build a body for the Lincoln head. "Walt was very clear in his aim that the Lincoln figure was to stand up and sit down in the course of the presentation," said Rogers. The team came up with a design for realistic facial movement by using small, pneumatically powered tubes in the lips of the Lincoln figure. The figure itself was electronically powered.

"Walt insisted on having a fully operable mouth on the figure, which would be able to shape the sounds A, E, I, O, and U. I worked with the guys in the machine shop and we designed a mouth that would do that. The corners of the mouth, and the areas all around the mouth, had a series of little actuators. That had never been tried before. That method was all made completely from scratch, and we had to develop animated movement for the figure itself, too."

Marty Sklar remembers the night before the Lincoln figure was shipped to New York for the Fair. "It was pouring rain, with all kinds of thunder and lightning, and we couldn't get Mr. Lincoln to work. Marc Davis remarked that God didn't want Lincoln to come back to life. But of course Walt had another idea, and Wathel's team made it happen—they made that Lincoln figure work!" The team ran the Lincoln figure several times before the scheduled inaugural show to ensure that the figure was working correctly. Walt was in the audience for the first preview, as were the mayor of New York City, the state governor, and numerous celebrities. Mr. Lincoln gave a great performance until the very end, when a broken wire caused him to end his speech with a sweeping bow, an unanticipated movement to Rogers but one that was well-received by the crowd. "They went crazy," said Rogers, "you wouldn't believe the applause." The unrehearsed bow was so popular, Walt considered making it permanent. "Ultimately, says Rogers, "Walt decided that Mr. Lincoln should remain upright at the end of the show."

Programming the numerous Audio-Animatronics figures that followed Mr. Lincoln was often an arduous task. While programming Carousel of Progress figures, Wathel spent four-hour periods strapped into a harness fitted with sensors, which relayed Wathel's movements to the static figure. His artistic and technical abilities impressed John Hench, who recalled that time working on the figures. "In those days, you had to strap an actor up in a harness-like device, and the actor's movements would make the figure move. Well, one day we found Wathel in the harness—he just jumped in and did it. He loved it. He had a particular knack for knowing what movements the figures should make and when. He had a good eye and a great sense of animation."

"I had to overreact in the harness," said Wathel, "to get the right movements from the figure. Another problem was that there was always a tiny delay between me and the figure. When we finished a 'take,' I had to be able to return to the position where we left off, or there would be a jerk in the motion because of that, too." The recording tape used at the time could not be spliced, so the programming sequence for each figure had to be taken in one sitting, without interruptions or mistakes. This exhausting show programming method was replaced by joystick controls in the late 1960s, and later, by the computer console system used today.

OPPOSITE TOP: Rogers's work often sent him back to the drawing board, where he had spent much of his early career in Disney's Animation Department.

OPPOSITE BOTTOM: Rogers fabricated the models for Ward Kimball's "Man in Space" episodes of the Disney TV show. His work for this project is now in the National Air and Space Museum of the Smithsonian Institution in Washington, D.C.

BELOW: Rogers wired "Project Little Man" in the early 1950s, Walt himself built the proscenium.

BOTTOM: Every day in the development of the Lincoln figure brought Rogers new problems and new innovations, even after the figure went on public display at the New York World's Fair.

No matter the methods, Rogers saw that all of his work and that of his colleagues had a single point of origin. "The actual specifications of what a figure was to do, the scope and style of the movements, would usually come from Walt himself. He would tell us what the figure was to do within the scene, and then we would set out to try and duplicate what he described. We would let the guys in the shop know what Walt wanted to accomplish, and then we would work together with them as they started drawing it up. We would check with them throughout the design stages until the figure was ready and could be combined with the rest of the show.

"I remember going down to Florida with Walt, when they were first starting to develop all of that land. We stood out there in the middle of Interstate 4, right on the highway. Looking both ways, there wasn't a car in sight, and I said, 'Walt, are you sure this is the place you want to put this thing?' And he said, 'Yes, don't worry about it, Wathel. They'll come from all directions, and we're putting it right here, because it's in the middle.' What a visionary he was."

After Walt's death, Rogers continued creating new attractions such as America Sings in Disneyland and The Hall of Presidents in Walt Disney World, with much of the show programming being done by Wathel and his staff of Audio-Animatronics specialists. "I was involved in the process from the very beginning, sometimes in the Art Direction part of it, sometimes in manufacturing, and sometimes in the development of the system controls and programming. I did every part of it over the years."

He also served as art director for Magic Kingdom Park after its opening and was the forerunner for what later became known as Show Quality Standards. Marty Sklar once remarked, "Any time a problem popped up in Walt Disney World, they would call Wathel and he always had a solution. They really loved him."

Following the opening of the Horizons pavilion in Epcot in October 1983 (for which Wathel supervised the field installation of more than a dozen Audio-Animatronics characters), he entered the hospital for heart bypass surgery. Complications resulting from the surgery kept him in the hospital for four months, followed by a long period of recuperation at home. "It was a difficult time for me," Rogers said, "but I received a lot of care and attention from my friends and co-workers. People went out of their way to let me know that they were waiting for me back at Imagineering. I wasn't allowed to forget that I had important reasons to get out of bed." By fall of 1984, Rogers was back at work.

Rogers retired in 1987 after forty-eight years with Disney, to Sedona, Arizona, where he joined a company of many artists and longtime Imagineering friends such as Blaine Gibson and art director Bob Jolley. "I'm going to paint landscapes, which I really enjoy doing," Rogers said at the time. It was there that he passed away on August 25, 2000.

Of working at Imagineering, Wathel said, "Each day presents new ideas to explore. If one has to work, there is nothing else I'd rather be doing."

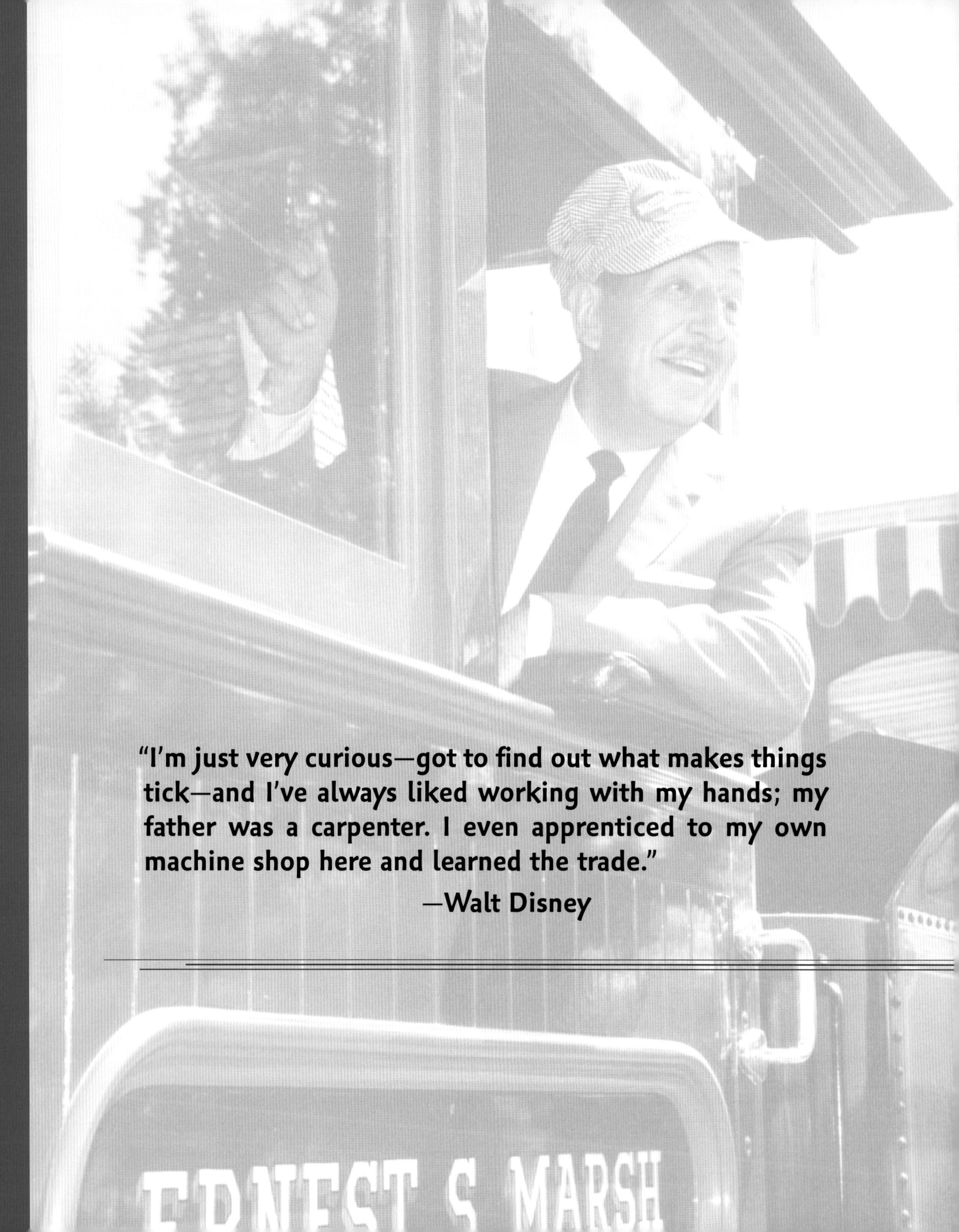

"I'm just very curious—got to find out what makes things tick—and I've always liked working with my hands; my father was a carpenter. I even apprenticed to my own machine shop here and learned the trade."

—Walt Disney

The Machine Shop

"Well, WED is, you might call it, my backyard laboratory, my workshop away from work," Walt Disney said in a 1964 interview. This was not just glib publicity chat—Walt enjoyed both the solace and the sense of accomplishment that working with his hands offered, and the reward in working with and learning from experts in departments like his own Studio Machine Shop. "Since my outlook and attitudes are ingrained throughout our organization," Walt believed, "all our people have this curiosity; it keeps us moving forward, exploring, experimenting, opening new doors."

Roger Broggie: The Machine Man

"Roger was one of those people Walt had absolute confidence in," said his close friend John Hench. "No matter what the project, Roger pulled it off. From original photographic devices to a small-scale steam train and full-sized locomotives, Walt Disney got what he asked for."

Roy E. Disney recalled fondly, "Any mechanical things you had to do, what you said was, 'Call Roger, he'll know how to fix it.' Without him, Disneyland would never have happened."

Roger Broggie, born in 1908 in Pittsfield, Massachusetts, was one of the most influential Imagineers to ever work with Walt Disney. Broggie lived in Worcester, Massachusetts, until he was eleven years old, when his father died. He was sent to the Mooseheart Child City and School, a residential child-care facility west of Chicago, Illinois.[1] "Which was I think probably a school similar to Japanese schools," said Broggie. "The school actually operated forty-eight weeks a year. [It] had scholastic classes in the morning, and vocational classes in the afternoon. And we went from one vocational class to another in the seventh and eighth grades, each one for three months: carpenter class, painting, drafting, and so on." When Broggie entered high school, he liked the machine shop class, and stayed there through the entire four years.

"At the end of that time, I qualified as a third-year apprentice in Western Electric in Chicago; [they] manufactured telephones for AT&T. Instead of that, I went to California. My first job there was working for a manufacturing company that was a heavy machine shop, which built equipment to build Boulder Dam. I realized I was qualified for the small work, and so I found out that there was a business in the Los Angeles area, and the first job I got went to work for a company that was making equipment to make color motion pictures."

He was initially employed as a precision machinist by Dupont Vitacolor Corporation,[2] then Technicolor, followed by Bell & Howell. In 1932, he built and operated a rear-projection system for Teague Process Company based at Metropolitan Sound Studios (now Hollywood Center Studios). During this period, he worked on films for Harold Lloyd, Walter Wanger, and other producers at Metropolitan. He also worked on *Modern Times* and *The Great Dictator* for Charlie Chaplin, and films produced by the David O. Selznick Studio in Culver City.

By 1937, Broggie was working at Universal Studios' special-effects department building process projectors housed in sound blimps.[3] Two years later, he had an opportunity to join the Walt Disney Studios. "The first cartoons crafted by Disney in color [were] done at the Technicolor lab," Broggie said. "When Disney wanted to have his own [color] camera department, Mickey Bachelor moved there from Technicolor. Bachelor hired [Dick] Jones. I was working at Universal in the special-effects department at that time. Jones called me and I thought, 'well, I'll go to Disney and find how they make these cartoons. I might learn something.'"

In 1939, he was hired at the Walt Disney Studios as a camera maintenance precision machinist, maintaining the camera equipment at the Hyperion Avenue Studio in Silver Lake. "I found out they hired me to fix their equipment, which was all right, I liked the company. I thought it was the best studio in town." Soon he joined the move to the

BELOW: Walt spent hundreds of hours in the Studio Machine Shop during the building of the *Lilly Belle* and the rest of the Carolwood Pacific. Broggie taught him to use the shop tools, and Walt became a proficient machinist.

1 Dedicated in July 1913 by the Moose fraternal organization, Mooseheart cares for youth whose families are unable, for a variety of reasons, to care for them.

2 Unrelated to the E. I. du Pont de Nemours and Company (duPont) petrochemical company, this company was named for cinematographer Max Dupont. After Broggie's departure, John Hench also worked for Vitacolor.

3 A blimp was a housing designed to muffle or deaden the sound of the mechanism inside.

new Disney lot in Burbank, where one of his initial tasks was to build and install the multiplane camera.

At the beginning of World War II, Roger established the Studio's Machine Shop, which was primarily used for creating special effects such as simulating airplanes and shops for military training films. He toiled happily in Camera and Effects at the Burbank studio, and recalled that he actually had no interaction with Walt Disney directly for the better part of a decade. That circumstance changed, however. "In 1949, Walt came down in the shop and wanted to find out about something called 'live steam equipment.' Walt knew that a draftsman in the shop, Eddie Sargent,[4] had built small locomotives and wanted help looking for equipment for himself, but what he saw was too modern to his liking. "So we dug up some photographs and found one that he liked, which turned out to be Number 172 of the Central Pacific Railroad, built about 1870. It was one of the first locomotives built on the West Coast, because there was no trans-continental railroad at that time."

From that photograph, Broggie secured a blueprint from the Southern Pacific Railroad. He and Sargent made drawings to a seven-and-a-quarter-inch gauge, which is one-eighth a full-size locomotive. A live steam engine of this type is large enough for the engineer to ride behind (sitting on the tender) while taking cars with passengers around the track. During its construction in the studio machine shop, Broggie taught Walt to use various shop tools so that he could help make some of the parts for the locomotive. "In the process of building the cars and the locomotive, he came down to the shop and said, 'Well, you gotta let me do some of these things, so show me how.' Walt spent many hours building parts for this engine, such as the smokestack, the flagpoles, and other small parts. He insisted on building the caboose on his own.

"I think we had something like twelve cars, cattle cars and freight cars and gondolas, and this caboose," Broggie recalls. "The first time the locomotive ran was on December 24, 1950. There was a party at the Studio and Walt said, 'Let's put this train on the track, and we'll give people rides.' Fortunately, the first time we fired it up, it ran."[5]

Soon, Walt's railroad, the Carolwood Pacific, was up and running on his property in the Holmby Hills neighborhood of West Los Angeles, where he and his family had moved in 1949. Walt's 2,615 feet of track included a 46-foot-long trestle, loops, overpasses, gradients, and an elevated earthen berm. A 90-foot tunnel was both a benefit and a compromise with Lilly Disney, to avoid having to run track through a favorite floral feature of her backyard landscaping and leaving a side of the house undisturbed by rail activity. He also named his steam locomotive the *Lilly Belle* in her honor.[6]

4 Sargent was hired in the Camera Department in October 1940; released only five months later, in 1941. In 1944 he was rehired as a draftsman, working there sporadically until August 1955.

5 Footage of the train running on its Studio trial can be seen in a promotional short of the time called *Operation: Wonderland*, a behind-the-scenes look at the making of *Alice in Wonderland*.

6 The story of the Carolwood Pacific is exhaustively documented in Michael Broggie's book *Walt Disney's Railroad Story: The Small-Scale Fascination That Led to a Full-Scale Kingdom* (1997, 2005, Donning Company Publishers; Virginia Beach, VA).

In 1950, Broggie was promoted to department head of the studio Machine Shop and its staff of a dozen machinists. "[Dick] Jones had died," Broggie said humbly, "and I became department head." This event, combined with Walt's increasing interest in miniatures and mechanics, saw Walt and Broggie spending more time together in the shop. Walt began his work on the elaborate miniature of Granny Kincaid's cabin, and sought Broggie's input on how to bring automated motion to the scene. "Walt built that set, and he had a laundry outside the window with clothes on it. We had to put a fan behind it to make the clothes move." He also discussed with Broggie making an automaton of Granny, who could rock in her chair by the cozy fireside, while a recorded narration by Beulah Bondi (the actress who had played Granny Kincaid in *So Dear to My Heart*) told the story of the diorama.

ABOVE: Cristadoro's sculpture of one of "The Drunkard" for the Disneylandia project. Note the beer mug in his right hand.

OPPOSITE, TOP: The backstage dwarfs the stage in this mechanical vaudeville scene, officially known as "Project Little Man" but dubbed "the telephone booth" by the Machine Shop staff.

Walt's curiosity about how things worked only seemed to grow. He brought home a number of mechanical birds from his travels, and gave them to several Studio colleagues to examine. "That was the bird in the cage. He wanted Sam Slyfield, [head of the] Sound Department and myself to take a look at it and, and find out how it works. Basically, it's a clock mechanism. The sound itself is a bellows. When you squeeze a bellows, air comes out, and it goes across the reed like a harmonica, and the bird makes the sound. I don't think it was anything on his mind that he wanted to make a lot of birds. He just wanted to know."

Walt's work on Granny's Cabin led to more elaborate and complex mechanical diorama ideas, including the well-documented Project Little Man. "We built the figure nine inches tall, with what I call cams and cables. We put springs up through the feet of this figure and operated these cables, and that made the figure dance. [It] was very cumbersome. The cam had to have a three-foot diameter for a two-minute show, and the controls that went up and down it had to be patterned around that perimeter. And we had to synchronize the sound with that cam.

"Then we also started a barbershop quartet. There was a barber, a man in the chair, and two other men in this set of an old-fashioned barbershop. We were going to have the barbershop, a little grocery store, the dancing man, and so on. The ultimate thought was that there might be some twenty or twenty-five scenes in miniature. There had been static exhibits of dollhouses. There's a very famous one that went around the country[7] that you'd walk through. [Walt's idea was] twenty or so small rooms, all done like dollhouses. His would be animated, in scale, an inch and a half to the foot, and that each one of these would be a piece of Americana.

"We started [the quartet], started programming four figures, all on three-foot cams, when I was asked what would it cost to operate that if we had, let's say, about a dozen of these little sets. And I said, 'Well, those figures are only nine inches tall. And if we build all those sets, everybody that goes through the ride looking at it will put a quarter in the slot. You'll never pay the maintenance costs, because everything is too small.' And on that basis, the whole project was killed. I finally said to Walt, 'What we're doing is the same thing that was done for the kings of the sixteenth and seventeenth centuries. We ought to be something better. We should get into large figures, big, full-size figures, and then we have better control on what we do."

Broggie continued his work in the Machine Shop while "moonlighting" on Walt's many miniature and mechanical fascinations. In fact, as the Studio ventured into full live-action production, television, and new animation technology, Broggie was busier than ever. "In 1954, we were converting to CinemaScope, with a shop of twelve men. I was on special effects on *20,000 Leagues* when Walt said, 'You gotta stop this now, because we now have a contract for this amusement park, and we got a year to do it in, and you've got to be making big dreams instead of little ones.'"

7 Broggie is probably referring to the famous Fairy Castle dollhouse of silent movie star Colleen Moore. The star owned several elaborate dollhouses as a child; her later fame gave her the resources to expand her collection. By 1935 more than 700 individuals had lent their expertise to produce a "Fairy Castle" of fantastic proportions (8'7" x 8'2" x 7'7") containing more than 2,000 miniatures, valued at nearly $500,000. In 1935, Moore organized a famous national tour of the Fairy Castle to raise money for children's charities. Moore donated the Fairy Castle to the Chicago Museum of Science and Industry in 1949, where it is still proudly displayed today.

A train, naturally, was a primary component of even the earliest concepts for Walt's amusement park, and Broggie was prepared to bring it to life. "Since we already had the drawings from which we made the railroad that went around his house, we just made the drawings five times larger, and that became the thirty-six-inch gauge railroad that went around Disneyland." Railroad engines weren't the only mode of power built in Burbank. "We also built the steam engines that drove the *Mark Twain* riverboat." By 1954, the Machine Shop had moved to a new larger facility on the Studio lot and was producing rides and shows for the park.

Under Broggie's direction, new processes and techniques were also being developed and introduced, such as Circarama, later renamed Circle-Vision 360, a format that creates a motion picture that completely surrounds the audience. The public first experienced Circarama at the opening of Disneyland in 1955. "That's a case of Walt walking in on us in the shop. He had just seen a three-screen film,[8] and he comes in and says, 'Look, there's three screens side by side. Why is it that you can't go 360 degrees, go all the way around?' Well, all we could say was, that's true, you can do it. And we did." The initial camera consisted of eleven Cine Special cameras equipped with 200-foot film magazines and 15mm lenses. The Circarama, U.S.A. attraction opened in Disneyland in 1955 with the 12-minute film *A Tour of the West*. A second Circarama short, a 16-minute film called *America the Beautiful*, was created for the 1958 World's Fair in Brussels, Belgium, and opened at the Circarama Theater in Disneyland in 1960.

Later that year, Broggie and Ub Iwerks rebuilt the entire camera system, changing the camera array to nine Arriflex 16mm units with 400-foot magazines and 12½ mm wide-angle lenses. In addition, each camera was operated by its own motor, all interlocked mechanically, and operated by a single control box. The box included a rheostat for adjusting speed, a tachometer, a footage counter, and a malfunction warning system.[9] This new Circarama was used to film *Italia '61*, for the Fiat Corporation exhibit at the Italia '61 Exposition in Turin, Italy.

The system was revamped yet again in 1964, for the making of *The Magic of the Rails*, sponsored by Swiss Federal Railways, and shown at the 1964 Swiss National Exposition in Lausanne, Switzerland (and later in Germany). The new system used an array of 35mm cameras instead of 16mm, which created a more solid, less grainy image when projected.

The Circarama process was also renamed CircleVision 360 at this time, at the gentle urging of the legal representatives of the Cinerama Corporation. Ten more films have been made using progressive improvements of this camera system.

By 1958, the studio machine shop was staffed with seventy employees, producing the Monorail system, Matterhorn Bobsleds, and dozens of other attractions and technologies for the expanding Disneyland. Broggie's suggestion that the Imagineers' work in automatons should "get into large figures, big, full-size figures" took almost a decade to see fruition, beginning with the development of a full-sized robotic Confucius figure. When work on the human figure didn't progress to Walt's standards, the show idea was reconceived as a dinner show in an enchanted South Pacific aviary. Creating credible birds was simply easier than making a believable human.

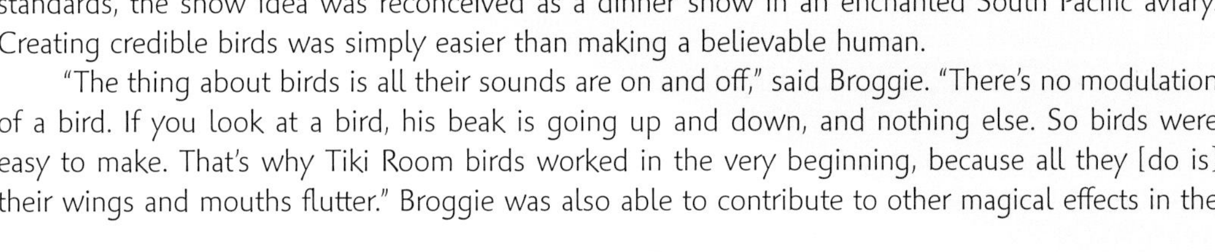

"The thing about birds is all their sounds are on and off," said Broggie. "There's no modulation of a bird. If you look at a bird, his beak is going up and down, and nothing else. So birds were easy to make. That's why Tiki Room birds worked in the very beginning, because all they [do is] their wings and mouths flutter." Broggie was also able to contribute to other magical effects in the

8 Walt had no doubt seen the Los Angeles premiere engagement of *This Is Cinerama* at the Warner Hollywood Theatre, which opened April 29, 1953.

9 With the earlier setup, when something went wrong it was often not discovered until it was too late to repair or reshoot.

attraction. "The engineering group was working on a fountain that was to shoot up about ten or twelve feet. Everything they tried to make the water go up failed, because water is heavy. I said all we have to do is get a six-inch tube of glass, fill it with water, and we pump it up. You see the water, but not the glass itself."

The success of Walt Disney's Enchanted Tiki Room only encouraged Walt that his team should and could create a convincing animated human figure, which they achieved at the 1964-1965 New York World's Fair. Walt Disney was delighted with Great Moments with Mr. Lincoln. Broggie, however, never seemed content with the first iteration of anything. Initially, the Audio-Animatronics figures had to be laboriously programmed by means of a harness fitted with sensors that relayed movements to the static figure. The animator had to "overact" to get the right movements and there were many tiny nuances and "cheats" that had to be learned and the programming sequence for each figure had to be done in one sitting. This complexity vexed Broggie. "On the New York Fair, the shows were programmed 'at speed.' I thought, if it's possible, we should look into a system that uses stop-motion electronically, which turned out to be a computer system. So the first thing I did was hire computer engineers who built equipment that animators could understand. In the cartoon business, I learned a lot of things. For example, when you speak, the first thing you do is open your mouth, and the time lapse between opening your mouth and the sound coming out is two frames. So we programmed stop-motion by computer systems, frame by frame. We could advance and play back, like today's equipment. But at that time it was all-new to program animated shows by computer rather than use real time."

This method not only created more detailed and credible animation, it was a much more efficient technique than the real-time recording done in the animation sensor harness. "On that basis,' Broggie continued, "we were able to build ten shows at one time, and opened up in Florida using the same two or three animators who had moved from the Studio over to WED." Nearly every major attraction at the Disney parks in Anaheim, Orlando, Tokyo, Paris, and Hong Kong, has an application of Audio-Animatronics, establishing the remarkable animation technique as a hallmark in the entertainment industry.

At the conclusion of the Fair, Roger was transferred to WED Enterprises in Glendale, California, and was promoted to vice president and general manager of Mapo, Inc., the manufacturing subsidiary of WED Enterprises. "The name Mapo was something Walt disliked very much. We asked, well, what does that mean, M-A-P-O? The accountant responds, we made $40 million off of *Mary Poppins*, so let's call this company Mapo. Walt says, 'That's a hell of a name.' I said, 'Well, the paperwork's already gone to Sacramento, and that's going to be the corporate name.'"[10]

After Walt Disney's death, like many of his colleagues Broggie found that without Walt's gyroscope, he was much less at ease. "I functioned much better when he was there than after he died. The ten years after he left, I discovered that I was facing committees making decisions and that it took a great deal of time as compared to [Walt] making his decisions about how things should be done." During that time, WED was beginning to design and produce shows and attractions for Walt Disney World, which was then the largest privately funded construction project in history. Starting with eighty employees in 1965, Mapo reached 285 by the opening of Walt Disney World in 1971.

In addition to mechanical animation and camera processes, Broggie directed the design and construction of all Disney conveyance systems including the monorail, WEDway PeopleMover, Skyway, and the narrow-gauge railroad that surrounds Magic Kingdom Park. Broggie had learned a little something between the hand-fabrication of the Disneyland and Santa Fe Railroad and the planning of the Walt Disney World counterpart. "It's cheaper to restore a locomotive than it is to build one from scratch. We built locomotives 1 and 2 in Anaheim from all new material. Then when Walt wanted another train, I looked into equipment that was for sale. I think I paid twelve hundred [dollars] for locomotive 3. To do the same thing would be more like twenty or twenty-five thousand. Then we bought a second one from a place in New Jersey, and put it in a boxcar, and shipped it to the studio, restored it, and had locomotives 3 and 4."

For the locomotives for Florida, Broggie found out that the country of Yucatan, Mexico, was changing from steam-gauge to standard-gauge diesel and they were junking equipment. "There was a boneyard, so I went down there to take a look at what they had. We bought about five locomotives from them and we moved them to Tampa. I was told on the Florida project, anything that we can manufacture in the state of Florida, we should do." Broggie found a shipyard that had been in the business of converting World War II–era freighters to use as

10 Mapo is still in business, although in the interim, a credible reverse-engineered source for its acronym was conceived: Manufacturing and Production Organization.

oil tankers. "They had a lot of machinery to do what we wanted to do to the locomotives. So we restored four locomotives. They're in Florida now."

In 1973, Broggie was named vice president of research and development for WED Enterprises, leaving Mapo to concentrate on development of Epcot and ski resorts in California. On October 1, 1975, he retired from the company under a mandatory program for employees reaching the age of sixty-five. He continued to act as a consultant to the Disney organization and was occasionally invited to represent the company at public functions.

Roger Broggie passed away on November 4, 1991, survived by his wife of thirty-five years, Mary, his sons Roger, Jr., Michael, and Brian, seven grandchildren, and nine great-grandchildren. Eight members and three generations of the Broggie family have worked for the Disney organization, including Garry Broggie, now a member of the Studio's Camera Department, where his grandfather started more than six decades ago.

As testimony to his unique contributions to the company, one of the four steam locomotives in Walt Disney World was dedicated in his honor. The *Roger E. Broggie* is one of two identical 4-6-0 engines with consecutive serial numbers originally built in 1925 at the Baldwin Locomotive Works in Pennsylvania. Its twin was named the *Walter E. Disney*. Two other locomotives are the *Roy O. Disney*, named for Walt's brother and co-founder of The Walt Disney Company, and the *Lilly Belle*, named for Walt's wife, Lillian Disney.

"I never said I couldn't do anything for [Walt]," said Broggie, "I said, 'Well, we'll try it.' I was able to gain his confidence. That's how I always got along with Walt Disney, because I've been asked lots of times, 'How was it to work for this man?' I never had any problems, because I was from a different field than he was. I was fortunate that I could interpret what he wanted to be done. I never had any opinions about how to make cartoons—that was his business, and mine was something else."

BELOW: Walt rides the prototype of the WEDway PeopleMover for Disneyland at WED in 1966. Sadly, he passed away before the system was installed.

Bob Gurr thinks that being a tenacious problem-solver was a great strength of Broggie's—one that was understood by Walt, but perhaps misunderstood by others. "A lot of people didn't understand him because he'd just look at you and he wouldn't say a word. Or you'd say hello to him, and he'd just look at you. It bothered salesmen from the outside, because they wondered, what did they do wrong? But it was Roger's nature. He was very reticent, no-nonsense, and was totally focused on what had to be done—and he did it without explanation. In a way, it drove a lot of the people around him totally nuts because of that kind of a manner. But in the crunch, he always made—almost always—the right business decisions."

Broggie's own perception of his long and influential Disney career support Gurr's view of his taciturn perspective and manner. "I worked for the company thirty-six years, and all that time, I liked what I did. That's why I stayed there."

Bob Gurr: A World on The Move

"If it had wheels, Walt gave me the first crack at it," Bob Gurr says without a hint of conceit. "It was just, 'Bobby is the car designer.'"

Gurr shared a fundamental interest with Walt Disney—the technology and beauty of transportation. Born in Los Angeles, California, in 1932, Gurr said, "My first word, my dad says, was 'airplane' rather than 'daddy.' I was a little brat, and by five years old—I was living next to an airport—I decided I liked airplanes and cars, and that's what I wanted to do at five years old. I'm the kind that, at five years old, would crawl under a hole in the fence and climb into an American Airlines DC-3 and play with the controls until the mechanics came and threw me out. So the interest in doing something with vehicles was established very early on.

"Through junior high and high school, I pursued designing airplanes, but my math was so bad that I said, 'Well, I'd better design cars.' So I took architecture in high school, because the drafting teacher would let me draw cars." Gurr's teacher also suggested that he attend Art Center College of Design, which he did after leaving high school in 1949. He received his bachelor's degree in industrial design, and although he attended Art Center on a General Motors scholarship, he went to Detroit and wound up working for the Ford Motor Company.

"After going to a four-year college to design automobiles, I could see after two weeks that being a California native living in Detroit was a dead end—this was not going to be a life. Try to visualize it—twenty years old, out of college, your mind's made up, you get there, and it's not it. That meant my antenna was up, and I was open to anything to see what's coming."

Gurr was invited to work for George Walker Industrial Design in Detroit, where he "got to do tire treads and garbage trucks and all the other exciting stuff," and also worked on the Lincoln Continental Mark II project, which Walker was doing in competition with four other companies. "The car that I helped design came in number two in the competition with the Ford Motor Company for the Lincoln Continental Mark II, which was a 1955 car—and that was in 1952." Gurr soon returned to Southern California. In 1953, he bought a rubber stamp and an invoice pad, and inaugurated R.H. Gurr Industrial Design—a company of one, whose first big job was to consult with WED Enterprises on the design of a project called Autopia. "I still have the stamp." Gurr said.

R. H. GURR
INDUSTRIAL DESIGN

"That was in October of 1954. I was a good friend of Ub Iwerks, because I went to high school with his son and I went to their formal Sunday dinner every month. Of course, sitting around the Iwerks' house, Ub would always tell us about interesting things. Then Ub says, 'Yeah, we got a little car running around in the back lot and it doesn't have a body on it.' A few days later, I got a phone call saying, 'Meet me at the Disney Studios in twenty minutes.' So I waved at my boss and walked out the door without explanation and drove to the Studio, and that was the start of the career. I got out there and met Dick Irvine. In fact, he came out to the gate to meet me. I thought that was pretty cool. Sure enough, he took me into a room and said, 'Can you draw a body for this little car?'"

ABOVE: Walt and a young Bob Gurr test out one of the later generation Autopia cars (note the introduction of a track guide rail).

OPPOSITE: Bob Gurr designed and oversaw the construction of the original Disneyland Monorail, seen here at its June 14, 1959, dedication with Walt and the Richard M. Nixon family. Television host Art Linkletter peeks out from inside the bubble.

Gurr joined the Disneyland team, but wasn't especially surprised that he wasn't ushered into Walt Disney's office for a personal meeting. Walt was, after all, the head of the whole operation, and the fact that he had been greeted personally by Dick Irvine was impressive enough for the young Gurr. His first encounter with Walt was the antithesis of Hollywood glamour. "I was working on the body for this little Autopia car for Disneyland," Gurr said. "We were working Saturdays in those days. Of course, when you have a whole automobile with no body on it, there are tires and guys will walk up, put their foot on a tire and then lean with their elbow on their knee. We had a spare tire available and this guy walks up. He was unshaven and I remember he had something like a Roy Rogers belt on, with little silver painted fake bullets and a funny-looking tie, and I thought he was probably a father of one of the night guards, because he just sort of oozed into the conversation. Then I noticed the other guys were calling him Walt, and, when everybody walked away, I thought, 'Gosh, that's Walt Disney.'"

Walt was so impressed with Gurr's work that he hired him as a permanent employee at WED. "When I went to the Studio, people said, 'Oh, you have to have a business card. What's your title, Bob?' I thought Director of Special Vehicle Development sounded kind of fancy. It's a title that just came out of thin air. I never was aware of titles or positions in the company because we were always working on stuff, but something had to go on the card." Gurr began to design and supervise a fleet of Autopia vehicles. "When we built the first forty cars, two of them were planned as police cars. They had sheriff's badges on their hoods, and red lights. There was a third one, which I insisted should be a 'special,' and it became known by everybody as 'Walt's car.' It was our 'show car.' The rest of the cars were standard, designed for the public to drive, while the three were used for promotional stuff. The standard cars didn't have windshields (just 'grab bars') but Walt's car had a plastic windshield and special upholstery. We made special spun wheel covers and a pattern for some brass knockoffs to hold the spinnings over the wheels. That car's bumper was an actual 1953 Pontiac upper bumper bar that we sliced, rewelded, and rechromed to look like a new bumper. Otherwise, the car was mechanically the same as the others. I patterned those earliest cars after the Ferrari."

Walt had an inescapable faith in the people he put his trust in, and on the opening day of Disneyland, Gurr found himself in a peculiar position for a twenty-three-year-old: completely supported and endorsed on the basis of someone else's instinct. "I found out later how much I didn't know about designing cars. When Walt said, 'Hey, Bobby, you gonna design the body of the car?' he naturally assumed that if I drew the bodies, I [also] did the mechanical part. I never had the courage to say I didn't. So this was a learning experience, to get those cars running. By the end of [Disneyland's] first day, about half the cars were out of commission, and within a week, I think two out of the forty cars were the only ones left running."

Gurr expected the worst. "You know, [Walt] never really got upset. I was out in the field with my own tools and my own Cadillac, sitting outside Autopia trying to fix these cars as fast as they would fall apart. And after a week and a half or so, Walt came by and sat there in the shade looking at the whole thing, not any real strong emotion or anything, but he indicated, 'Well, we got to do something.' In other words, he wasn't critical. He wouldn't jump on you and say, 'You designed junk, make these things work!' I said, 'We don't have anything designed here to maintain the cars with.' So he went away, and about a half hour later, comes a guy driving an old tractor dragging this little wooden building on a sled down the dirt road. 'Where do you want your damn garage? Walt just sent this over here.' Walt would see something, and though he wouldn't be really critical, he'd go make sure it got fixed."

Gurr's career at WED ultimately spanned more than three decades. He worked on more than a hundred designs for vehicles and attractions, including the second Disneyland and Walt Disney World monorails, Matterhorn Bobsleds, and the memorable Disneyland Flying Saucers.

"In those days, Walt was gathering people almost like instruments in an orchestra. He put us all together, but he never passed out the music. Oddly enough, I think he was the only one who knew where he was going to go. He knew the different skills that all the different folks had, and I think that was the method he used to pick people—put them all together, and only he knew what the outcome was generally going to be.

"What we were asked to do generally didn't exist, and in a way, that's a blessing. You don't waste any time researching because there was nothing to research. You just grab your pencil and you start. And I think that was the thing that taught everybody how to do their craft really well. An MBA would say it's cross-utilization, and that 'cross' is just far enough. It's like I would work in a machine shop, and I could nose into high-voltage electrical power, or DC power, or I could nose into the Camera Department, or I could go over and nose into the Welding Department or watch the guys machine stuff or watch the pattern maker work, building wood patterns for steel castings, even though that's not my level of expertise. But I could get education by going over and talking to these other guys.

"Learning by doing" was a credo of Walt Disney's, and it couldn't have suited young Gurr better. "A number of us worked on the [Disneyland] railroad. I worked on the first excursion train, which was the Narragansett open-type car. Roger [Broggie] had me design a car out of steel so it would look like it was built out of wood. So again, that was a new experience, because I'd never worked on a railroad, but I learned about historic railroad construction by doing that job.

"This all goes to the fact that I think [Walt] was inherently extremely curious, and when he would get curious about something, he'd go at it quite thoroughly. I'm never quite sure how he did all that, because all the stuff that was going on at the Studio at that time was a massive amount of stuff. I think he did it by walking around. Walt would simply walk over to the machine shop, walk up behind the guy building something on the bench, and stand and watch. Walt was totally informed by informing himself—if he was curious, he would ask a guy about something. That's a very crucial thing."

Since his earliest fascination with railroads, transportation was a passion of Walt's. On a trip to Germany, he and Lilly encountered the Alweg Monorail—and Walt was utterly enthused. Gurr remembered, "If you look at the original sketches made up for Disneyland, in some of these original sketches, there was a monorail. It was kind of an overhead, hanging type of monorail. After [Walt] saw the Alweg train in Germany, 1958, [he] got hold of Roger Broggie and myself and said, 'Fellows, I just found the monorail, and I would like to have you get started and see if you can figure out how we can do this.' I had never seen this type of train before, and I got all excited, and started figuring out how we were gonna do it, because it would be what we call the German 'saddlebag' type of train that sits on a beam rather than hangs. I had never seen that before. But the shape of the German trains was so ugly. Like a loaf of bread with a slot in the bottom, sitting on a stick. I can remember thinking, 'How am I going to hide the beamway with the slot in the bottom of the train?' I remembered the old Buck Rogers rocket ship of the 1930s, which had a pointed front, and had two fans acting like sled runners down the side, and I thought, 'A-ha! That would hide the beam. The train would look pointy and really neat-looking, [with a] wraparound windshield.' Walt took one look at that thing, tapped on it, and said, 'Bobby, can you build that?' and stupidly I replied, 'Yes.' I found out later I had drawn some parts that were almost impossible to build. But that's all it was, to go from an idea that he wanted, and now we had something that was really neat."

Gurr joined the Disney team during an idyllic and creatively prosperous time in company history. Unlike many of his colleagues, Gurr had not experienced the Hyperion Studio, the days when animation was king; the early, more detached and intellectual fame of Walt Disney. As projects such as the New York World's Fair and Walt's vision of a planned city came to the fore, Gurr began to spend more and more time with Walt. The Walt that Gurr got to know was one of the first major celebrities of the television generation.

"I remember one day, he came over to my office and he just sat down with a big sigh, and he said something like, 'Oh, Bobby, I made a mistake. I can't pump my own gas, and I can't go to the drugstore to get my own medicine anymore. Everybody wants an autograph. Before the television program, nobody knew me.' The way he said it, he was truly sad that something was slipping away. I never forgot that because I felt it must be painful to not be able to do what you want anymore." Gurr noticed and appreciated the efforts Walt made to "step down from the Mount," and diffuse the intimidation often caused by his celebrity. "I think Walt was always very aware that, to a lot of people, he was kind of a god-like figure, but from a practical standpoint, when you're working with people and you're communicating with them, you've got to have a natural ease with that communication. We were visiting Westinghouse in Pittsburgh, and Don

Burnham, the chairman of the board of Westinghouse at that time—the key figure in Westinghouse—met Walt—the key figure at Walt Disney Productions—at a cocktail hour. I noticed that Don Burnham's lower lip began to quiver and he was having a hard time talking, the closer that Walt got to him. Walt would deliberately do things, little motions, like loosening his tie and making his clothes kind of askew so that you felt kind of friendly, he was more approachable figure. I saw this all the time. He would take a few minutes to calm everybody else down, that it's okay, it's only me, and these are ideas, and we want to talk about them.

"He had a little funny porkpie type of hat that he would stuff in a side pocket, and when we'd go outside of a building to look at some equipment, he'd pick this little hat up and simply plop it on his head and not even rearrange it. Wherever it hit, that was it, and I think that, in combination with keeping his tie sort of askew, always made him look sort of semi-ratty and I think that was the signal that he was subtly sending to everybody

LEFT: Walt rides a 1965 Ford Mustang convertible through the Magic Skyway at the 1964–1965 New York World's Fair. The Mustang made its public debut at the Fair.

BELOW: Despite everyone's best efforts, mechanical problems would ground the Disneyland Flying Saucers in 1966, after just five years.

that, yeah, I might be Walt Disney, but I'm really an easy guy to talk to."

Gurr remembers an even more unusual incident. "The three of us [Walt, Gurr, and Joe Fowler] walked into the drugstore at the Sheraton Hotel in Pittsburgh to get a cheeseburger. In the store, Walt noticed that the merchandise rack had the Disney merchandise down on the bottom. So he said something like, 'Come on, boys. Let's fix this!' If you can, imagine the three of us fully grown men, down on our knees, picking up the Disney merchandise and the sales tags off the bottom racks, and putting them up on the top, and then putting whatever merchandise was up there back down on the lower one. And a saleslady comes over and, very obstinately, says, 'May I help you?' Walt says, 'No, we're all done here.' And then we went over to get our cheeseburgers."

As Walt's interests expanded and evolved, so did Gurr's. The 1964–1965 New York's World Fair brought a whole new generation of transportation technology with the OmniMover system initially created for the Ford Motor Company's Magic Skyway ride.

"I was asked to participate in all four of the attractions," Gurr said. "The State of Illinois exhibit started quite late in the job, and unbeknownst to the lot of the people in the Studio, Walt had a little secret room at the machine shop, where some guys were working on this animated human—and it wasn't working well at all. One day, Walt called Roger [Broggie] to get me to come over and take a look at it, and I was surprised to see there was something going on that I didn't know about. Walt was really upset. He showed us this Lincoln, which was very heavy and had hydraulic leaks in it. I remember he looked at this thing, and he said, 'Bobby, I want twice as many motions and half as much weight. Can you do that?' It was obviously another one of the jobs where you say, 'Yeah, I'll start.' I drew up all the parts in that thing, and had it all figured out, in about ninety days, not knowing that there was a lot of electronics that had to be figured out by everybody else, all the rest of the staging, and what not, until it finally worked. You could see that Walt had that twinkle in his eye like, 'Look, world—look what I just did!'"

The most exciting notion at the end of Walt's life was his EPCOT concept. Gurr and his boss, Roger Broggie, and a core company of other stalwarts were often invited to meet, discuss, and research technology and industry for application to what Marty Sklar adroitly dubbed "Waltopia." "In January 1966," Gurr recalled, "Walt took twelve of us on the company plane on a sales junket, to Pittsburgh to meet with Westinghouse. This was really one of the first official go-out-and-sell-it junkets, one of the very first. We had a Gulfstream G-1 in those days, turbo powered. And [Walt would] make us travel on Sundays, and I finally figured out why. You can work on Sunday. He would drag along the proposed designs for EPCOT and unfold the plans on a big table and gather us all around. We're sitting there at 21,000 feet, banging along in turbulence, on a Sunday, and he's got all these ideas going, and he's sketching away like mad on the drawings with us all afternoon.

"The EPCOT that Walt had in his mind, to me, was very, very clear. Literally, Walt was going to provide the playground, and he was going to invite all kinds of companies with their products and their ideas, to come to this playground and participate with the guests that would come to EPCOT. This obviously meant that the people who were going to come from different companies were going to be living there, almost like a sabbatical. EPCOT would be the great demonstration of how tomorrow's communities could evolve by actually being a community, albeit temporary in the nature, that the participants from the various companies would have people who would stay there, work there every day for a temporary period of time, almost as if they were citizens, because that meant it could always be evolving, there's always fresh people, fresh ideas. Then the idea I think Walt always had was the observers, the guests, would now be able to go back to their communities and say, 'You know, some of this might work. We were there, we saw how some of this is starting to work.' That was the idea. This would be the genesis place of where, truly, we as a big world civilization could actually make a really nice place to go live."

EPCOT, in Walt's mind, was already as real a place as his Studio, or Disneyland, or his own home. Gurr agreed, "In fact, several of us remember Walt said, 'Nighttime. Lilly and I are going to sit on the bench and we're going to watch people right there.' So I knew there was a place that was going to have a human touch right smack in the middle of it."

Late in 1966, Gurr began to notice that Walt was out of sorts. "He was more irritable. For example, we were working on the body for the Monsanto OmniMover. I did a design and I didn't really like it, but Walt came over and he approved it, and then the guy that was president of Monsanto came along and he wanted it done differently. I remember [Walt] was very pissed that the president of Monsanto changed something he'd already agreed to.

"I don't know how much might have been the irritability because he wasn't feeling as good. Everybody knew he wasn't feeling well, and he had spent a lot of time down at Smoke Tree Ranch[11] down by Palm Springs. Right up to two weeks before he died, we all knew he was over at the hospital getting a lung repaired, but at no time did anybody have any inkling that this was fatal. It was just a case of when he was going to review stuff next, based upon when he came back up from Smoke Tree Ranch after he left St. Joseph's. He was going to go back down to the ranch then. And then—boom. Gone."

Gurr continued his work for WED; the transportation and ride systems for Walt Disney World all bear the mark of his expertise. In 1981, he took an early retirement from WED to start his own firm, GurrDesign, Inc. Then in 1984, he teamed up with two former Imagineers to form Sequoia Creative, Inc. This firm

11 Established in 1936, this Palm Springs, California, enclave of homes and guest cottages situated in 375 acres of pristine desert had been a favorite retreat for Walt and other celebrities.

LEFT: Walt's vision for EPCOT, the Experimental Prototype Community of Tomorrow. Gurr dispelled the notion that Walt's plans for EPCOT were impractical, or that his aspirations clouded the feasible reality of what a planned city would entail. Gurr saw Disney with his head in the clouds, and his feet firmly on the ground.

BELOW LEFT: Bob Gurr on the construction site of the new Autopia in Disneyland, in early 2000.

created such fantastical beasts as Universal's King Kong and Conan the Barbarian's serpent. Two of Gurr's all-time favorite projects were the mysterious UFO that flew over the closing ceremonies of the 1984 Los Angeles Summer Olympics and the animated "spiders" for the Jacksons' "Victory" tour. Director Steven Spielberg asked Bob to assist with the T. Rex animated figure for the film *Jurassic Park*. He was the mechanical designer of the sinking ship at Treasure Island's pirate battle show in Las Vegas, and a design consultant on the Cirque du Soleil "Mystere" show, also in Las Vegas. Gurr often returned to Walt Disney Imagineering, consulting on new attractions for the R&D Department. He recently contributed to giant animated effects for the Tokyo DisneySea nighttime spectacular BraviSEAmo. In 1999, Gurr was honored with the Themed Entertainment Association's Lifetime Achievement Award.

"You never come to an end in this business, because there's always a new gig. Every day is a kind of discovery. Duplicating things that have been done before is no fun, and I don't do that. On the other hand, if it hasn't been done, I'm immediately interested. So much for having objectives and having a course set in life. What happens, happens. Take advantage as it comes. See the opportunities. No grand plan at the time."

Bob Gurr's personal motto comes from Malcolm Forbes: "While alive, live."

"Music has always had a prominent part in all our products, from the early cartoon days. So much so, in fact, that I cannot think of the pictorial story without thinking about the complementary music which will fulfill it."

—Walt Disney

The Music Makers

"Some people will tell you that music was a key ingredient of Walt Disney's success," Leonard Maltin wrote in 1988. "Don't you believe it. Music was the *foundation* of Walt Disney's success." From the first strains of "Turkey in the Straw" in *Steamboat Willie* through the bold musical innovation of *Snow White and the Seven Dwarfs* and the pioneering concert feature *Fantasia*, music was a primary element of Disney storytelling. In many ways, the dimensional and environmental storytelling of Disneyland relied on the evocative qualities of music more than any Disney project before, tunefully transporting park visitors to other times, other places, and other worlds.

Richard M. and Robert B. Sherman

"Their effortlessly upbeat and optimistic bent made the Sherman Brothers a perfect fit in the Disney world," Disney historian Stacia Martin wrote in *The Sounds of Disneyland*. "Bright and breezy songs, sweet and sentimental ones, clever lyrics and melodies filled with heart and humor perfectly complemented—and often guided the direction of—the projects to which they were assigned."

The Sherman Brothers, Robert B. and Richard M. (Bob and Dick to nearly everyone), are well known as the leading composer/lyricists in family entertainment. Their career spans fifty years, and includes nine Academy Award nominations and two Oscar wins (for *Mary Poppins*, Best Score and Best Song, "Chim Chim Cher-ee"). Other honors include three Grammys, twenty-four gold and platinum albums, and a star on the Hollywood Walk of Fame.

During their phenomenal seven-year association with Walt Disney, they composed more than 150 songs for his films, TV shows, and even the 1964–1965 New York World's Fair. Of course, their boss being who he was, they also brought their musical storytelling flair to Disneyland.

If musical talent is hereditary, the Shermans can credit part of their success to their dad, Al Sherman, who wrote such perennially successful hits as "You Gotta Be a Football Hero," "Pretending," "Potatoes Are Cheaper," "No, No, A Thousand Times No," "Save Your Sorrow (for Tomorrow)," and "Me Too!"[1] Both boys were attending Beverly Hills High School when their father was turning out top tunes. Dick wanted to be a composer of Broadway musicals, Bob a writer. But Uncle Sam had other plans for both of them.

Older brother Bob was sent to Europe to fight the Germans, where he won the Purple Heart and three battle stars in the infantry. Dick was drafted during the Korean War and spent two years with the Army Special Services. Between wars, the Sherman brothers attended Bard College, New York, where they graduated in 1949. Dick majored in music, Bob in English.

In 1950, Al Sherman bet his boys that if they would get together and pool their talents, they could "write a song a kid would spend his lunch money on." He was right. They wrote their first hit, "Things I Might Have Been," which was initially recorded by seven artists, but made a standard by Kitty Wells. (Johnny Mathis, Willie Nelson, Kris Kristofferson, and Rita Coolidge have covered the song since.) The Shermans gained more recognition in popular music with a few top-ten hits—among them "You're Sixteen (You're Beautiful, and You're Mine)."

The partnership was temporarily suspended when Dick entered the Army. Neither brother was able to score a hit by himself. Then, in 1958, the boys teamed up again to compose "Tall Paul," a smash hit for Walt Disney's young star, Annette Funicello. The record sold 700,000 singles and brought them to the attention of Walt Disney.

Soon, the Shermans were working on one song after another for Walt, which led to their being hired as staff composers in August 1960. "Walt liked a lot of things about the Shermans," Roy E. Disney says. "On a personal level, I got the feeling he felt they were 'good kids.' He often referred to them as 'the boys.' He certainly liked their songs. He liked their 'stick-to-it-iveness,' and their 'can-do' style." Stacia Martin eruditely observes, ". . . [Walt] realized that in these brothers, he had found virtually his own musical voice."

Their Disney credits include the films *The Parent Trap; The Sword in the Stone; The Happiest Millionaire; The Jungle Book; The One and Only, Genuine, Original Family Band; The Aristocats; Bedknobs and Broomsticks*; the Winnie the Pooh films; and of course *Mary Poppins*.

The credo about songwriting that the Shermans had learned at their father's knee

TOP: Richard and Robert with their songwriting father, Al Sherman.

ABOVE: Robert and Richard at work on the anthem for "it's a small world."

OPPOSITE: Richard and Robert with fellow composer Buddy Baker.

1 Pop artist Cyndi Lauper recorded the 1928 Al Sherman (with Al Lewis and Abner Silver) hit "(S)he's So Unusual" in 1983, and released an album of the same name that year.

had particular appeal to Walt. "Simplicity, sincerity, and singability" was the rule of writing an effective song—and a good song should also be a story in miniature.

"A song should be like a poem set to music," Bob has said. "You can't use gingerbread. You can't be superfluous. You can't waste words. Each line should be like a drop of water on a still lake that makes ripples in every direction all the way to the shore. We can't do it all the time, but we can try."

It was natural that, after applying their songwriting abilities to solve story problems in several films and television programs, Walt would ask his enthusiastic young songwriters for their contribution to his newest storytelling enterprise in Anaheim.

"Walt's secretary called us up one day and asked us to come over to Stage 2 at the Studio," Richard recalls. There they were greeted by a cacophony of chirping birds, talking parrots, and singing flowers, all brought to life through Walt's new Audio-Animatronics technology. As a show, it was amazing. As a story, it was a mess. "Nobody knows what the damn thing is about," Walt explained. He turned to the Shermans and asked, "Any ideas, boys?"

On the spot, they suggested that one of the parrots be elevated to Master of Ceremonies, and sing a song that would set up the story of the show, and carry the audience through various "acts." Walt added to the idea, suggesting four hosts—Spanish, German, Irish, and French. "He always had a way of 'plussing' a good idea," Richard says.

The result was the theme song "In the Tiki, Tiki, Tiki, Tiki, Tiki Room," a lengthy, gag-driven calypso number, which serves as the structure of the show's story. Walt Disney's Enchanted Tiki Room opened in Disneyland on June 23, 1963—and continues to entertain new audiences today. Again, "the boys" had risen to Walt's challenge, and again earned his confidence. At the same time, "Dick and Bob Sherman created a new language for Disney theme park attractions," Marty Sklar says.

The Shermans were called for another attraction assignment, this time for the General Electric show for the 1964–1965 New York World's Fair. General Electric Progressland featuring the Carousel of Progress was a unique theater show extolling the virtues of progress through electric technology in the twentieth century. As a Walt Disney–produced show, however, it didn't stop there, but also looked to the promise of the future.

The resulting anthem was as much about Walt Disney's point of view as it was about binding together the different acts and eras of the show. "'There's a Great Big Beautiful Tomorrow' is really a song about Walt," Dick says. "This is really the way he thought—his vision of the future was great, big, and beautiful."[2]

The song also had to work technically with the format and operational requisites of the show, and had to change eras, from a turn-of-the-century rag, to twenties jazz, forties swing, and even as a sweet, mellow piece. "Now all this has nothing to do with writing the song," Dick says, "it's more like troubleshooting, which is what a lot of our assignments were."

That kind of troubleshooting serendipitously also resulted in what has been called the most translated and performed song on earth. For the Unicef Pavilion at the New York World's Fair (sponsored by Pepsi-Cola), "it's a small world" was planned as a boat ride with children of the world's nations, all singing their homeland's varied national anthems. On paper, charming. In execution—utter cacophony. Walt needed a rescue. "I need something and I need it right away," he

2 When the attraction moved to Walt Disney World in 1975, General Electric requested a new theme song. The result was "The Best Time of Your Life," which lyrically posited that whatever era one found oneself in was as good as it could be. In 1994, after GE's sponsorship ended, the theme song returned to the original.

told the Shermans. "It should talk about unity and understanding and brotherly love—but don't get preachy." "It's a Small World (After All)" is one of the most beloved (and, to some, one of the most annoying) songs ever written.[3]

One of their more unusual Disneyland assignments was creating an anthem about chemical research in molecular manipulation for industry, for a Disneyland attraction called Adventure Thru Inner Space. No big trick for these tried-and-true problem solvers, and "Miracles from Molecules" was the "simple, singable, and sincere" result.

After Walt's death, the Shermans found themselves without a champion at Walt Disney Productions, and left the Studio. They went on to compose song scores for *Chitty Chitty Bang Bang* (with its Oscar-nominated title song), *Snoopy Come Home*, *Charlotte's Web*, and the hit Broadway musical *Over Here!* They worked on unproduced musical versions of *Roman Holiday* (for Paramount Pictures), James Thurber's *The Thirteen Clocks* (for Warner Bros.), and an unproduced animated musical, *Sir Puss-in-Boots*, with the voices of Sammy Davis, Jr. and Karl Malden.

They created screenplays and song scores for *Tom Sawyer* (their music won First Prize at the Moscow Film Festival), *Huckleberry Finn*, the 1976 Royal Film Performance *The Slipper and the Rose* (with co-author Bryan Forbes), and James Stewart's final theatrical feature film, *The Magic of Lassie*, which earned them their ninth Academy Award nomination for Best Song.

In the late 1970s, the Shermans were called back to Imagineering by Marty Sklar, who remembered their unbounded enthusiasm and the trust Walt had placed in them. Their return was also encouraged by the "second generation" Imagineers who had grown up with Walt Disney's Enchanted Tiki Room, Carousel of Progress, and "it's a small world."

Sklar remembered what a perfect anthem "There's a Great Big Beautiful Tomorrow" had been for the Carousel of Progress, and when Imagineering began working on its behemoth Future World projects for Epcot in Walt Disney World, Sklar felt that there was no better team to bring the project's messages of optimistic futurism to the visitors through music.

For Journey Into Imagination, they composed the haunting "Magic Journeys," the ebullient "One Little Spark," and "Makin' Memories," which the composers admit was "a subliminal commercial pitch for [pavilion sponsor] Kodak—no doubt the 'softest sell' in the history of singing commercials."

The Shermans have the dubious honor of contributing the music and song for the shortest-lived show in Epcot history, The Astuter Computer Revue, which closed after less that a year. Computers were astuter (more astute, actually) than this show, which was quickly outpaced by a burgeoning technology called the "PC." Another short-lived contribution was the theme anthem to the nightly World Showcase parade, a song titled "There's No Place Like World Showcase," which likewise marched away after a year.

In 1981, Marty Sklar received a memo from Oriental Land Company, owners of Tokyo Disneyland. He called Dick and Bob into his office and read them the note, which asked, "If the people who wrote 'It's a Small World (After All)' are still alive, could you find out if they are available?" He put down the letter with a grin and asked, "So, how are you feeling?" After assuring Marty that they were, indeed, still alive, the brothers began work on music and lyrics for the carousel-theater attraction, Meet the World, for Tokyo Disneyland.[4]

When a new Tomorrowland was being designed for Disneyland in 1998, the Shermans were asked to bring some music to the mix. For the Rocket Rods attraction, new lyrics were written to the melody of their upbeat ballad "Detroit," from *The Happiest Millionaire*. When Innoventions was slated to occupy the former home of Walt Disney's Carousel of Progress, "There's a Great Big Beautiful Tomorrow" became the equally optimistic anthem, "There's a Bright New World of Innoventions."

In 2004, the Shermans wrote several new songs for the stage version of *Chitty Chitty Bang Bang*, which opened on Broadway in April 2005 (while it continued in London as the longest-running musical ever to play the London Palladium). The stage production of *Mary Poppins*, co-produced by Disney and Cameron

ABOVE: From left: Robert Sherman, Walt Disney, artist Don DaGradi, Richard Sherman, and writer/producer Bill Walsh.

3 Dick's longtime pal Milt Larsen, owner of the world-famous Magic Castle in Hollywood, has had the urinal in the men's room there rigged with a motion sensor, so that hapless gentlemen hear the song while tending to their "private" business.

4 Originally intended for both Tokyo Disneyland and the Japan Pavilion in Epcot, Meet the World was a nineteen-minute staged chronicle of Japan's history and relations with other countries using a combination of film and Audio-Animatronics. It opened with the Tokyo Park on April 15, 1983, and closed on June 30, 2002, but never made it to Florida.

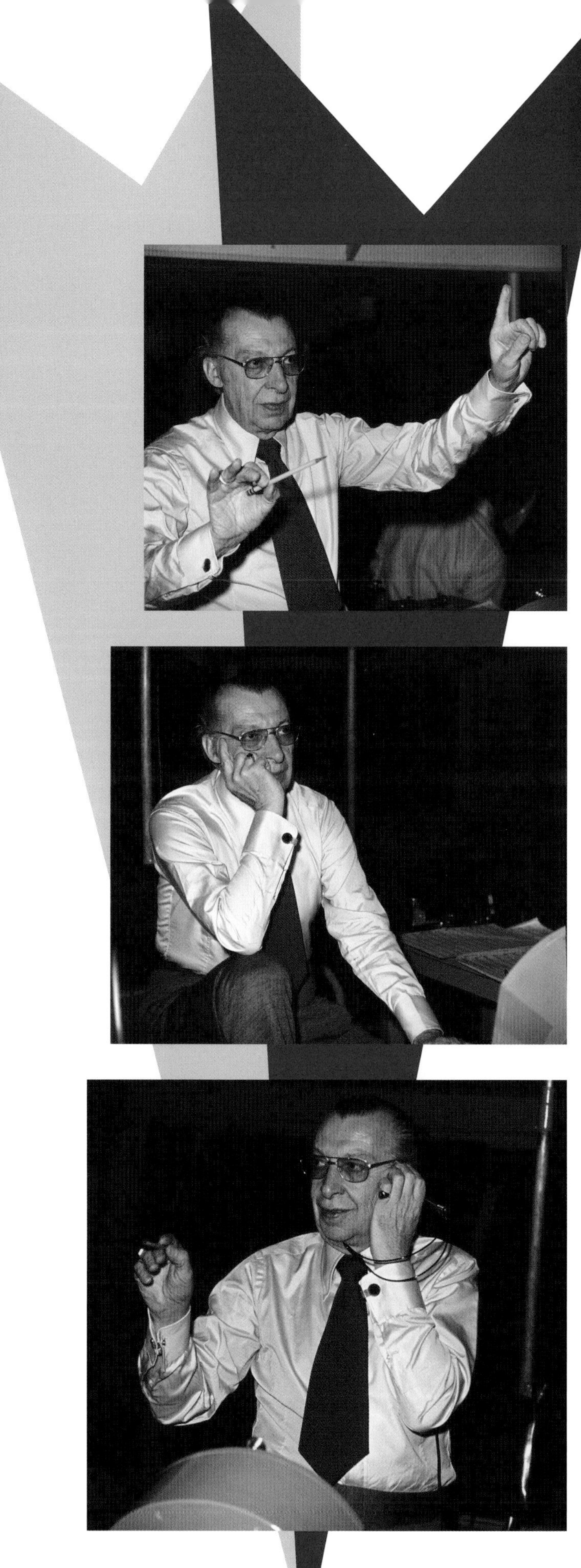

Mackintosh, opened to critical acclaim in London on December 15, 2004, immediately winning two Olivier Awards, and playing to packed houses. It repeated its success on Broadway, opening on November 16, 2006, at the New Amsterdam Theater.

After this lengthy and hugely successful career, the Sherman Brothers still feel they owe a great deal of credit to Walt. In him, the Shermans found a second father, who offered the same kind of encouragement, confidence, and praise that Al Sherman had. "We credit whatever success we have attained to two people," Richard Sherman says, "our father and Walt Disney."

In addition, the Sherman Brothers recognize and treasure what great value there was in having Walt Disney's confidence. "He trusted their instinct as storytellers," Roy E. Disney agrees, "and appreciated their attentiveness and enthusiasm. Most of all, I think he liked their unflagging optimism."

Buddy Baker

Whether it was a sad song, a happy song, a slow or a fast tune, a tune to evoke childhood memories of a certain part of the world—Norman D. "Buddy" Baker could compose it. In many ways, Baker was an adjunct in melody to the Sherman Brothers in songwriting: a "can-do" guy to whom every challenge offered up by the boss was something of a delight, and so a natural resource for Walt and his creative heirs in the development of Disneyland and other Disney parks.

"Music has to fit like the proverbial glove, as it has to complement so many factors: story, atmosphere, the action," said Baker. Born on January 4, 1918, Buddy[5] was raised in Springfield, Illinois, and it was said that he learned to read music before he could read words. He began piano lessons at age four, trumpet lessons at age eleven. In high school, he started his own band, as well as playing in his school and Boy Scout bands.

He studied music at Southwest Baptist University with Dr. John Bucholtz, and earned both an AA and doctorate of music.[6] There he became fascinated with harmony, and eventually devised his own system, which intrigued no less an expert than the great Nadia Boulanger, teacher of Elmer Bernstein, Aaron Copland, and Quincy Jones.

Buddy moved to Los Angeles in 1938, where he played trumpet for bandleaders Harry James, Kay Kyser, and Stan Kenton, among others. He soon began writing arrangements for the bands, and became so busy that he gave up performing altogether.

He composed and arranged music for Harry James, Stan Kenton, Phil Harris, Charley Barnet, Kay Kyser, Jack Teagarden, Bob Crosby, Glen Gray, and the Casa Loma Orchestra. Moving to

5 Baker got his nickname because his sister could not pronounce the word brother; instead the word came out as "buddy."

6 He also studied privately with E.W. Peters at Drury College and with Dr. Frank Hubbell in Los Angeles.

I probably learned more

from Walt Disney

than I have ever learned

from any formal education.

Walt was a great teacher.

—Buddy Baker

network radio, he composed, arranged, and conducted music for *The Bob Hope Show, The Jack Benny Show, Kay Kyser's Kollege of Musical Knowledge, The Eddie Cantor Show*, and *The Standard Symphony Hour*, with Robert Armbruster.[7]

In 1954, a former student named George Bruns, who was working as a composer at the Walt Disney Studio, found himself overloaded with work and asked Buddy to help out with the studio's new *Davy Crockett* television show. Buddy stayed at Disney for the next twenty-nine years, and composed more than two hundred scores for Disney's films, television shows, and theme parks.

Baker's fifty-plus film scoring credits include *Summer Magic, The Monkey's Uncle, The Gnome-Mobile, The Apple Dumpling Gang* (and its sequel), and *The Fox and the Hound*. His 1972 score for *Napoleon and Samantha* was nominated for the Academy Award. He scored the three original Winnie the Pooh featurettes and the Cannes Award–winning animated featurette *Donald in Mathmagic Land*, as well as the Donald shorts *Donald and the Wheel* and *The Litterbug*, Goofy's last short cartoon, the Academy Award–nominated *Aquamania*, and the special short subject *Disneyland After Dark*.

As the Studio ventured into new areas, Buddy was right there. He wrote for a wide variety of Disney television series, including *The Mickey Mouse Club* (on which he served as musical director) and provided music for nearly a hundred episodes of Disneyland and its successor programs *Walt Disney Presents, Walt Disney's Wonderful World of Color*, and *The Wonderful World of Disney*.[8]

In 1964, Walt invited Baker to apply his skills to the new world of attractions, and the magnificent scoring of Great Moments with Mr. Lincoln for the 1964–1965 New York World's Fair was the result. "The close collaboration between Jim Algar and Buddy Baker provided the Audio-Animatronics Mr. Lincoln with a heart," music historian Alexander Rannie says, "but it was Buddy Baker's music that gave Mr. Lincoln his soul." A complex and multilayered score created an emotional musical vehicle that carried fairgoers from the entry of the Lincoln show through a rousing patriotic finale.

"On January 20 and 27, 1963, *Johnny Shiloh*, a two-part historical drama, based on the life of a drummer boy for the Union Army during the Civil War, was televised on *Walt Disney's Wonderful World of Color*," Rannie explains. "While the score contained a newly written title song by the Sherman Brothers, the main body of the music was a thoroughly researched, highly authentic homage to music from the time of the Civil War. No fewer than eight period songs were incorporated into the score, including 'Dixie's Land (Dixie),' and 'The Battle Cry of Freedom.' Additionally, the music department acquired copies of two noteworthy, but unused, songs: 'The Drummer Boy of Shiloh' and 'Beauregard's Retreat from Shiloh.' The mood and era evoked by Buddy Baker in 'Johnny Shiloh' became the basis for Mr. Lincoln's musical accompaniment."

Most visitors vividly remember the exhilarating finale of "The Battle Hymn of the Republic," which had been planned as the show's climax since its conception. During testing, Baker had used a version recorded by the full Mormon Tabernacle Choir, using the arrangement of popular composer, arranger, educator, and choral director Peter J. Wilhousky, which they all had (unfortunately) become quite used to. When cost and rights issues precluded the use of the recording (Baker also wanted to create a directional stereo effect impossible with the existing record), Disney obtained permission to adapt the Wilhousky arrangement for the Lincoln show. Allan Davies, Disney's primary vocal arranger, reworked Wilhousky's choral writing, while Baker adjusted the orchestral parts, to suit the needs of the pavilion.

"When it came time to record the singers, Baker ingeniously made thirty-two singers sound as big as and perhaps even better than the Mormon Tabernacle Choir," Rannie reveals. "This aural illusion was created by recording the singers, or a portion thereof, nine times, each time in a slightly different configuration."

First, Baker recorded the full chorus. Then speakers were placed on the soundstage, and a second pass was made with the first recording played back through the speakers, reinforcing the live chorus. Then several takes were recorded with microphones hanging in the back of the soundstage, far away from the singers, in order to emphasize room ambience. Baker then recorded one pass each of the sopranos, altos, tenors, and baritones and basses. "When these multiple tracks were mixed down and played back through the specially designed speaker system at the Illinois pavilion," Rannie reports, "the effect was that of being immersed in the middle of the largest chorus you had ever heard. It elicited a thrilling and memorable, visceral response."

---

7 Late in the 1940s, Baker also found time to teach arranging and orchestration at Los Angeles City College, where future Oscar winner Jerry Goldsmith was one of his students. He also taught at USC.

8 Later television work included the milestone Children's Television Workshop educational series *The Electric Company*.

From then on, Baker included theme-park-attraction music in his varied repertoire. Walt soon came to Buddy with his New York World's Fair musical problem child, "it's a small world." Walt had already solved the basic problem of the noisy national anthems with Richard and Robert Sherman's memorable tune. "Can you imagine, in that big, open ride space?" Baker said. "It would have been like putting five marching bands in a gymnasium and trying to figure out what tune they're playing!"

Richard Sherman admits that although he and Bob quickly wrote the tune, the hard part fell to Buddy Baker "to arrange the song so that each repetition of the tune would match each featured country as the boats passed by." Baker solved the problem by creating synchronized one-minute repeating segments, each with different orchestral treatments for each country. Orchestrating for this new kind of entertainment proved not only a creative challenge, but a logistical one as well. Baker's desk was often strewn with papers covered not with musical notes but algebraic equations, which were necessary to ensure that all the music tracks throughout an attraction were heard in sync. Said Baker, "I had to come up with new formats that never existed in film music."

On loan from the Studio to the WED Imagineers, Baker also scored the General Electric Carousel of Progress for the New York World's Fair, and for G.E. Progress City when the attraction moved to Disneyland. Other Disneyland attractions under his baton included the Swiss Family Tree House, Adventure Thru Inner Space, the People Mover, and the Circle-Vision 360 film *America the Beautiful*. Baker cowrote "Grim Grinning Ghosts" with X. Atencio for The Haunted Mansion, and worked closely with Marc Davis on America Sings in Disneyland.

For Walt Disney World, Baker scored the original Country Bear Jamboree, If You Had Wings, and the Circle-Vision 360 film *Magic Carpet 'Round the World* attractions. But Baker's biggest role came with the opening of Epcot in Walt Disney World, where he was charged with overseeing its music development. He worked on seven attractions: Universe of Energy, The American Adventure, World of Motion, *Wonders of China*, The Land (including Kitchen Kabaret and Listen to the Land), the Mexico pavilion, and his personal favorite, the film *Impressions de France*. Combining original music and classic pieces by French composers such as Debussy, Ravel, and Satie, the film score was recorded in London with a 100-piece symphony orchestra.

He also had the opportunity of conducting his Disney theme park music and motion picture scores with The Philadelphia Orchestra, the Royal Philharmonic Orchestra of London, and the Graunke Symphony Orchestra of Munich. Baker conducted Disney programs at the Hollywood Bowl and Radio City Music Hall, and for many years was the musical arranger for the *Disney on Parade* arena show.

ABOVE: Buddy's last theme park–music project: The Many Adventures of Winnie the Pooh in Walt Disney World.

The last composer on staff at any studio in Hollywood, Buddy retired in 1983. Not one to spend his golden years idly, he became program director for the Advanced Studies Program "Scoring for Motion Pictures and Television" at the University of Southern California, widely considered the best in the nation.

Baker won many awards during his long career. He was honored by the Country Music Association for his Outstanding Contribution to Country Music, and received the Diamond Circle Award from the Pacific Pioneer Broadcasters for his many years of radio and television broadcasting. He received the 1996 President's Award from the Film Music Society for outstanding contribution to film music education at the USC Thornton School of Music. In 1999 the American Society of Composers, Authors and Publishers (ASCAP) presented him with their Lifetime Achievement Award. Other awards include those from the Southern California Motion Picture Council for *Napoleon and Samantha, The Best of Walt Disney's True-Life Adventures, The Bears and I,* and *$1,000,000 Duck*.

In 1999, he returned to the Hundred-Acre Wood to score The Many Adventures of Winnie the Pooh attraction in Walt Disney World, Tokyo Disneyland, and Disneyland in California.

When Baker orchestrated the Sherman Brothers' song "Heffalumps and Woozles" for *Winnie the Pooh and the Blustery Day* in 1968, he wanted the unusual, crazy, and silly-sounding instruments for the sequence to give it an off-kilter, colorful, nightmarish feel. In addition to instruments such as ocarinas and accordions, Richard Sherman suggested a kazoo—and Baker readily agreed. "And when I came in to help him re-record the score for the Walt Disney World Winnie the Pooh ride in 1999," Dick smiles, "Buddy had a kazoo ready for me to play."[9]

He created a new arrangement of the Carousel of Progress anthem by the Sherman Brothers, "There's a Great Big Beautiful Tomorrow" for Innoventions in Disneyland, as well as music for the Journey to the Center of the Earth and Seven Voyages of Sinbad attractions in Tokyo DisneySea. He said at the time, "It feels good to be back home!"

Shortly before his death on July 26, 2002, Baker said, "I probably learned more from Walt in the years that I was there than I have ever learned from any formal education or any other means of broadening my scope. He was a great teacher."

George Bruns

George Bruns burst onto Disney's musical scene in 1953 when hired by Walt Disney to score the animated feature *Sleeping Beauty*. "Can you adapt Tchaikovsky's ballet for the film score?" Walt asked the big, bearish Bruns. "Why not?" he answered. "I've been rewriting Tchaikovsky for my own music for years now!"

At the same time, Walt also asked the newly hired composer/conductor to "make up a little something" for a three-part television series for the Disneyland TV program. Soon, George's "little something," the catchy "Ballad of Davy Crockett" (with lyrics by Tom Blackburn) was on the lips of every Disney fan, young and old alike. The down-home ditty soared to the top of the hit parade for six months and sold more than eight million records, while the music he developed for *Sleeping Beauty* received an Academy Award nomination, the first of three he received during his twenty-two-year career with the Walt Disney Studio.

Born in Sandy, Oregon, on July 3, 1914, George began piano lessons at six, mastered the tuba and trombone by high school, and later added another dozen instruments to his mind-boggling repertoire. In 1934, he cut short his engineering education at Oregon State University to play with popular bands of the day, including Jack Teagarden and Harry Owens' Hawaiian Band, and was musical director of radio stations KOIN and KEX in Portland, Oregon. In the late 1940s, he played trombone with the Rose City Stompers and the Castle Jazz Band, and also played tuba with the Webfoot Jazz Band.

George moved to Los Angeles in 1950, where he began arranging and conducting for Capitol Records and UPA Studios, while playing with bands including that of Tennessee Ernie Ford and Turk Murphy's Jazz Band, doubling tuba and bass. After leaving Murphy's group, Bruns stayed in Southern California, working at a nightclub with his wife, vocalist Jeanne Gayle.

Three years later, he landed at Disney where he contributed to such hit films as *The Absent-Minded Professor, One Hundred and One Dalmatians, The Jungle Book, Robin Hood, The Love Bug*, and a dozen more. George received two more Oscar nominations, for his work on Disney's first live-action musical *Babes in Toyland*, followed by the 1963 animated feature *The Sword in the Stone*.

9 The score of "Supercalifragilisticexpialidocious" in the film *Mary Poppins* also features the exquisite kazoo stylings of Richard Sherman.

Beginning in the 1950s, George also contributed to Disney's pioneering television series *Disneyland, The Mickey Mouse Club,* and *Walt Disney's Wonderful World of Color*. In all, he contributed to more than twenty motion pictures, sixty television shows, as well as specials, short subjects, and attractions. His 1957 theme from the *Zorro* TV series (with lyrics by Norman Foster, the show's director) sold more than a million copies.

His association with the Studios led to work with the Banjo Kings and the Firehouse Five Plus Two, the Disney Artists' Jazz Band led by Ward Kimball, becoming the full-time tuba player with the Firehouse Five when Ed Penner died in 1956. He also led the Wonderland Jazz Band, which included several of the Firehouse Five musicians.

Like the Shermans and Buddy Baker, Bruns was soon summoned by Walt for musical duties on attractions. He scored Walt Disney's Enchanted Tiki Room in Disneyland, and created suitable international, futuristic, prehistoric, and automotive environments for the Ford Wonder Rotunda at the 1964–1965 New York World's Fair.

For Pirates of the Caribbean, he wrote the rousing and jovial "Yo Ho (A Pirate's Life for Me)" (1967) with lyricist and Imagineer X. Atencio, adding to this music a spirit of fun in what is actually a rather grim and violent story.

"Great sense of humor," Bruns's colleague Buddy Baker told film music authority Jon Burlingame in 2001. "He also had what I thought was a terrific dramatic sense."

In 1975, George retired from The Walt Disney Studios, returning to his Oregon hometown where he continued conducting and playing in bands, composing and arranging music, as well as teaching at nearby Lewis and Clark College. Bruns died at the age of sixty-nine on May 23, 1983, in Portland, Oregon.

Legendary animators Frank Thomas and Ollie Johnston recalled in their book *Disney Animation: The Illusion of Life*, "George Bruns worked equally well in either medium (television or film), writing 'Davy Crockett' for the live TV show at the same time he was adapting Tchaikovsky's ballet score for *Sleeping Beauty* to our animated version of the classic fairy tale. George was big and easygoing, but he worked very hard and produced a seemingly endless string of fresh melodies and haunting scores."

Theme From ZORRO
Words by NORMAN FOSTER
Music by GEORGE BRUNS
WALT DISNEY MUSIC COMPANY

X Atencio: The Reluctant Tunesmith

It was in 1938 that Xavier Atencio startled the neighbors by running from the original Hyperion Avenue studio to his aunt's house shouting, "I got a job at Disney! I got a job at Disney!"

Landing a job as an in-betweener[10] for animated shorts almost didn't happen. The eighteen-year-old artist's instructors at Chouinard had to prod him into submitting a portfolio, because Atencio thought a job at Disney was out of his reach.

OPPOSITE, BOTTOM LEFT AND RIGHT: George conducting the Disney orchestra, and working out an arrangement in his office at the Disney Studio.

ABOVE: Bill Justice (left) and X Atencio at work on stop-motion animation for *A Symposium on Popular Songs* (1962).

ABOVE RIGHT: Yo ho, yo ho, a parrot's life for me! Atencio at WED in 1967.

The young boy from Walsenburg, Colorado, whose friends shortened his name from Xavier to simply X, first saw his work on-screen at the premiere of *Pinocchio*, and was moved by the audience's reaction. He was promoted to assistant animator for *Fantasia* in 1940, but left temporarily to join the Army Air Corps in the war effort.

"I was in England most of the time, on an RAF base in Photo Intelligence," Atencio told John Frost of LaughingPlace.com in 1999. "I was drafted to Greenland. I said, 'Is there anyway to get out of Greenland?' They said, 'Apply to OCS and join the Air Corps.' I got my commission down in Florida, and from there they shipped me off to England."

Upon his return in 1945, he picked up where he left off, returning to the Studio to work for the next eight years on animated subjects. His first screen credit was for *Toot, Whistle, Plunk and Boom* in 1953, an Oscar-winning film that related to the history of music, as well as *Jack and Old Mac* (1956). He also started gaining story and layout experience while working on the I'm No Fool series for the original *Mickey Mouse Club*.

10 In-betweeners produce the drawings between previously completed key poses, in order to complete the illusion of movement and action. This is often an entry-level role in the animation department.

Atencio was part of the trio with Bill Justice[11] and T. Hee[12] involved in the creation of special stop-motion animation used in the short *Noah's Ark* (1959) and the featurette *A Symposium on Popular Songs* (1962), both Academy Award nominees. "Bill was very good at this stop-motion stuff, I didn't have the patience for it myself," Atencio admitted. "But he had all the patience in the world. You had to. You moved this piece over, move that one, move that one, click."

Atencio and Justice animated the opening titles for *The Parent Trap* (1961), sequences for *Babes in Toyland* (1961), and the nursery sequence in *Mary Poppins* (1964). "Bill and I were working together on stop-motion films. Walt assigned us to do the scene tidying up the nursery. Bill had done the toy sequence in *Babes in Toyland*. We used some of the toys we had from *Babes in Toyland*—the soldiers, for instance. The soldiers marching into the toy box in *Mary Poppins* were from *Babes*."

In 1965, Atencio grudgingly transferred to WED Enterprises at the request of Walt Disney, to work on the Primeval World diorama for Disneyland. "I hated to leave the studio. I had a nice office there. Then when I got over to WED I had a couple sawhorses and a piece of plywood for my desk. That's the way it was until I got my feet wet. They didn't have posh offices then." He eventually came to enjoy the close-knit feeling among Imagineers, which reminded him of the old days at the Studio.

"When I got over there, well, nobody knew what I was supposed to be doing. Then one day [Walt] called and said, 'I want you to do the script for the Pirates of the Caribbean.' I had never done any scripting before, but Walt seemed to know that's what I could do.

"I did one scene, the auctioneer scene, and sent it over to him. He said, 'That's fine, keep going.' And then after the script was done, I said 'I think we should have a little song in there.' I had an idea for a lyric and a melody. I recited it to Walt, I thought he'd probably say, 'That's great, get the Sherman Brothers to do it.' Instead he said, 'That's great, get George Bruns to do the music.' So that's how I became a songwriter."[13]

"Yo Ho (A Pirate's Life For Me)" has become an honest-to-goodness classic; its inclusion in the epic motion pictures based on the attraction was both sentimental and essential.

---

11 Justice joined Disney in 1937, serving as an animator on many Chip and Dale shorts, as well as *Fantasia*, *Saludos Amigos*, *Victory Through Air Power*, *The Three Caballeros*, *Make Mine Music*, *Alice in Wonderland*, and *Peter Pan*. Walt Disney tapped Bill to join Walt Disney Imagineering in 1965, where he programmed Audio-Animatronics figures for such Disneyland attractions as Great Moments with Mr. Lincoln, Mission to Mars, Pirates of the Caribbean, The Haunted Mansion, Country Bear Jamboree, and America Sings. After forty-two years with the company, Bill retired in February 1979

12 Thorton Hee (1911–1988) was an animator, director, and teacher. He is most recognized for directing the "Dance of the Hours" segment of *Fantasia*. He left Disney after the 1941 animator's strike, and went on to work for United Productions of America. He was later one of the two founding teachers, along with Jack Hannah, of the Character Animation program at California Institute of the Arts.

13 Atencio also voiced the Jolly Roger talking skull at the top of the first waterfall in the Disneyland Pirates attraction: "Ye come seekin' adventure with salty old pirates, eh? Sure, you've come to the proper place."

FAR LEFT: X (at right) confers with fellow tunesmith George Bruns on the theme for Pirates of the Caribbean.

LEFT: A 1966 gathering of legends reviews concepts for the "Bear Band" that would become the Country Bear Jamboree. From left, Marc Davis, Richard Irvine, Claude Coats, and X Atencio.

BELOW: X and friend brave the frights at The Haunted Mansion thirtieth anniversary celebration in 1999.

Atencio was another of the many talents on whom Walt Disney took a calculated risk, with joyous results for everyone concerned, and Atencio was profoundly moved by Walt's death. "I remember the day he died. How I was affected by it. They dismissed us at noon that day and I came home. Traditionally I always bought my Christmas tree on the fifteenth of December. Since I had the afternoon off, I came home but felt real bad just sitting around. So I thought, Oh, I'll go out and get the tree. I bought the Christmas tree and came home. As evening fell, I started thinking about Walt being gone again. I sat in the living room and started to cry. I cried and cried, just bawled my eyes out. It was as if I'd lost my father, you know? I really got choked up.

"I started getting amazing Christmas cards. People from all over—even friends I had in England—all wrote a little note in their Christmas card. A note of condolence, as if someone in my own family had died. In essence, someone in my family had died. That's how I felt about Walt's passing."

Atencio's next WED project was The Haunted Mansion. "I guess it was Dick Irvine and Marty Sklar. They knew I had done Pirates, so they wanted me to move onto the next assignment. And there again, Claude Coats and Marc Davis had worked out the continuity of the ride, and everything like that, as they did on Pirates. My job was to figure out what was going to be said in it.

"As opposed to Pirates, where I had to use a pirate's dialogue, this was just straight narration. I had to try and get it in a kind of spooky frame of mind—but not too spooky. I hired Paul Frees to do the narration—he was a great voice.

"When Buddy and I did the music for this, the graveyard, for instance, we had a cacophony of sound, because each little vignette had its own little music bit in it. But it didn't work, so finally Buddy had to put a general sound throughout."

As had happened with Pirates of the Caribbean (and as Richard and Robert Sherman had done for "it's a small world"), Atencio and Buddy Baker created a unifying song for The Haunted Mansion, "Grim Grinning Ghosts."[14]

Atencio contributed to many attractions in Walt Disney World as well, and in 1982 supervised the recordings for the Haunted Mansion in Tokyo Disneyland.

Atencio also worked on Adventure Thru Inner Space in Disneyland, and If You Had Wings and Space Mountain in the Walt Disney World Magic Kingdom, and the Spaceship Earth, World of Motion, and Mexico pavilions in EPCOT Center.

X retired in 1984 and continues to work as a consultant for Walt Disney Imagineering. Throughout his career, his reward, as it was in the days of *Pinocchio*, "is still the audience's reactions."

14 Atencio's voice can also be heard in the Disneyland Haunted Mansion when the attraction vehicles need to make a temporary stop. He announces, "Playful spooks have interrupted our tour . . . please remain seated in your Doom Buggies."

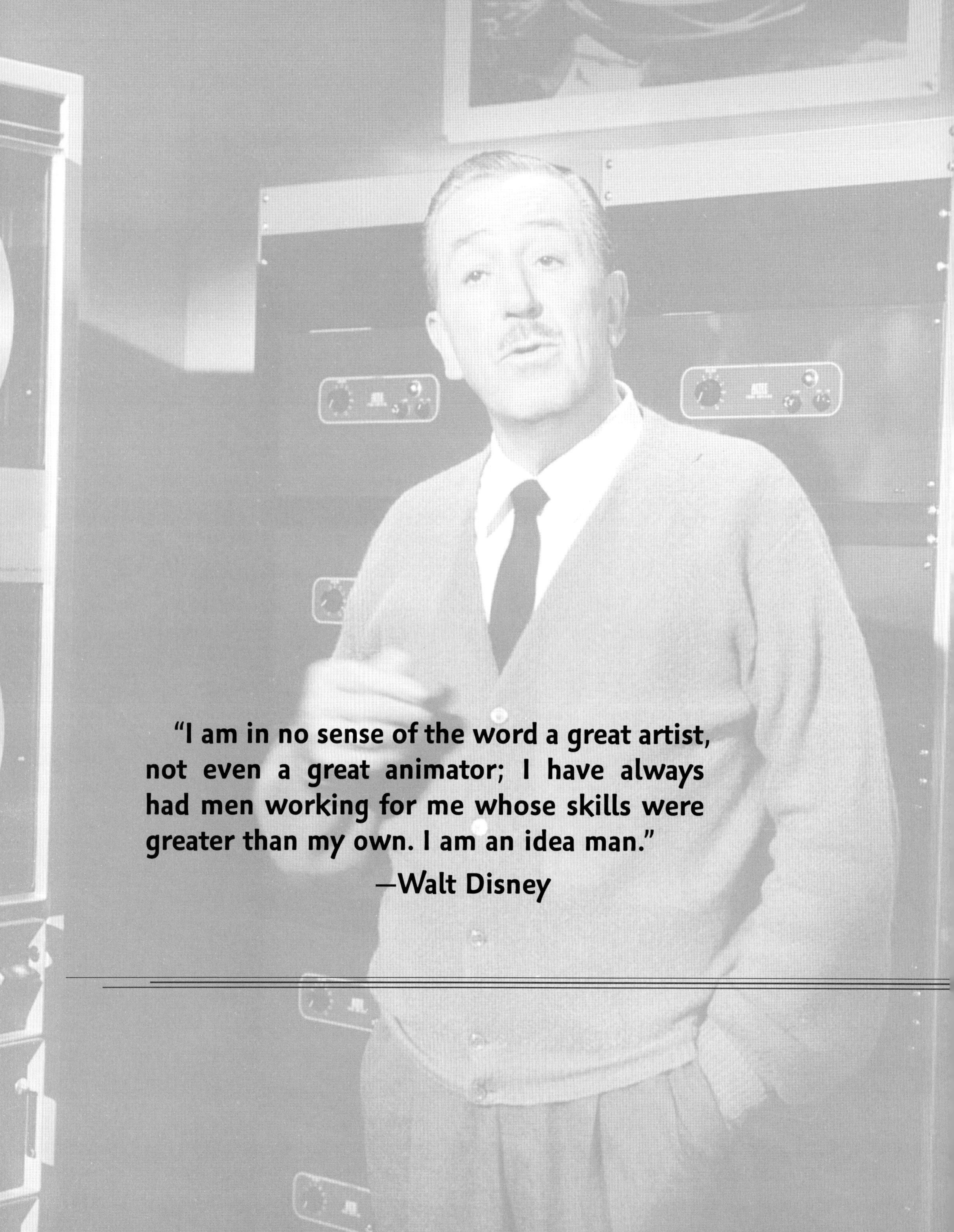

"I am in no sense of the word a great artist, not even a great animator; I have always had men working for me whose skills were greater than my own. I am an idea man."

—Walt Disney

The Unofficial Imagineers

In the creation of Disneyland, Walt worked in earnest with a few initial team members. However, in the beginning, and throughout the rest of his life, Walt frequently called upon Studio employees to contribute to Disneyland. They were not officially Imagineers, as their professional commitment was to the film and television businesses. No matter what the role or commitment, if an employee possessed a talent Walt required for Disneyland (or any other project outside their job description), he called upon it.

Ub Iwerks

As Disneyland evolved, it was natural that special technical challenges would fall to the Studio's resident "tinkerer" and one of Walt's oldest and closest colleagues, Ub Iwerks.

Born in Kansas City on March 24, 1901, Iwerks met Walt when they were both still teenagers. The two formed the Iwerks-Disney Commercial Artists Company in Kansas City, but it was rough going for the two youngsters, so Walt took a job at the Kansas City Slide Company as a cartoonist, while Ub held down their personal business. Ub soon joined Walt at the Kansas City Slide Company, and the two continued experimenting with animation in their off time. Two years later Walt established Laugh-O-gram Films, and Iwerks joined him as chief animator. Again, success proved elusive, and Walt went West to join his brother Roy, where they formed the Disney Brothers Studio in 1923. Iwerks joined the Disney brothers soon afterward.

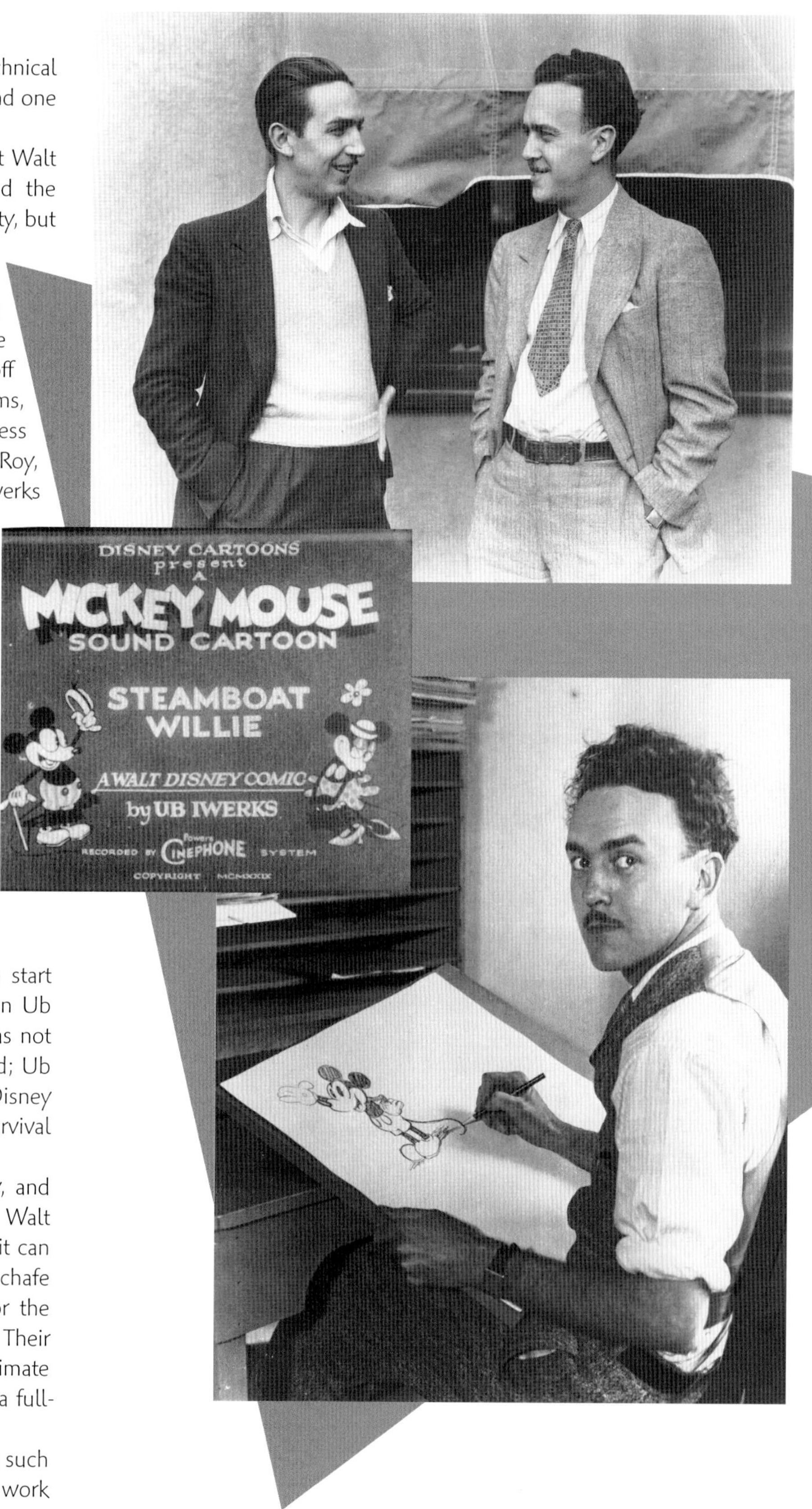

In 1928 Iwerks turned Walt's concept of Mickey Mouse into reality when he created Disney's most beloved character. Although Walt may certainly have come up with the concept of Mickey's physiognomy and personality, he realized that the requisite draftsmanship skill and animation talent for the character's success belonged to Iwerks. In fact, on the first Mickey Mouse cartoon short completed, *Plane Crazy* (1928)[1] Iwerks drew all of the animation—and at the phenomenal rate of seven hundred drawings a day! Iwerks continued to contribute the lion's share of the actual drawing to the first several Mickey Mouse short subjects, and then served as chief directing animator for the Silly Symphony cartoon series before branching out on his own.

Iwerks left the Disney Studio in January 1930 to start his own animation company. "Walt was devastated when Ub left the Studio," Disney archivist Dave Smith states. It was not simply Iwerks's technical proficiency that would be missed; Ub had come to be regarded by the staff as the father of the Disney animators, and the loss of this key position called the survival of the Studio into question.

Walt had a deep and well-known sense of loyalty, and many have expressed the belief over the decades that Walt never recovered from this early betrayal. While possible, it can be observed that each of the two men may have begun to chafe in their relationship, each holding a mild resentment for the other that may actually have made their parting timely. Their separation may have been a firebreak in their long and intimate personal and professional relationship, one that stopped a full-blown conflagration.

Iwerks's new studio created animated shorts starring such characters as Flip the Frog and Willie Whopper. Ub's solo work

1 *Steamboat Willie* was the first Mickey Mouse short released, but *Plane Crazy* and *The Gallopin' Gaucho* were completed first.

was technologically innovative and technically proficient, but he needed the various supports provided by his friend and partner, including fiscal security and good story guidance, as well as the Disney aptitude for "good taste." For instance, in the Willie Whopper short *The Air Race*, airplanes buzz by a cloud from which St. Peter is thumbing for a ride. The holy hitchhiker exhibits his disdain for the daredevil aerialists—by extending his middle finger toward them.

TOP LEFT: Producer and director Walt Disney and chief animator Ub Iwerks in a moment of shared amusement outside the Hyperion Avenue studio, circa 1928.

MIDDLE: In the title card for the first Mickey Mouse cartoon to be released, Walt Disney gives billing to the talented and prolific Iwerks.

BOTTOM LEFT: Iwerks drew every frame of Mickey's first film—storyboards, extremes, in-betweens, and backgrounds—and did so in just two weeks.

After the failure of his own venture and several years as a journeyman and animation instructor, Iwerks rejoined the Disney Studio in 1940. While many have assumed that he returned in sheepish defeat, Iwerks had spent more than a decade in animation production, and told his colleague, animator Hugh Harman, "I can't go on any longer in this business." He sought a different kind of challenge in returning to Disney, one that allowed him a large degree of autonomy to utilize his talents as an engineer, a technician, and inventor; and to apply his natural problem-solving skills to just about any technical or production application that might arise.

Iwerks initially came back to fix what Studio executive Ben Sharpsteen called "a weakness here in our technical setup, especially in our checking department." (The checking department made sure that technical problems in an animated production did not reach the camera, such as the numbering on animation cels, the colors used, and exposure sheet instructions for background and camera moves. Problems not caught and dealt with by the checking inspectors at this stage could prove expensive if re-shoots were required later.)

But animator Ollie Johnston recalled that when the animation staff heard of Ub's return, they knew he wouldn't be confined to a single job. "We knew he'd be into everything. He was an important figure and genius at what he did with technical and mechanical stuff."

ABOVE: Ub's fascination with technology harmonized with Walt's. Here he checks the view on the newly designed camera used for Color Traveling Matte Composite Cinematography.

In addition to refining the production control process (the stage between the animation drawing and ink and paint process), Iwerks developed the Special Process Laboratory, which handled the technical photographic processes for the animated cartoon features (and later live-action productions). Over the years, Iwerks received two Academy Awards for his inventive genius.[2]

Disneyland (and later, Walt Disney World) occupied much of Iwerks's technical attention in the 1960s. From his foundation in the film industry, Iwerks naturally had a hand in the development in motion picture technologies used in the Disney attractions. Most prominent among these was Circarama, a 360-degree motion picture process, later known as Circle-Vision 360.

Iwerks also developed an automated, continuous loop projection process for use in attractions that removed the need for constant human attention. This system also substantially reduced film wear by eliminating film reels and replacing them with a series of film rollers that carried the film in an endless ring, where the film never touches another surface or itself.

Iwerks worked closely with Imagineers Wathel Rogers and Roger Broggie developing the Audio-Animatronics technology for Great Moments with Mr. Lincoln, first for the 1964–1965 New York World's Fair, then for its new iteration in Disneyland. It was Ub who created the finale lighting effect that became a signature of the attraction, where the cloud-filled sky behind the United States Capitol Building transforms into a stylized American flag.

For The Haunted Mansion, Ub (more or less accidentally, according to legendary

2 For his technical contributions to the motion picture industry, Ub was given an Academy Award in 1959 for the design of an improved optical printer for special effects and matte shots, and received an Oscar again in 1965 for advancements in the traveling matte system.

Studio cameraman Bob Broughton) discovered a memorable effect with the use of a white Styrofoam wig stand. From this humble beginning, the original "Madame Leota" and the singing busts in the mansion graveyard came to life. (Imagineers Yale Gracey and Rolly Crump are known to have stumbled on to a similar effect while developing illusions for the Mansion.)

He frequently assisted the Imagineers in research and development for even the most mundane visual and lighting techniques and other special processes. At the time of his death on July 7, 1971, Iwerks was in charge of technical design for the film presentation for The Hall of Presidents attraction in Magic Kingdom Park in Walt Disney World.

Author Lawrence Watkin observed that "Ub was like Walt in many respects, but in nothing more than in his answer to a challenge. Both loved their work and both were stubbornly persistent when facing the impossible."[3]

BELOW: Walsh was that rare breed of Hollywood producer, a solid combination of an imaginative and resourceful creative mind, and pragmatic and organized thinking.

RIGHT: Producer Walsh and director Norman Foster confer prior to staging a keelboat contest for *Davy Crockett and the River Pirates*, 1956.

Bill Walsh

Bill Walsh spent three decades at the Walt Disney Studio, most of that time as a producer and screenwriter. As Disneyland came closer to a final concept, Walt relied on Walsh's talents to give written cohesion to the many different and disparate ideas that had come about during the creative evolution of the Park.

Walsh was beloved as a generous, witty, and creative colleague, and seemed to be a genuine fit into the "one genius/many hands" culture created by Walt. Walsh's talents were varied and formidable; his ego seemed satisfied by doing excellent work and enjoying the regard it generated. He certainly made the Studio pleased with him, with career box office grosses exceeding $200 million.[4] Walsh was an engine behind varied and beloved motion pictures such as *The Absent-Minded Professor, The Shaggy Dog, The Love Bug, Blackbeard's Ghost, Mary Poppins,* and *Bedknobs and Broomsticks*.

Walsh began his career at Disney in 1943. Although he was still in his twenties, he had already spent half his life in show business. He was amiably vague about his childhood. "I was born in New York City on September 13, the year escapes me somehow.[5] It always sort of goes blank there," Walsh says. "I lived there about two weeks. I could see the city was starting to fall apart, so I moved to Cincinnati, Ohio, where I grew up with an aunt and uncle who were in a tent show."

Their names were Agnes and William Newman, and Walsh traveled with them summers (and whenever he could, as he said, "pooch off" during the school year), selling tickets and candy and peanuts, playing small parts, and helping load the tent after performances. His formal education suffered, but he learned much about the back roads of Ohio, Kentucky, Indiana, and Tennessee.

Walsh was thirteen years old and attending Purcell High when he got an afternoon job as sports reporter on the *Cincinnati Commercial* (since defunct). He also found time between classes to play football and write songs, including Purcell's stirring anthem "Onward Cavaliers."

Walsh entered the University of Cincinnati on an athletic scholarship.

---

3 Watkin was the author of *On Borrowed Time* (1943), and a book that became a classic Disney project: *Marty Markham* (1942), which became the 1955 TV serial "Spin and Marty." Watkin also adapted Herminie Templeton Kavanagh's tales of Darby O'Gill into a new novel at the time of that Disney film's release in 1959.

4 Back in the day when $200 million was an admirable lifetime accomplishment and not a two-week gross for a single summer blockbuster.

5 It was 1913.

Although he promptly sank to the bottom of his class scholastically, he wrote a show during his freshman year for The Fresh Painters, a campus musical club, and "got notices which were as laudatory as my grades were poor," he recalled.

At the same time, Frank Fay and Barbara Stanwyck, stars of the New York stage who also were popular in films, happened to be barnstorming their footlight musical *Tattle Tales* through town en route to Broadway. They read the reviews of Walsh's show and invited him to join them as rewrite man and script doctor at twelve dollars a week.

"I thought Fay was under some kind of influence or something," said Walsh. "Twelve bucks a week! This was the Depression, so I left that night with the Stanwyck-Fay troupe, and that was the end of my life in Cincinnati."

Tattle Tales expired on Broadway in five weeks ("despite the Cincinnati touch," Walsh quipped), although this was a fair showing in 1934, a year hardly noted for its ticket sales. Walsh followed the two stars back to Hollywood, where he discovered "everybody was unemployed and starving." He found a "temporary" job as press agent with the Ettinger Company "which I kept for fifteen years," he said. "I publicized everything from the Brown Derby restaurants to Technicolor to diamonds to Elizabeth Arden face cream, and a group of people such as Irene Dunne, Loretta Young, and Edgar Bergen."[6]

At Bergen's suggestion, Walsh tried his hand writing jokes and gags. They were so well-received that in 1943 he was put on salary by Walt Disney Productions, writing for the Mickey Mouse comic strip, something Walsh could do off the lot while continuing as a press agent. But gradually he phased out that side of his career and joined the Studio full-time.

Walsh had been working in various departments there when Walt decided to experiment with the promotional possibilities of television with an hour-long Christmas show, *One Hour in Wonderland*, which aired on Christmas Day 1950.[7] The program was to be a test of the effectiveness and potential of the new medium, and the program was built around a behind-the-scenes look at the upcoming animated feature *Alice in Wonderland*. When Walt selected Walsh to head the television production, he surprised everyone—no one more than Walsh.

Nobody ever really knew why Walt chose him for the job. "I kept bumping into him in the hall, which is not a bad place, or in the parking lot. So Walt, in his strange way said, 'You, you be the producer of TV.' And I always said, 'Huh? But I don't have any experience as a producer,' and Walt would always say, 'Who does?'"

Walsh helped write and produce both *One Hour in Wonderland* and its successor, *The Walt Disney Christmas Show*, which aired on Christmas Day 1951.[8] Both programs were highly successful, and established Walsh as Disney's in-house television producer. In August 1953,[9] Walsh sent Walt five dummy scripts for a proposed half-hour weekly Disney TV series, and included ideas for eight additional shows. Encouraged, Walt had Walsh prepare scripts for a full thirty-three-episode season of what was to be called *The Walt Disney Show*.

By early 1954, the TV show idea had coalesced into the weekly hour-long anthology program titled *Disneyland*, and the purpose of the program was to promote public awareness and anticipation for the Disneyland Park in Anaheim, through the regular programming of Disney material as well as frequent updates on the design and construction of the park.

Walsh's work in developing the nascent TV medium led him to produce one of Disney's legendary (and as he admitted, unexpected) successes, the Davy Crockett stories on the weekly *Disneyland* TV series. Though the series proved a blockbuster hit, Walsh recalled, "You know, I didn't think we'd get through that first year. Doing a new show every week, that was murder."

---

6 Bergen was later the de facto "host" of the 1947 Disney "package feature" *Fun and Fancy Free*, and was a social friend of Walt's as well as a professional client of Walsh's.

7 Walt's co-star in this first TV venture was none other than Edgar Bergen.

8 With this second TV special, Walt had gained enough confidence in his public profile to host solo. It is also said that he chafed at articles and reviews that called his first special a "Bergen Show" rather than a "Disney Show."

9 Walt was then in New York for meetings with all of the television networks about the possibility of entering the new medium on a regular and permanent basis.

The new project Walt assigned was hardly a relief. He put Walsh in charge of *The Mickey Mouse Club*, which was planned as a daily hour-long program. "An hour show every day!" Walsh later exclaimed. "And with children!"

Walsh developed Walt's original "clubhouse" concept and the specific content for *The Mickey Mouse Club*, and the show proved to be another huge success. Walsh was credited producer from 1955 until the program's last first-run airing in 1959, but by then he was ably supported by a cadre of associate producers, coordinators, and directors who helped relieve the daily grind.

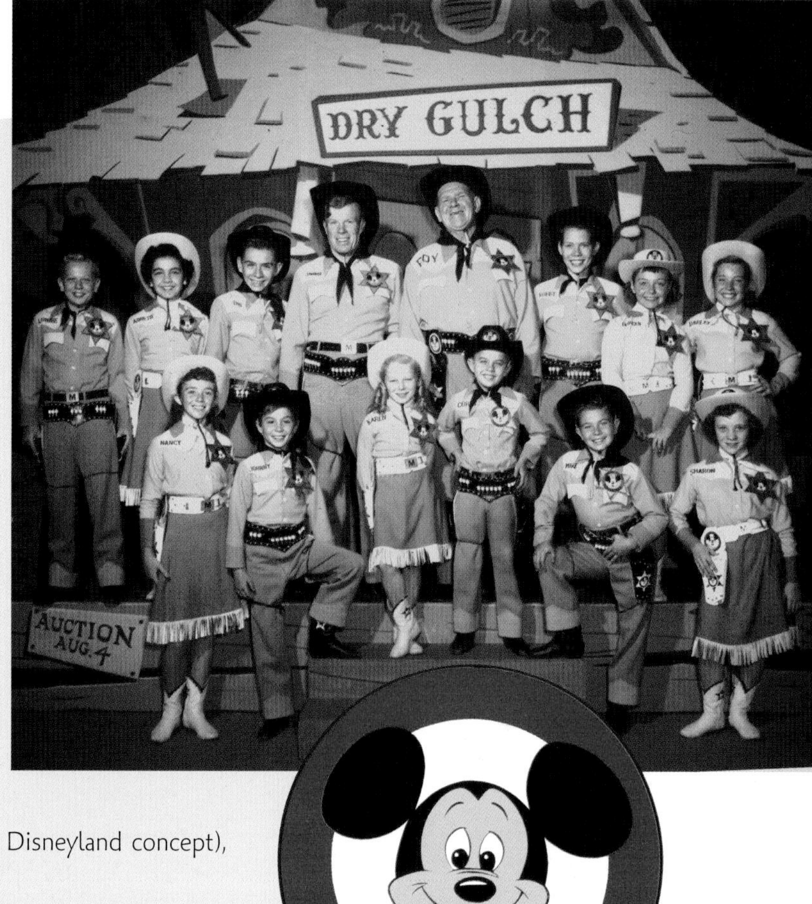

At that point, Walsh recalled, Walt told him he had paid his dues. "You'll never have to do any more TV shows," Walt said. Shaking himself free of television, Walsh produced *Westward Ho the Wagons!* in 1956, followed by *The Shaggy Dog; Toby Tyler, or Ten Weeks with a Circus; The Absent-Minded Professor; Bon Voyage; Son of Flubber; Mary Poppins; That Darn Cat!; Lt. Robin Crusoe, U.S.N.; Blackbeard's Ghost;* and *The Love Bug*.

A proven team player with a successful track record such as Walsh's would naturally be a resource to Walt, no matter the medium. As the ideas for Disneyland took form in Walt's mind, he called upon Bill Walsh to give them written life. "Walsh had a style that was as concise as it was enticing," Disney archivist Robert Tieman says. "He had proved his ability to 'sell' an idea with the TV show pitches, providing enough solid background to work from—and enough vagueness to allow continuing creative evolution while staying on an established overall path." It was only natural for Walt to call on such a talent in creating the first publicly released written materials for his new park concept.

Less well-known than the legendary drawing that Herbert Ryman famously created over the weekend of September 26 and 27, 1953 (and which was used time and again in the "sale" of the Disneyland concept), is Bill Walsh's accompanying written summary.

> *The idea of Disneyland is a simple one. It will be a place for people to find happiness and knowledge.*
>
> *It will be a place for parents and children to share pleasant times in one another's company: a place for teachers and pupils to discover greater ways of understanding and education. Here the older generation can recapture the nostalgia of days gone by, and the younger generation can savor the challenge of the future. Here will be the wonders of nature and man for all to see and understand.*
>
> *Disneyland will be based upon and dedicated to the ideals, the dreams, and the hard facts that have created America. And it will be uniquely equipped to dramatize these dreams and acts and send them forth as a source of courage and inspiration to all the world.*
>
> *Disneyland will be something of a fair, an exhibition, a playground, a community center, a museum of living facts, and a showplace of beauty and magic.*
>
> *It will be filled with accomplishments, the joys and hopes of the world we live in. And it will remind us and show us how to make those wonders parts of our own lives.*

Over the next decade, Walsh occasionally contributed to the development and execution of Disneyland attractions; however, these contributions were essentially minor

ABOVE: The Mouseketeers are joined by host Jimmie Dodd and "Big Mooseketeer" Roy Williams (back row, center) for a first-season portrait.

RIGHT: James Algar researches the Grand Canyon for Disney's True-Life Adventure series.

and not well documented.[10] Walsh continued at Walt Disney Productions after Walt's passing in 1966, helping supervise filmed entertainment and producing successful motion pictures until his own passing on February 3, 1975.

Echoing his boss's high regard for the innate intelligence of his audience, Walsh said, "I respect the public. You can't con them. The minute you think you're smarter than the public you'll find yourself very quickly in the real estate business. They're the only ones who know."

James Algar

During his forty-three years of service with Disney, producer-writer-director James Algar was involved in every imaginable type of film production, from features to shorts, featurettes to television, in animation and live action. His versatility, abundant knowledge, and intellectual passion were called upon for several projects during the first decade of Disneyland.

Algar's most highly acclaimed work was probably in the wildlife area, writing and directing Oscar winners such as *The Living Desert* and *The Vanishing Prairie* in Disney's renowned True-Life Adventure series. As a result of his close association and deep personal involvement with nature and conservation, Algar was considered among the best-informed American natural scientists.

Born on June 11, 1912, Algar was a native of Modesto, California, where he spent his boyhood years. He graduated from Modesto High School and studied at Modesto Junior College before transferring to Stanford University. There he met and married his wife, Persis, in 1938.

As editor of Stanford's humor magazine, *The Chaparral*, in the early 1930s, Algar gained a following as a campus cartoonist. Although he earned a master's degree in journalism, it was his cartooning that attracted the attention of the Walt Disney Studio recruiters. Upon his graduation in 1934, he joined the growing Disney staff of animators, and was immediately assigned to *Snow White and the Seven Dwarfs*. A few years later he became animation director on a Mickey Mouse short, *The Sorcerer's Apprentice*, which evolved into the cartoon feature *Fantasia*. Algar went on to direct sequences in *Bambi, Victory Through Air Power, The Adventures of Ichabod and Mr. Toad*, and Disney-produced health films for the U.S. Armed Services and Latin American countries during World War II.

Although Algar continued to be interested in art, "I used to be a Sunday painter, something I dearly loved, but I don't have time for that anymore," he admitted, he found his interest in the visual image being supplanted by his fascination with words.

"He spent most of his spare time reading," Roy Disney says. Algar admitted to completing an average of fifty books a year, in addition to countless magazines, scripts, and story treatments. He also collected books, mostly on early Americana. Later in his career, he confessed that he found nothing as relaxing as "sitting at the typewriter and knocking out a few pages of script."

10 Walsh's final contribution to the history of Disneyland might have been his most interesting: an unproduced screenplay (with Don Da Gradi) titled *Kruschev Visits Disneyland*, a character comedy built around the furor caused when the Soviet leader was denied a visit to the park in 1959. Peter Ustinov was slated to play Kruschev, but Walt died before it went into production, and the project was cancelled.

As he concentrated on a growing family at home (he and Persis had four children: Bruce, John, James, and Laurie Elizabeth, between 1941 and 1951), he also found professional support in an ever-evolving career at the Studio.

In 1948, he helped conceive and directed *Seal Island*, which won the Academy Award (as Best Two-Reel short subject) and spawned the internationally acclaimed True-Life Adventure series. "There were reels and reels of film—hundreds of 'em—that [nature photographers] Alfred and Elma Milotte had shot during two seasons in Alaska," Roy Disney recalls. "Walt just wanted the story of the seals. Jim Algar and Ben Sharpsteen honed all that film to a tight twenty-seven minutes that really captured people's attention and imagination."

For the next decade, Algar devoted most of his energies to nature and wildlife shorts, features and television shows. He functioned as writer-director on such Oscar-winning True-Life Adventures as *Beaver Valley, Bear Country, The Living Desert,* and *White Wilderness*. In all, he shared in the winning of nine Academy Awards, plus twenty-two other awards.

Combining his experience on *Fantasia* (which wed image to music) and his skill with compelling narrative nature photography, Algar directed the Academy Award–winning 1958 CinemaScope short subject *Grand Canyon*, which featured the beloved "Grand Canyon Suite" by composer Ferde Grofe.

Algar was not a deskbound producer, writing memos and lunching in the executive dining room while his production crew did all the work. As a filmmaker, he actively pursued the action and adventure in person, in a dozen remote corners of the world to bring authenticity to his Disney audiences. He lived among the lions of Kenya and other jungle animals during the making of *African Lion*, and challenged the raging white-water rapids of the Colorado River to film *Ten Who Dared*. For the Oscar-winning *The Vanishing Prairie*, he participated in the filming of a buffalo stampede on the Crow Indian reservation in Montana.

When Disney nature films evolved to the dramatic stories starring animal characters, Algar again set a standard with *The Legend of Lobo*, which he wrote and co-produced. He followed it with *The Incredible Journey*, for which he wrote the screenplay based on the book by Sheila Burnford. It became one of the biggest box office hits of 1963.

Beginning to concentrate more on television production, Algar produced many highly regarded episodes of *The Wonderful World of Color*. In all, he worked on twenty-six one-hour episodes of the Disney TV anthology, serving as producer of fourteen episodes. Seemingly ever-versatile, Algar also produced the highly successful comedy fantasy *The Gnome-Mobile*, which starred Walter Brennan, and *Rascal*, an adaptation of Sterling North's tale about a boy and a raccoon.

Besides his many contributions to motion pictures and television, Algar worked on several significant projects for Imagineering. Algar wrote the script for the first Circarama 360-degree film, *Circarama, U.S.A.*, and wrote and produced *America the Beautiful* for the 1958 Brussels World's Fair, as well as the remake of that film that enjoyed popular runs in Disneyland and Walt Disney World. In 1973, Algar returned to the circular format as producer and writer of *Magic Carpet 'Round the World*, which ran almost exactly a year from March 16, 1974, to March 14, 1975, in Magic Kingdom Park in Walt Disney World, followed by a three-year run, from 1983 to 1986, in Tokyo Disneyland.

There is no doubt that Algar's greatest legacy at Imagineering was as writer and co-producer of Great Moments With Mr. Lincoln, which came to life in the Illinois Pavilion at the 1964–1965 New York World's Fair, and subsequently enjoyed a decades-long run in Disneyland. Algar had begun creating the show for Disneyland in 1958 as part of a

THESE PAGES: Dramatic advertising sheets for six of the True-Life Adventures, all directed by James Algar, all but one written by him (*Beaver Valley* was written by Ted Sears and Lawrence Watkin).

concept called "One Nation Under God," which was to have featured all of the American presidents in a stirring patriotic program. When the State of Illinois expressed an interest in the Lincoln figure—sans the other chief executives—for their presentation at the Fair, Walt moved mountains in both cost concessions to the state[11] and in preparing the still-untried Audio-Animatronics technology in an ambitious multimedia presentation.

"With the State of Illinois wanting the figure, we created the Great Moments with Mr. Lincoln show, which was really taken out of The Hall of the Presidents[12] idea," Algar recalled. "This is the way Walt would work. He would do whatever idea could be brought to fruition."

In a perfect example of Walt's felicity for matching people to projects, the concise and focused writing of Jim Algar was combined with his love of American history. "What you have to understand about Jim is that he was an absolute Lincoln freak," Roy E. Disney recalls. "It was Jim who combed all of the Lincoln speeches and letters and cobbled together what became the seamless and contiguous speech used in the Lincoln show. People always ask, 'Which of Lincoln's speeches is that?' Well, it's four speeches—and a piece of a eulogy!"[13]

Algar finally completed the initial "One Nation Under God" concept when he produced and wrote The Hall of Presidents attraction, which opened in October 1971, in Magic Kingdom Park in Walt Disney World. Finally, the original concept of all the presidents of the United States appearing together on a single stage in the form of three-dimensional Audio-Animatronics figures was realized, and is still running today.

Algar's last works for Disney were the 1975 *The Best of Walt Disney's True-Life Adventures*, a compilation of highlights from the nature series; and "Race for Survival" and "The Bluegrass Special," a racetrack story, both for the Disney television show.

"Forty years isn't that long a period of time," he said in 1976, pondering his career, and although he retired the following year, he mused, "I think I still have a good, productive decade ahead of me." Among his many awards were the Thomas Edison Foundation's National Media Award, two Diploma of Merit awards at the International Edinburgh Festival, the *Look* Magazine Movie Award for Outstanding Achievement in Production, and two Certificates of Award from the Southern California Motion Picture Council.

Algar died after a brief illness at the age of 85 on February 26, 1998, at his home in Carmel, California.

Ward Kimball

Ward Kimball was a pioneering giant of animation who became one of Walt Disney's trusted Nine Old Men and was closely associated with such memorable characters as Mickey Mouse, Jiminy Cricket, and the Mad Hatter.

Kimball was known for his edgy eccentricity, wildly varied avocations, interests, and relationships, and a carefully cultivated persona as an irreverent but benevolent artistic and intellectual rebel. "To the end of his days, Ward had a pixieish spirit that was irresistible," animation historian/author and film critic Leonard Maltin says. "He had the soul of an artist and an innate sense of humor that came through in his work, his hobbies and his outlook on life. And he was always fun to be around."

The iconoclastic artist joined the Walt Disney Studio in 1934 and worked there until his retirement in 1973. He animated, or served as directing animator, on a dozen classic films, from *Snow White and the Seven Dwarfs* to *Bedknobs and Broomsticks*.

Kimball was born in 1914 in Minneapolis, Minnesota, and had a somewhat peripatetic childhood due to his father's ever-changing career path. Kimball began drawing as a child, and after two correspondence courses (and family relocations to Kansas, Oklahoma, Los Angeles, West Covina, and Ventura) he ended up attending

11 The president of the Fair, Robert Moses, was so enthusiastic about the prospect of the show, the Fair finally contributed the lion's share of the funding for the Lincoln show in New York, the first and only time financial support was given to any exhibitor at the Fair.

12 The show was often referred to as "Hall of the Presidents," which was the finale of the larger Constitutional drama "One Nation Under God."

13 At Walt's request, Algar also created a never-used "Special Script," another "anthology speech" (this time containing elements from four speeches and a tariff discussion), "for presentation on the patriotic holidays" of Memorial Day, Independence Day, and Labor Day.

Santa Barbara School of the Arts in 1932. In March of 1934, a recruiting ad for the Studio in a magazine caught his eye, and with the encouragement of a teacher and his mother, Kimball set out for Hollywood.

"On or about April Fools' Day,"[14] Kimball always said, the young artist (with his mother at the wheel) motored down from Santa Barbara in the family Buick with just enough gas to reach Los Angeles. The Disney recruiter was impressed by Ward's portfolio (Kimball is said to be the first applicant who ever brought one) and offered him a job as an assistant animator. Ward had not only fulfilled a longtime ambition of working at the Walt Disney Studio, but he "didn't have to bum gas to get back to Santa Barbara."

When Kimball first came to the Disney Studio, it was his interest in Mickey Mouse shorts that led him to apply for a job there. "Mickey was six years old and a world-famous movie star when I started working for Walt as a fledgling animator in 1934," recalled Kimball. Following a stint as an animator on *Snow White and the Seven Dwarfs*, he developed the character of Jiminy Cricket for *Pinocchio*, and was then promoted to animation supervisor on *Dumbo, Fantasia, Saludos Amigos, The Three Caballeros, Alice in Wonderland, Cinderella*, and *Peter Pan*. Two of the animated shorts Kimball created for Disney—*Toot, Whistle, Plunk and Boom* and *It's Tough to be a Bird*—won Academy Awards.[15]

In the 1956 book *The Story of Walt Disney*, Walt is quoted as saying, "Ward is one man who works for me I am willing to call a genius." This was a blessing and a curse for both the usually taciturn Walt and the equally cavalier Kimball. Walt realized that it undermined his own authority and monotheistic doctrine at the Studio (and often used his very public compliment against Kimball later); many of Kimball's Studio colleagues were hostile to or terrified of Kimball thenceforth.

After almost two decades, Kimball was becoming bored with animation, since he had always preferred the wilder possibilities of the medium to the sincerity of personality performances. "He was good at making fun of things, doing something that was satirical," Milt Kahl once said. "He didn't have the feel for getting into a character's personality and making him believable like Frank [Thomas] or Ollie [Johnston] or I did." So Walt Disney maneuvered Kimball, like Bill Walsh before him, into the nascent television medium. Walt wanted some programs about space travel and assigned the animation director to produce and host them, calculating (correctly) that Kimball would be personally challenged by the task, and would appear as enough of a "regular Joe" on television that viewers wouldn't be intimidated by the subject matter.

As a result, Kimball wrote, directed, and co-hosted three landmark shows for the *Disneyland* TV series that explored the science (and fantasy) of space travel. Working with scientists Willy Ley, Heinz Haber, and Wernher von Braun, Kimball's first effort was the 1955 program, *Man in Space*. *Man and the Moon* followed later that year, and *Mars and Beyond* landed in 1957. This trilogy of shows is often credited with giving impetus to the government's space program and popularizing the feasibility of manned space travel with the American public.

14 Although this sounds suspiciously convenient, Kimball's official hire date actually is April 2, 1934.

15 In addition to his major accomplishments in the field of animation, Kimball was a founding member of the popular jazz group, The Firehouse Five Plus Two. He played trombone and led some of his fellow Disney employees (including Harper Goff on banjo and Frank Thomas on piano) in the legendary Dixieland band, which recorded albums, played concerts, and appeared both on television and in films.

RIGHT: Ward works, watched by Ward, Ward, and Ward.

BELOW LEFT: Ward monkeys around.

BELOW CENTER: Ward's sketch of the Dixieland band, The Firehouse Five Plus Two. He founded the band and played trombone.

BELOW RIGHT: Walt looks over Ward's work for the Mad Tea Party from *Alice in Wonderland* (1951).

"Those were the days," Kimball recalled, "when [Walt] didn't have any contact with the picture. He was too busy getting ready with Disneyland and we had free rein. This was the most fun we ever had 'cause no one bothered us."

Although phrased in a self-serving manner and disingenuous on its face, Kimball's statement contains a greater truth. There was never a "Walt Disney" project—especially one as important as this series—that Walt Disney "didn't have any contact with." The greater compliment to Kimball's reputation and the more important fact is that Walt trusted Kimball to execute the project. Walt created an idea, assigned people based on their talent—and his own level of confidence in them—and allowed them what must have at least felt like "free reign."

In 1961, Kimball contributed to the Disney live-action musical fantasy *Babes in Toyland* and it was during this period that Kimball's relationship with Walt reached its nadir. Kimball had written a complete screenplay and was given the impression that Walt wanted him to direct the picture. Kimball disagreed with Walt on several points, especially casting, feeling that there was a better strategy in bringing fresh talent from Broadway in the juvenile leads. Ward's vision of the film and that of his boss never matched up, and Jack Donahue, a tried-and-true TV director, landed the assignment. Ward was given a shared screenplay credit, and directed the animated toy sequence (without screen credit).

In retrospect, Kimball's eccentric sensibilities probably would have rescued and invigorated the leaden, amateurish feature that resulted.[16] Instead—perhaps because all of his criticisms and instincts about the film's potential shortcomings had been correct—Ward found himself banished from the "inner circle."

He was relegated to animating (not even directing) the character of Donald Duck's pseudo-scientist uncle, Ludwig Von Drake, for *The Wonderful World of Color*. His anger and lack of interest actually resulted in wildly funny and unusual animation, but Kimball spent the remainder of Walt's life in the doghouse with the boss.

After Walt's death, Kimball was granted more responsibilities, working on special subjects such as *Scrooge McDuck and Money, Music For Everybody, A Salute to Alaska*, and *Man on Wheels*; designing and contributing to the kinetic and unique title and interstitial segments for *The Adventures of Bullwhip Griffin*, and creating and directing the popular, critically acclaimed, and award-winning short subjects *It's Tough to be a Bird* and *Dad, Can I Borrow the Car?*

He produced a refreshing television special, *The Mickey Mouse Anniversary Show*, in 1968, which ultimately led to his producing, writing, and directing forty-three episodes of the syndicated TV show *The Mouse Factory*, which began airing in 1972.

After enjoying a two-season run with that program, Ward retired to "start enjoying some of the things my wife and I had been too busy for."

Some of those "things" included a best-selling book on art called *Art Afterpieces*, teaching action analysis drawing at various art schools and universities, and adding to his impressive collection of railroad memorabilia.

Kimball, with his wife, Betty, built America's first privately operated full-size backyard railroad, called Grizzly Flats R.R., in 1938. Starting with a 64,000-pound coal-burning locomotive, a wooden passenger car, and more than 900 feet of track, Kimball added to the collection over the years, and went on to build a museum of miniature trains as well.[17]

This is probably where Ward Kimball exacted his most primal influence on the development of Disneyland. Although he did not work on the initial design of the Park, and would not consult with WED until years after Walt's death, as a railroad enthusiast,

ABOVE: Ward relaxes in his Disney Studio office—though his neighbors probably didn't.

RIGHT, TOP AND BOTTOM: Rail man Ward. Although during Walt's lifetime he did not work on the conception or design of Disneyland, Kimball has come to be recognized as a primal force in inciting interests in Walt that became fundamental in the creation of the Park.

BELOW: Ward with the RM-1 spaceship from his *Man In Space* series.

16 Richard Sherman reports that after the first screening of the *Babes in Toyland* rough cut, Walt dejectedly left the screening room, muttering, "I guess Disney doesn't know how to make musicals." This terrified the Shermans, as they were waist-deep in developing the song score and story for *Mary Poppins*.

17 In 1992, he donated part of his railroad to the Orange Empire Railway Museum in Perris, California.

he was among a tight-knit group at the Studio who fired Walt's innate interest in trains.

Kimball (like Walt) had been mad about trains since childhood, and one day in August 1948, he got a call from the boss, asking the dumbfounded Kimball to join him for a trip to Chicago. The Railroad Fair on Chicago's Lakefront that year celebrated "the hundredth anniversary of the opening of the West by rail transportation." Sponsored by America's leading railroads, it opened July 20 and continued through Labor Day. For the burdened and depressed Walt, "the trip to the Chicago Railroad Fair, accompanied by one of his most lighthearted, impish employees, was literally what the doctor ordered," author John Canemaker reports.

The pair traveled to the Fair on the Super Chief from Pasadena, and in Chicago Walt found his great loves of railroading and Americana combined. Walt was given the VIP treatment—he and Ward were even able to operate some of the steam locomotives assembled for the spectacular "Wheels A-Rolling" Pageant. "We had the time of our lives!" Kimball enthused.

In Dearborn, Michigan, the pair visited the Henry Ford Museum and Greenfield Village, an assortment of historic American buildings and artifacts collected and restored by the auto magnate. The Wright brothers' bicycle shop, George Washington Carver's cabin, and Thomas Edison's laboratory were some of the original buildings that Ford had relocated to Greenfield Village, and Walt was utterly charmed by the nostalgia and presentation of history. After seeing this collection, Walt began to imagine something along the same lines that suited his interests and desires.[18]

Returning home with a "Rail Fever," Walt soon began work on his own scale railroad for his Holmby Hills property, working on his train in the Studio machine shop with Roger Broggie, and hiring the famed Evans brothers to landscape his backyard rail right-of-way. Walt named his finished engine "Lilly Belle" (after his wife, Lillian), and the Carolwood Pacific Railroad (Walt lived on Carolwood Avenue) had its first run on May 15, 1950.

This sequence of events was in large part stoked by the enthusiasm and encouragement of Kimball (as well as Ollie Johnston and his hobby rail line)—and absolutely essential in the procedural development of Disneyland, as it has been described.

Kimball did contribute to the Disney parks—eventually. "We brought Ward in to help us on World of Motion for Epcot in the early 1980s," Marty Sklar recalls. The GM-sponsored transportation pavilion was at that point primarily the work of Claude Coats, but the overall feeling was that the show was a little too academic, and lacked the Disney spark of wit and fun. Several of the Imagineers recalled that Ward had produced and directed some innovative and funny shows on transportation for the Disney television programs *Magic Highway, U.S.A.* (1958) and *Man on Wheels* (1967). It was felt that this less conventional approach might invigorate the vignettes within the World of Motion.

Although retired, Kimball lent a hand, with great success. Some of his scenes within this attraction were as memorable as those created by Coats and Marc Davis for Pirates of the Caribbean (although memories are what they are—World of Motion was replaced by Test Track in 1996). "That big city scene was brilliant," Sklar recalls. "The literal and figurative collision of the horse-drawn era and the motor age was succinct in its story and memorably funny."

Kimball passed away on July 7, 2002, from natural causes in Arcadia, California. He was eighty-eight years old.

In the end, rather than any specific work, Kimball seems to have made a mark with his persona. "He was a wonderful character himself and as entertaining in real life as the ones he created on screen," Roy E. Disney agrees.

Perhaps just as Kimball would have liked to be remembered.

---

18 In fact, the August 31, 1948 memo detailing his "Mickey Mouse Park" was composed on the Super Chief back to California from his vacation with Kimball.

"I think all artists—whether they paint, write, sing, or play music, write for the theater or movies, make poetry or sculpture—all of these are first of all pleasure givers. People who like to bring delight to other people, and hereby gain pleasure and satisfaction for themselves."

—Walt Disney

The Renaissance Imagineer

If there was a defining artist at Walt Disney Imagineering, one who embodied both the skills of an Imagineer and Walt Disney's attitude toward his artists' creative skills, it was John Hench. To many, he defined the aptitudes and interests of the perfect Imagineer, and was an idealization of the philosophies and legacy of Walt Disney himself. "Other than Walt Disney himself," says Marty Sklar, "no one symbolizes The Walt Disney Company more than John Hench."

John Hench: The Essence of The Disney Legacy

By definition, a "renaissance man" is a modern scholar who is in a position to acquire more than superficial knowledge about many different interests, the term ostensibly based on the concept that a true scholar during the Renaissance (because knowledge was limited) could know almost everything about many topics.

Both tracks of definition have application to John Hench, who, during his sixty-five-year Disney career, worked in a wide variety of departments and media, with varied personalities and personnel, from art design and animation to camera and effects, to his midcareer move to WED. There, he relentlessly pursued both creating and designing Disney parks, while persistently striving to understand, quantify, explain, and comprehend the methods and meanings of the Disney culture and its consequence to humankind. His interest and expertise in the field of color styling is the stuff of legend, and his initiative and love of his work—he drove to the office every day until two weeks prior to his death—was the envy of men a third his age.

Hench was born in Cedar Rapids, Iowa, on June 29, 1908, and grew up in Southern California. After attending the Art Students' League, Otis Art Institute, California School of Fine Arts, and the Chouinard Institute, he entered the motion picture industry, and researched color processes at Vitacolor Studios in Hollywood—the beginning of his fascination with color theory. Hench also worked in special effects at Republic Studios. In May 1939, he was hired at Disney's old Hyperion Studio.

He actually wasn't at the Studio itself, but rather on the top floor of a two-story apartment behind it. In one of the back bedrooms, John joined a group that was at work on *Fantasia*, as a sketch artist on "The Nutcracker Suite." He experimented with pastels on black paper, creating underwater effects for the "Arabian Dance" sequence. "The wall in the bedroom where I worked was plastered with a sandy finish," Hench said in a 1990 interview, "and by holding black paper up against it and rubbing pastels over the paper, it produced a sparkle effect, suggesting unusual underwater lighting." In those days of growth and experimentation, Hench's varied interests and abilities were a perfect fit. He found that he was not restricted to simply banging out story sketches. "When they found out I could draw sexy girls, they told me to take a stab at sexy fish. After a lot of work, we were finally able to get something satisfactory."

The apartment building was "hot as hell in the summer," John recalled, but he savored the environment created by the constant strains of classical music that permeated the building. "The walls of the apartment were quite thin, and everybody set their record players on loud, so you could hear what was playing in the next room, and the next. The 'Toccata and Fugue in D Minor' group was in the next bedroom; there was a lot of collaboration between their group and ours." Hench particularly remembered the Sibelius tone poem "The Swan of Tuonela," which was being developed as an additional segment of *Fantasia*; "a desperately sad piece, which drove everyone crazy." He was relieved when the segment was shelved, and the constant, heartbreaking concert ceased for good.

In the midst of production, the *Fantasia* teams were moved to Walt's new Burbank studio. The facilities were certainly a step up from the stuffy, crowded, and beat-up apartment building, but John also noticed a cultural change—one that even Walt would come to miss in his efficient, modern animation plant. "We lost some of the musical and personal contacts. Since the rooms were more soundproof, we couldn't hear the other Music Rooms[1] playing, and the groups became more and more isolated," Hench recalled. "In Hyperion, [Walt] was all over the place, and his enthusiasm was, of course, infectious." Still, the culture of the new Studio continued to rely most on the man at the top, and Hench was another artist who was given abundant opportunity by Walt to expand his horizons and develop his skills. "He was always looking for talent," Hench remembered. "Walt was always one to respond to people's enthusiasm. He really was an enthusiastic man himself, and if somebody was really interested in the work they were doing, as most of us were, we got to do other things.

"I guess I've been in most departments," Hench said. "I didn't get a chance for character animation, but I did do effects animation, and I worked through story and layout, background painting, and multiplane background painting.

1 "Music Room" was an in-house Disney term for the director's room, or the common area outside a director's office, which was often furnished with a piano, radio, and record player.

Then I wanted to go down to Camera and see what happened to all this stuff, so I spent three years in Camera and Special Effects. And the Studio, at that point, was able to do things like that. I asked Walt, and he said, 'Sure, go ahead.'"

Hench had, at first, been incredulous about the Disney organization. "I was appalled! I didn't think the company would be open six months. [Animation] was so hard to do—it was like engraving pinheads or something. Hard to do, and not much value I could see, but Walt was the key to all this, of course." Hench's recognition of Walt's galvanic nature, and his appreciation of enthusiasm and lack of rigidity, led Hench to stay on at the Studio where he worked on such legendary Disney animated films as *Dumbo*, *The Three Caballeros*, *Peter Pan*, and *Cinderella*, and live-action efforts such as *So Dear to My Heart*, and *20,000 Leagues Under the Sea*.

ABOVE: Hench, Claude Coats, and Walt confer about art-design work for *Alice in Wonderland*, c.1950.

In 1945, Walt Disney met Spanish painter Salvador Dalí at a dinner party hosted by Warner Bros.' Jack and Ann Warner. Dalí, who was then working on the dream sequence of Alfred Hitchcock's *Spellbound*, had previously collaborated on two short films with the Spanish master Luis Buñuel. The artist believed that he and Walt could create what Dali called "the first motion picture of the Never Seen Before." "I have come to Hollywood and am in touch with the three great American surrealists," Dali had written to his friend Andre Breton,[2] "the Marx Brothers, Cecil B. DeMille, and Walt Disney."

Walt assigned Hench, along with layout artist Bob Cormack, to work with Dalí, who had selected the Mexican ballad "Destino" by Armando Dominguez as the subject and score for his Disney project. Destino is the Spanish, Portuguese, and Italian words for "destiny." "I think that was why he chose it," Hench said. "Not because of the music, but because he liked the notion of Destiny." Hench and Dalí collaborated at the Studio for eight months in late 1945 and 1946. Dalí spent his time painting, drawing, and discussing with Hench the challenges of adding motion to what he described as his "hand-colored photographs." Walt had intended for the Dalí piece to be part of a musical compilation feature, but the project never sufficiently pulled together, and was shelved in 1947 after eight months of work. Hench compiled an eighteen-second animation test, in the hopes of rekindling Walt's interest in the project, but the production was no longer deemed financially viable.[3]

In 1954, Walt Disney asked Hench to leave the Studio and join the small team at work on Disneyland. "Well, I was really told," Hench said to writer Brian Sibley. "Walt said, 'I want you to work on Disneyland—and you're gonna like it.'" Hench worked first on the creation of Tomorrowland, and in the process discovered a new career as a Disney park designer. As usual, he became fascinated not only with the projects, but also with the processes, and with the underlying psychological, sociological, historic, and cultural underpinnings of the work. With John Hench, there was never an end to knowledge, never a limit to intellectual pursuit, and never more pleasure than that of discovery.

Hench enthusiastically supported and collaborated with the cadre of "movie men" Walt assembled to envision Disneyland. "That came from his neighbor who was a practicing architect," he recalled. "That was Welton Becket. I guess it's still Becket Associates. [Walt] spent time going to every amusement park in the United States—big ones—talking to the owners and operators. . . . Some time later, he talked to Becket, and Becket said, 'You've got to use your own people. We can't help you. We don't have any kind of a background for this. Just use your own guys.' And so that's the way it started. We did use some architects here, but we found that people who had spent time in the

2 A French writer, critic, and editor, Breton's 1924 Manifeste du surréalisme provided a definition of Surrealism, of which he was the chief intellectual advocate—and Dalí was perhaps the best-known public promoter.

3 Dalí died in 1989. In 1999, Roy E, Disney decided to bring the dormant project back to life. With the consultation of John Hench, Walt Disney Feature Animation France, under the direction of Dominique Monfrey, finished *Destino*, which premiered on June 2, 2003, at the Annecy International Animated Film Festival in Annecy, France. Destino won several awards, and was nominated for a 2003 Academy Award for Animated Short Film.

motion picture business were much more understanding of what we were trying to get out of them. It was because they knew something about theater, and basically, a big part of it was 'show business' as a way of communicating."

In the Disneyland project, Hench found new interests, new skills, and new fascinations, particularly a renewed enthusiasm for color theory and a deeper understanding of communication well beyond the page, the stage, and the screen. "Hench was a master of the 'Art of the Show,'" Sheila Hagen, a longtime contributor to the MousePlanet.com Web site wrote in 2004, "a philosophy that demanded that every design element contributed to the story or helped to create a natural visual segue from one themed land to another. His philosophy was that the parks were like movies, and the designer must provide transitions between one 'scene' to another; gradual changes in color and design helped to avoid making the changes abrupt. He did this most often through his legendary gift of color sense."[4]

"Even as a kid, I was always aware that the amount of space occupied by a color was critical, as well as the kind of light falling on the color," Hench recounted. "Color, being like most everything else in the world, is highly relative and doesn't have any absolute value (except in a lab). When it's used in combination with other colors it takes on different appearances—and meanings."[5]

"Disneyland was the first park to be designed for this kind of experience—to go through a series of sound/color themes—though most people aren't aware of how it was achieved," Hench said. "I think that's the way good communication should work. People shouldn't be able to detect the creaking of the machinery. But people do feel things, they do get the message."

Hench became the "color guru" of Disney for the parks, hotels, and resorts—even the builders of new offices at the Studio sought out Hench's consultation, insight, and approval. "Employees happily adapt," Hench admitted, "though I believe the daily color experience rubs off to become a part of their lives."

"Hench also was a master in utilizing cultural icons in theme park design," Sheila Hagen wrote. "He understood how to use images and colors that people see on a daily basis to create an instant comfort and immediate understanding of the design elements in the parks. One of his earliest successes was the design of the Moonliner. In the 1950s, people had seen various images, both real and imaginary, of spacecraft. His job was to incorporate all the images seen before into the design of the Moonliner, which would be new in design but that when people saw it, they would instantly 'recognize' it."

This recognition had some unusual, though entirely understandable, results. "We had letters over and over again from little towns in Nebraska and Kansas that said they wanted to make their Main Street 'authentic' like ours," Hench said. "Would we help them to do it? And ours wasn't authentic at all. Nothing about it was authentic. It just seemed to be to people—they felt that this was the truth about main streets. "No color-coordinated main street had actually existed in the world up to that point—Disneyland's was the first. People thought that Walt had perhaps copied the street from his hometown of Marceline, Missouri. Marceline never looked like that."

This idealization, as a result of efficiently communicated ideas and simple, yet sophisticated design principles has led to backlash of what is bemoaned as "cleaned-up, standardized, rendered safe for the whole family, replica of something rather than something."[6] This was a complaint leveled against any successful Disney project—such things are "Disneyfied." Hench dismisses such simplified intellectualism.[7] "It's the same thing that happened to painters like Van Gogh. Nobody can paint sunflowers without reference to Van Gogh. And nobody can paint ballet without reference to Degas. So when you make a strong statement about it, you own that from then on."

"It would be difficult to overestimate the importance of Disneyland in the American imagination,"

ABOVE: Hench surveys a model at WED, c. 1979.

TOP RIGHT: Hench's twenty-fifth anniversary portrait of Mickey Mouse, 1953. Walt insisted that Mickey appear in his best-known wardrobe—Hench had wanted to dress the mouse in more contemporary costume.

BOTTOM RIGHT: Hench with an early concept for Spaceship Earth in Epcot.

4 Against Hench's arguments, the head of a corporation once insisted on white for the walls of an Epcot attraction. A frustrated Hench replied, "Well, I have thirty-four shades of white. Which one do you want?"

5 The search for meaning was a theme in Hench's life; he and his wife were both longtime devotees of the Hindu saint Ramakrishna and members of the Southern California Vedanta Society.

6 Tom Vanderbilt, "On Place: It's a Mall World After All," *Harvard Design* Magazine; Constructions of Memory Number 9, Fall 1999.

7 Vanderbilt agrees, "In Manhattan, where the clarion against Disneyfication has recently been sounded, one wonders at the precise cause for alarm. Fears of lost authenticity sound hollow in a city where themed restaurants (for instance, Murray's Roman Gardens) have existed since the turn of the century and a favorite museum is a reconstruction of a twelfth-century Spanish cloister." Ibid.

wrote Alexander Wilson in *The Culture of Nature*. No surprise to John Hench, who stated simply, "There's order about it, and there're some other kinds of things about it that speak to [the visitors] and where they live. It is reassurance. And it's beyond something that they have to rationalize or think about intellectually. They can just feel this."

The castle icon is a primary example of the Imagineers' ability to speak to the public unconscious. "We carry these so-called myths, and they're part aspiration, part dream, and it's something we share, on a fundamental basis, of course, with every living person. The castle was a strong point, and I suppose it actually has something to do with the relationship with mountains, too—with a high point in the landscape. It's a place of safety. I think the medieval churches also played up that same kind of feeling. It was a large architectural statement and it said something to people about a rallying point, a safe place, a protector. Also an orientation point, they could always refer to it." Such is the function of the Magic Kingdom castles even today, and the success of their appeal to millions of visitors to the parks.

Another part of this success is a torch that Hench carried for decades, one that came from Walt, and that Hench passed on to future generations: say what you want to say, and don't contradict your own message. "Walt had accomplished this in the pictures, that we would have to have a kind of visual literacy. We should say things, use the forms to communicate, but it shouldn't be contradictory. It should say one thing. And, of course, architecture is full of visual contradictions and cities are nothing but contradictions, because we understand how they're put together. They're put together by sheer accident."

Walt saw the source of this "Architecture of Reassurance" in an innate respect for the public. "I worked in two other studios, and I know what most motion picture people think about their audience. When something was really good and it looked fine, he'd say, 'I think they're going to like that.' And when he said 'they,' he meant the whole rest of the world. He said, 'If they don't get it, it's because you're a poor communicator. Because people are okay. Just remember that. They're okay.'"

Part of Walt's respect for his audience was his insistence that the Imagineers leave their Glendale offices frequently and get a guest's-eye view of their work. "It's quite different than being in the film business, where you don't get to see the film over and over again with different audiences," Hench explained. "Walt expected us to go down there—in fact, he required us to go to Disneyland when it was finished. I think it was twice a month that we would go there and check the rides that we'd worked, as well as others, and stand in line. He didn't want us to go in the back way, he said we should walk in, stand in line in front, and walk in and have the same experience as our guests and with our guests. Listen to and watch them—how they reacted. I don't know any other design firm that's had that privilege. Again, it relates to something that you can't read, that you have to experience."

Hench's varied talents were applied to other Disney projects. In 1960 Hench and his team of WED artists and designers created the backdrop for the VIII Winter Olympic Games at Squaw Valley, California, helped stage the opening and closing ceremonies, and oversaw production of "snow statues" and other elements seen throughout the Olympic village.[8] Hench also helped develop the four Disney shows that debuted at the 1964–1965 New York World's Fair: Great Moments with Mr. Lincoln, Carousel of Progress, "it's a small world," and Magic Skyway.

Although Hench once said he hated working on the Fair, he looked on the experience as one of the projects in which Walt was most deeply immersed, making immediate decisions and guiding every element. Hench cites "it's a small world" as an example. "The music was given to the Sherman Brothers. They came back the next morning with

8 One of Hench's most recognizable works is the modern Olympic Torch. Nearly all of the recent versions have been modeled after his design for the 1960 Winter Olympics.

"It's a Small World (After All)," played it on the piano, and Walt said, 'That's great. That's it.' So decisions were being made all the time because Walt was there, and he made those fast decisions. Even with Lincoln, who just wouldn't work—I had lost faith in the man. I thought he'd never work. To me it was just like Walt had willed him to. He just said he was going to, and by God, one morning he did—absolutely perfectly. Walt had to apologize to the press two or three times, saying, 'We're just not ready yet'—and one day we were ready."

One of Hench's more renowned accomplishments was his career as Mickey Mouse's "Official Portrait Artist." Hench completed portraits for Mickey in 1953 (twenty-fifth anniversary), 1978 (fiftieth), 1988 (sixtieth), 1998 (seventieth), Millennium Mickey (2000), and for the fiftieth anniversary of Walt Disney Imagineering in 2003.

John was also long fascinated by Mickey's worldwide appeal and acceptance. "As a graphic representation, Mickey is a symbol of life. He is a series of round shapes that have a distinctive relationship characterized by the flow of one curve into another, creating lines that relate to each other in the musculature of a human being. Curves typically indicate movement typical of the living human figure. I see Mickey as a record of dynamic movement."

By the mid-1960s, Hench was a trusted lieutenant of Walt's and there was a building perception (which only grew later) that John had somehow attained some kind of knighthood in Walt's "court." Hench deflects the idea that there was some sort of bequest of Walt's aesthetic authority, he always simply considered himself a disciple of the Master. "Well, obviously he was a very intuitive person," Hench said. "He had a sense of direction. He seemed to know where he was going. He certainly knew quickly and positively where he didn't want to go. We had, really, quite a bit of freedom. I always had an idea. I had a lot of freedom. But in looking back, we were generally going the direction Walt wanted us to go. The only way I could really describe the way I thought freedom worked around here was that we had rather long leashes, and if Walt was walking north, why, we could go east or west considerably—but none of us could go south!"

After Walt Disney's death in 1966, Hench became one of Imagineering's chief designers and played a key role in the creation of every one of Disney's eleven existing theme parks.

With his clipped mustache and ascot tied neatly around his neck, he resembled a character actor in a 1930s movie. Dapper, articulate, and charming, Hench (although happily married for more than six decades to his wife, Lowry) was well known for his appreciation of the fair sex, even to the point of being kidded on-screen about it in the 1964 television program *Disneyland Goes to the World's Fair* by Walt himself. Hench also had a passing resemblance to Walt, which occasionally led to awkward encounters. "He was very close to Walt Disney and sometimes was mistaken for Walt in the Disneyland Park," says Martin Sklar.

BELOW: Disneyland Ambassador Julie Reihm, Walt, and Hench admire John's work on the interior design for the Plaza Inn Restaurant, 1965.

OPPOSITE: One of Hench's illustrations for the 1952 Golden Book, *Walt Disney's Peter Pan*. Hench did the staging and pencil work, Al Dempster provided the color.

"But the resemblance to Walt didn't end just there," Sheila Hagen wrote. "He also had the same philosophy as Walt on how to operate Disneyland—not everything had to make money. He would point out that a popcorn wagon by itself would not make money, but in the long run, it would all even out. It was all about 'show,' about creating an environment that when the sum of its parts was totaled up, would create a richer and more satisfying experience."

Hench saw this as an extension of Walt's qualities of honesty and artistry, which he greatly admired and proselytized throughout his life. "He was a very modest guy, in a way. He, you know, he had quite a simple life, really, private life. His private life was exactly like his public life. There wasn't anything he had hidden. He was an extraordinarily honest guy. I never knew anyone to be more honest, you know? And he was an artist. And he was one artist that never had a creative block. I think that's astonishing."

Hench helped oversee the creation of Walt Disney World in Florida in 1971 and the addition of Epcot in 1982. He helped supervise the design of Disney's first overseas park, Tokyo Disneyland, which opened in Japan in 1983. Hench continued to work with and inspire new generations of Disney designers in the creation of the Disney Studios in Florida (1989); EuroDisney, now Disneyland Paris, (1992); Disney's Animal Kingdom Park in Florida (1998); Disney's California Adventure (2001); Tokyo DisneySea (2001); Walt Disney Studios in France (2002); and Hong Kong Disneyland (2005).

In 1998, Hench was presented a Lifetime Achievement Award by the Themed Entertainment Association, an industry trade group and in early 2004, John was honored with the Winsor McCay award from the International Animated Film Society in recognition of lifetime career contributions to the art of animation. Hench's 2003 book, *Designing Disney: Imagineering and the Art of the Show*, chronicled the years John spent working side by side with Walt Disney, and the lessons he learned.

John Hench died of heart failure after a brief illness, on February 5, 2004. He was ninety-five years old.

John's greatest achievement may have been his inspiration to others. "He was an accomplished artist, designer, and stylist who had a tremendous influence not only on the movies and theme parks he worked on," Marty Sklar says, "but on the thousands of people he worked with during his many years with the Company." Said Michael Eisner, past chairman and chief executive officer of The Walt Disney Company: "John Hench taught me and so many others about the essence of the Disney legacy. He was at Walt's side during the creation of so much classic entertainment and continued to be a vital creative force for our company right up until the end."

"I don't look on myself as a replacement for Walt," Hench had deferred. "But I do think that the thing that has held us together is a kind of momentum. Walt, again, going north, and we are more separated, of course . . . but we're still taking, instinctively, the same direction."

Imagineer Tom Morris says, "More than anything, John was the Philosopher of Imagineering, and I look to him, and his teachings, to always remember why 'Disneyland is good for you.'"

Selected Bibliography

Bright, Randy. *Disneyland: Inside Story.* New York: Harry N. Abrams, 1987.
Canemaker, John. *The Art and Flair of Mary Blair.* New York: Disney Editions, 2003.
——. *Before the Animation Begins: The Art and Lives of Disney Inspirational Sketch Artists.* New York: Hyperion, 1996.
——. *Paper Dreams: The Art And Artists Of Disney Storyboards.* New York: Hyperion, 1999.
——. *Walt Disney's Nine Old Men and the Art of Animation.* New York: Disney Editions, 2001.
Cotter, Bill. *The Wonderful World of Disney Television: A Complete History.* New York: Hyperion, 1997.
Dunlop, Beth. *Building a Dream: The Art of Disney Architecture.* New York: Harry N. Abrams, 1996.
Gordon, Bruce and David Mumford (editors). *A Brush with Disney: An Artist's Journey.* Santa Clarita, CA: Camphor Tree Publishers, 2000.
Gordon, Bruce and David Mumford. *Disneyland: The Nickel Tour.* Santa Clarita, California: Camphor Tree Publishers, 1995.
Hench, John with Peggy Van Pelt. *Designing Disney: Imagineering and the Art of the Show.* New York: Disney Editions, 2003.
Imagineers, The. *The Imagineering Way: Ideas to Ignite Your Creativity.* New York: Disney Editions, 2003.
——.*Walt Disney Imagineering: A Behind the Dreams Look at Making the Magic Real.* New York: Hyperion, 1997.
Iwerks, Leslie and John Kenworthy. *The Hand Behind the Mouse.* New York: Disney Editions, 2001.
Kurtti, Jeff. *Since the World Began: Walt Disney World, The First 25 Years.* New York: Hyperion, 1997.
——with Bruce Gordon. *The Art of Disneyland.* New York: Disney Editions, 2005.
Marling, Karal Ann (Editor). *Designing Disney's Theme Parks: The Architecture of Reassurance.* Paris-New York: Flammarion/CCA, 1997.
Martin, Stacia with Bruce Gordon. *The Sounds of Disneyland.* Burbank, CA: Walt Disney Records, 2005.
Murray, R. Michael. *The Golden Age of Walt Disney Records 1933–1988.* Dubuque, Iowa: Antique Trader Books,1997.
O'Day, Tim and Bruce Gordon. *Disneyland: Then, Now, and Forever.* New York: Disney Editions, 2005
O'Day, Tim and Lorraine Santoli. *Disneyland Resort: Magical Memories for a Lifetime.* New York: Disney Editions, 2002.
Queens Museum. *Remembering the Future: The New York World's Fair from 1939 to 1964.* New York: Rizzoli, 1989.
Smith, David R. *Disney A to Z: The Updated Official Encyclopedia.* New York: Hyperion, 1998.
——. *The Quotable Walt Disney.* New York: Disney Editions, 2001.
Sklar, Martin A. *Walt Disney's Disneyland.* Anaheim, CA: Walt Disney Productions, 1969.
Surrell, Jason. *The Haunted Mansion: From the Magic Kingdom to the Movies.* New York: Disney Editions, 2003.
——. *Pirates of the Caribbean: From the Magic Kingdom to the Movies.* New York: Disney Editions, 2005.
Thomas, Bob. *Walt Disney: An American Original.* New York: Hyperion, 1994.
——. *Building a Company: Roy O. Disney and the Creation of an Entertainment Empire.* New York: Hyperion, 1998.
Walt Disney Productions. *Disneyland: The First Quarter Century.* Anaheim, CA: Walt Disney Attractions Merchandise, 1979.
Watts, Steven. *The Magic Kingdom: Walt Disney and the American Way of Life.* New York: Houghton Mifflin,1998.

PERIODICALS

Anderson, Paul F. "Illinois 'Land of Lincoln' Pavilion," *Persistence of Vision* Issue 6 & 7, 1995, pp. 83–98.
Bonner, Marcel and Stephen Daly. "Remembering Fred Joerger." *The "E" Ticket,* Summer 2006, pp. 6–17.
Janzen, Jack and Leon Janzen. "Disneyland Art Director Bill Martin," *The "E" Ticket,* Winter 1994–95, pp. 10–19.
——. "Disneyland on Wheels: An Interview with Bob Gurr," *The "E" Ticket,* Summer 1997, pp. 29–41.
——. "Flair and Versatility: A Visit to Walt's Original WED Model Shop," *The "E" Ticket,* Summer 2006, pp. 28–41.
——. "An Interview with Harper Goff," *The "E" Ticket,* Winter 1992–93, pp. 6–11.
——. "An Interview with Rolly Crump," *The "E" Ticket,* Summer 1990, pp. 28–32.
——. "The Mighty Eye: Disneyland's Adventure Thru Inner Space," *The "E" Ticket,* Winter 1992–93, pp. 12–21.
——. "Tomorrowland 1967," *The "E" Ticket,* Winter 1993–94, pp. 6–15.
——. "Wathel Rogers and Audio-Animatronics," *The "E" Ticket,* Winter 1996, pp. 26–34.
Janzen, Leon J. "Rolly Crump and the Museum of the Weird," *The "E" Ticket,* Summer 1990, pp. 24–27.
O'Boyle, J.G. "Mindsetter: A Cultural Analysis of Main Street, U.S.A." *Persistence of Vision,* Issue 10, 1998, pp. 31, 85–93.
Richman, Betsy. "The Color Whiz: A Conversation with John Hench," *WDEye magazine,* Winter 1990, pp. 5–9.
Smith, Hal. "Yerba Buena Tuba," *Frisco Cricket*, Summer 1998.

SPECIAL PUBLICATIONS

Richman, Betsy. Wathel Rogers Retirement Announcement, WED Enterprises Company Release, October 1987.
The Walt Disney Company. *The Art of Disneyland 1953–1986* (Exhibit Catalog, The Disney Gallery Inaugural Exhibition 1987–1988), 1987.
The Walt Disney Company. *From the Kingdom of Dreams: The Art of Disneyland, The Magic Kingdom, and Tokyo Disneyland* (Exhibit Catalog, The Disney Gallery Tokyo Disneyland), c. 1988.
Walt Disney Productions. *Walt Disney's Pirates of the Caribbean.* Anaheim, CA: Disneyland Merchandise, 1969.
Walt Disney Productions. *it's a small world: A Disneyland Pictorial Souvenir.* Anaheim, CA: Disneyland Merchandise, 1969.
Walt Disney World: Background and Philosophy. Compiled by Martin A. Sklar, September 21, 1967.

INTERVIEWS

Greene, Richard and Katherine. Unedited interviews with Bill Cottrell, Marvin Davis, Bob Gurr, Sam McKim recorded for biographical CD-ROM project. © The Walt Disney Family Foundation. Used with permission.

Horan, Jay. Walt Disney Imagineering Key Employee Interviews with Ken Anderson, Herb Ryman, Bill Cottrell, John Hench. © Disney Enterprises, Inc. Used with permission.

Hubler, Richard. Interviews with Roger Broggie and Dick Irvine; recorded for an unpublished biography of Walt Disney (May, 1968). © Disney Enterprises, Inc. Used with permission.

Mannheim, Steven. Unpublished interviews with John Hench, Bob Gurr, Bill Evans, Ward Kimball, Bill Martin; recorded for *Walt Disney and the Quest for Community.* Burlington, VT: Ashgate Publishing, 2002. Interviews © The Walt Disney Family Foundation. Used with permission.

Peri, Don. Interviews with Harriet Burns, Fred Joerger, and Bill Martin, ©The Walt Disney Family Foundation. Used with permission.

Thomas, Bob. Unedited interviews with Harriet Burns, Rolly Crump, and Dick Irvine; recorded for *Walt Disney: An American Original.* New York: Simon & Schuster, 1976. © Disney Enterprises, Inc. Used with permission.

Walt Disney Family Foundation. Unedited interviews with Harriet Burns, Rolly Crump, Bob Gurr, and Sam McKim; recorded for *Walt: The Man Behind the Myth*. ©The Walt Disney Family Foundation. Used with permission.

WEB SITES

http://www.laughingplace.com/
http://www.mouseplanet.com/
http://www.soundofmagic.com/

In addition, countless back issues of *Disneyland Line, Eyes & Ears of Walt Disney World, WDEye,* and *Disney Newsreel* (all Disney employee newsletters), were referenced in researching this book, as well as dozens of park guides, souvenir brochures, promotional pamphlets, and souvenir maps.

It is fortunate for the goals of this project to have had the cooperation, collaboration, recollections, and insights of Marty Sklar, whose professional, personal, and profound relationships with the featured Imagineers brings a degree of expertise, credibility, and discernment to the narrative that would otherwise have been impossible. He is a large part of the continuity of the legacy of Walt's Imagineers with those of today. Without his mindfulness of his responsibility to this legacy, much of the history of this organization and its creative philosophy and intellectual engine might have been lost to posterity.

The Walt Disney Company is the professional home of smart and passionate people who likewise watch out for the legacy of its founder every day. My eternal thanks to Dave Smith and the Walt Disney Archives staff; Brian Hoffman, Ed Ovalle, and Rob Klein. Robert Tieman and Rebecca Cline rate a special mention for silly questions (answering, not asking), research on demand (not permitted, but often performed), and generally putting up with me with great good humor.

The staff at the Walt Disney Photo Library is similarly enthusiastic and cooperative, thanks to Ed Squair, Shelly Graham, Andrea Recendez-Carbone, and Michael Buckhoff.

At the Walt Disney Imagineering Art Library, the collaborative nature and convivial spirit of Mike Jusko, Denise Brown, and Vanessa Hunt made my work there a pleasure.

Across the hall at the Walt Disney Imagineering Slide Library, Diane Scoglio was her typical helpful, supportive, and warmhearted self.

Ken Shue of Disney Publishing Worldwide generously (and quickly!) furnished the beautiful *Peter Pan* book illustration for the John Hench chapter.

Jonathan Garson at Disney remains a stalwart support, a great pal, and "one of the good ones."

My friends and colleagues in the wonderful world of documenting Disney could not have been more distinctive in their kindness and aid. Sincere thanks and affection to John Canemaker, Brian Sibley, Richard Holliss, Malcolm Prince, Paula Sigman-Lowery, and Tim O'Day.

Colleague, collaborator, boss, and best of all, loyal friend and staunch supporter—proper credit for Tom Schumacher requires too many adjectives for my word count.

Wendy Lefkon, Jody Revenson, and Jessica Ward at Disney Editions are patient, understanding, and as always, cheerfully collaborative, helpful, and fun to work with.

The Disney family was generous and cooperative with their time and resources, and my thanks go as always to Roy E. Disney for his amicable and accommodating nature, and enthusiasm for my work.

Ron Miller, Diane Disney Miller, Walter Miller, and the Walt Disney Family Foundation have my lasting gratitude and sincere fondness for all the wonderful and joyous things they have brought to my life and work.

It's been another memorable project with Bruce Gordon. Another lasting memory of Diet Cherry Vanilla Dr. Pepper™, grouchiness, arguments, disagreements, demands, lost discs, re-sent documents—and camaraderie, shared passion for Disney, lots of laughter, joyous friendship—and a beautiful book design.

Most of all, I love home, because that's where I live with Ken and Brendan and Baby Joseph.

Index

SYMBOLS

$1,000,000 Duck 114
20,000 Leagues Under the Sea 2, 3, 7, 80, 96, 137

A

Absent-Minded Professor, The 89, 115, 124, 126
Adventureland Bazaar 68
Adventures in Music: Melody 49
Adventures of Bullwhip Griffin, The 132
Adventures of Ichabod and Mr. Toad, The 54, 127
Adventure Thru Inner Space 58, 110, 114, 119
African Diary 49
African Lion, The 128
Algar, James 16, 113, 126-128
Alice in Wonderland 6, 22, 28, 48, 49, 54, 74, 85, 88, 94, 110, 111, 125, 130, 131
American Broadcasting Company x
America Sings 51, 52, 58, 91, 114
America the Beautiful 97, 114, 130
Anderson, Ken 3, 6-9, 11, 39, 54, 55, 75, 82
Aristocats, The 8, 108
Art Center College of Design xiii, 39, 100
Astuter Computer Revue, The 110
Atencio, X 114, 116, 117-119
Audio-Animatronics vii, 3, 16, 23, 30, 43, 49, 50, 52-53, 70, 88, 98, 109, 123,129
programming 90-91
Autopia 43, 101, 105

B

Babes in Toyland 115, 118, 132
Baker, Buddy 111-115, 116
Bambi 28, 42, 48, 74, 88, 127
Baxter, Tony 8, 55, 58, 59, 64
Bear Country 128
Bears and I, The 114
Beaver Valley 128
Becket, Welton v, 19, 39, 112, 137
Bedknobs and Broomsticks 108, 124, 129
Bertino, Al 43, 52
Big Red 36
Big Thunder Mountain Railroad 50, 82
Blackbeard's Ghost 124
Blair, Mary xii, 23, 50, 70
Blank, Dorothy Ann 27
Bon Voyage! 36, 126
Bradbury, Ray 38
Broggie, Garry 99
Broggie, Roger 3, 53, 55, 94-99, 102, 104, 123, 133
Broggie, Roger Jr. 43, 76, 99
Broughton, Bob 124
Bruns, George 113, 115-116, 118
Burbank Daily Review x
Burns, Harriet 80, 83, 84-87, 89

C

California Institute of the Arts xii, 24, 26, 112
Campbell, Collin 40
Canemaker, John xii, 8, 28, 48, 49
Carolwood Pacific Railroad ix, 62, 95, 133
Carousel of Progress 16, 52, 57, 70, 74, 86, 90, 109, 114, 115, 139
Carson, Tom viii
Château de la Belle au Bois Dormant 65
Chicken of the Sea Pirate Ship 7, 12
China Pavilion 12, 13
Chouinard Art Institute xii, xiii, 2, 11, 15, 20, 24, 39, 49, 66, 72, 108, 112, 117, 136
Cinderella 6, 28, 48, 49, 54, 85, 88, 130, 137
Cinderella Castle 12, 44
Cinderella Castle Mystery Tour 59
Circarama 97, 123
Circarama, U.S.A. 128
Circle-Vision 360 97, 123
Coats, Claude 7, 28, 52, 54-59, 66, 68, 82, 96, 119, 133, 146
Comstock, Paul 65
Cottrell, Bill 12, 26-31, 86, 114
Country Bear Jamboree 26, 52, 57, 77, 114
Crump, Roland "Rolly" 50, 66-71, 72, 74, 81, 83

D

Dad, Can I Borrow the Car? 132
Dalí, Salvador 137
Darby O'Gill and the Little People 89
Davis, Marc vii, xii, 23, 39, 48-53, 58, 62, 76, 86, 90, 114, 119, 133
Davis, Marvin 12, 21, 24, 26, 34-39, 114
Davy Crockett 36, 124, 125
Disneylandia x, 3-4, 85
Disneyland TV show 4, 36, 94, 116, 125
Disney, Lillian 42, 95, 99, 133
Disney on Parade 71
Disney, Roy E. xii, 7, 12, 16, 49, 88, 94, 108, 129, 136
Disney, Roy O. 23, 24, 26, 36, 39, 77, 109, 111
Disney's Polynesian Resort 83
Disney, Walt v, vii, 18-19, 32-33, 46-47, 60-61, 77, 78-79, 80, 88, 92-93, 106-107, 120-121,134-135
Dodd, Jimmie 126
Donald in Mathmagic Land 113
Duck Pimples 49
Dumbo 10, 27, 54, 130, 137
Dumbo the Flying Elephant 75

E

Earle, Eyvind xii, xiii, 7
Edison Square 12, 17
Education for Death 10
Eisner, Michael 143
Ellenshaw, Peter xiii, 57
Elliott, Maggie 20-23, 108, 109, 110
Epcot 9, 10, 12, 13, 45, 59, 66, 71, 74, 99, 110, 140
EPCOT 38, 39, 104, 105, 112
Evans, Morgan "Bill" 15, 20, 62-65

F

Fantasia 6, 10, 54, 72, 74, 107, 128, 130, 136
Ferdinand the Bull 54
Ferges, Jack 76
Firehouse Five Plus Two 116, 130, 131
Flight to the Moon 12
Flying Saucers 101
Ford Wonder Rotunda 10, 57, 116
Ford's Magic Skyway 12, 16, 17, 53, 57, 103, 139
Fowler, Joe 23, 43, 103, 111
Frees, Paul 119
Fun and Fancy Free 49, 54

G

Gibson, Blaine 55, 58, 62, 68, 69, 74-77, 82, 88
Gnome-Mobile, The 16, 113, 128
Goddess of Spring 6
Golden Horseshoe Revue, The 15
Goff, Harper 2-5, 12, 50, 80
Gracey, Yale 57, 67, 72-74
Grand Canyon 128
Grand Canyon Diorama, The 56
Granny's Cabin 7, 81, 96
Grant, Joe xiii, 27, 48, 113
Great Moments with Mr. Lincoln 16, 50, 74, 76, 86, 88, 90, 91, 98, 99, 113, 123,128, 131, 139
Great Mouse Detective, The 28
Great Movie Ride, The 16
Green, Howard 6
"Grim Grinning Ghosts" 114, 119
Gurr, Bob 20, 73, 81, 83, 99, 100-105, 109

H

Haber, Heinz 57
Hall of Presidents, The 12, 16, 77, 88, 90, 91, 124, 129
Happiest Millionaire, The 108, 111
Haunted Mansion, The 16, 44, 45, 52, 58, 67, 69, 70, 73, 80, 119, 123
Hauser, Tim vii
Hee, T. 30, 118
Hench, John viii, x, 7, 17, 28, 34, 69, 73, 88, 94, 135, 136-141
Henry Ford Museum and Greenfield Village 133

I

If You Had Wings 58, 114, 119
Impressions de France 114
Incredible Journey, The 128
Indiana Jones™ Adventure 12
Irvine, Richard F. 20-24, 28, 33, 34, 43, 71, 101, 104, 119
"it's a small world" 16, 57, 69, 70, 71, 76, 84, 108, 109, 139
It's Tough to Be a Bird 130, 132
Iwerks, Ub 7, 97, 122-124

J

Joerger, Fred 80-83, 85, 89
Johnny Shiloh 113
Johnny Tremain 16
Johnston, Ollie xii, 116, 123, 130, 133
Journey Into Imagination
Jungle Book, The 8, 27, 108, 115
Jungle Cruise 4-5, 12, 52, 53, 63, 65, 76, 83, 89
Justice, Bill xiii, 117, 118

K

Kahl, Milt xii
Kimball, Ward xii, 57, 66, 89, 91, 116, 129-133
King Arthur Carrousel 81
Kuri, Emile 82

L

Lady and the Tramp 7, 55, 66, 75, 88
Land Pavilion, The 71
Lantz, Walter 26, 114
Legend of Lobo, The 128
Liberty Street 12
Lilly Belle 95
Living Desert, The 127, 128
Love Bug, The 115, 124, 126
Lt. Robin Crusoe, U.S.N. 126

M

Magic Carpet 'Round the World 114, 128
Magic Highway, U.S.A. 133
Magic Kingdom Park 12, 16, 74, 98
Magic Skyway 16, 17, 53, 57, 139
Make Mine Music 30, 54
Malmberg, Melody 64-65
Maltin, Leonard 107
Man in Space 89, 91, 130
Mannheim, Steve 44
Man on Wheels 133
MAPO vii, 98, 99
Marceline, Missouri viii
Mark Twain riverboat 97
Mars and Beyond 130
Martin, Bill 39-45
Mary Poppins 86, 98, 108, 111, 115, 118, 124, 126
McKim, Sam 14-17, 33
Meet the World 111
Melody Time 6, 22, 28, 54, 110
Melton, Mel 23, 111
Mickey and the Beanstalk 22, 110
Mickey Mouse Club, The 28, 29, 80, 84, 89, 113, 116, 117
Mickey Mouse Park x
Mickey Mouse Revue 59, 86
Miller, Diane Disney vii
Miller, Walter Elias Disney vii
Mineral King 52
Mine Train Through Nature's Wonderland 49, 88
Monkey's Uncle, The 113
monorail vii, 12, 42, 97-98, 100, 102
Moon Pilot 36
Morris, Tom 8, 35, 55, 142
Moses, Robert 129
Mr. Toad's Wild Ride 7, 55, 73, 75

N

Napoleon and Samantha 113, 114
Natwick, Grim 48
New Orleans Square 12, 44
New York World's Fair 12, 16, 22, 37, 43, 50, 57, 70, 74, 76, 84, 86, 98, 102, 103, 109, 110, 113, 114, 128, 139
  Carousel of Progress 16, 52, 57, 70, 74, 86, 90, 109, 114, 115, 139
  "it's a small world" 16, 57, 69, 67, 70, 71, 76, 108,109,139
  Ford's Magic Skyway 12, 16, 17, 53, 57, 103, 139
  Great Moments with Mr. Lincoln 16, 50, 74, 76, 86, 88, 90, 91, 98, 99, 113, 123,128, 131, 139
Nikki, Wild Dog of the North 16
Noah's Ark 118

O

O'Boyle, J. G. xi
O'Brien, Ken 76
Old Mill, The 54
OmniMover system 104
One and Only, Genuine, Original Family Band, The 108
One Hundred and One Dalmatians 7, 49, 66, 75, 115

P

Palmer, Terry 63
Parent Trap, The 108, 118
Parinella, Joe 65
Partners statue 77
Peter Pan 6, 7, 22, 28, 55, 66, 74, 110, 130, 137, 140
Peter Pan's Flight 7, 41, 55
Pete's Dragon 8
Pinocchio 6, 10, 28, 54, 74, 85, 88, 117, 119, 130
Pirates of the Caribbean 12, 16, 23, 28, 30, 44, 51, 52, 56, 57, 58, 75, 76, 82, 86, 116, 118, 119, 133
Plane Crazy 122
Pluto's Judgement Day 27, 28
Price, Harrison "Buzz" 36
Primeval World diorama 96, 118
Project Little Man 7, 20, 80, 85, 89, 91, 94, 96, 99, 103, 110

R

Rainbow Caverns Mine Train 42, 56, 71
Rannie, Alexander 113
Redmond, Dorothea 40
Red Wagon Inn 15
Reluctant Dragon, The 6, 28
Rescuers, The 8
Retlaw Enterprises vii, 30-31
Richard F. Irvine riverboat 111
Rinaldi, Joe 75
Rivers of America 12
Robin Hood 8, 115
Rocket Rods 111
Rogers, Wathel 66, 76, 80, 83, 88-91, 123
Rouse, James 38
Ryman-Carroll Foundation 13
Ryman, Herbert xiii, 8, 9, 10-13, 16, 20, 33, 44, 108, 109, 126

S

Saludos Amigos 10, 28, 54, 130
Sargent, Eddie 95
Savage Sam 36
Seal Island 128
Shaggy Dog, The 16, 124, 126
Sherman, Al 108
Sherman, Richard M. and Robert B. 108-111, 114, 115, 116, 118
Sibley, Brian 137
Sklar, Martin v, 2, 13, 16, 17, 45, 55, 59, 64, 65, 90, 91, 104, 109, 110, 119, 135, 140, 141
Skyway 98
Sleeping Beauty xiii, 7, 28, 48, 49, 66, 75, 88, 89, 115, 116
Sleeping Beauty Castle 12, 44, 64, 81, 85, 89
Smith, Dave 122
Snow White and the Seven Dwarfs 6, 26, 27, 28, 48, 54, 107, 115, 127, 129, 130
Snow White's Scary Adventures 7, 55
So Dear to My Heart 6, 49, 98, 137
Song of the South 6, 48, 54, 67, 74
Son of Flubber 126
Space Mountain 74
Space Station X-1 57
Stanford Research Institute x, 36
Steamboat Willie 107
Steinmeyer, Jim 71
Storybook Land 7, 80, 85
Submarine Voyage 12, 42, 56, 57, 78, 82, 83
Summer Magic 113
Swamp Fox 36
Sword in the Stone, The 8, 108, 115
Symposium on Popular Songs 117, 118

T

Ten Who Dared 128
That Darn Cat! 126
The American Adventure 12, 114
Thomas, Bob 24, 28, 48, 112
Thomas, Frank xii, 9, 28, 116, 130
Three Caballeros, The 10, 30, 54, 72, 137
Three Little Pigs, The 48, 85
Three Little Wolves 27, 28
Three Orphan Kittens 6, 27, 28
Tieman, Robert 126
Tiger Walks, A 36
Toby Tyler, or Ten Weeks with a Circus 126
Tokyo Disneyland 12, 31, 59, 63, 111, 114, 119, 140
Tokyo DisneySea 115, 140
Toot, Whistle, Plunk and Boom 49, 117, 130
Tower of the Four Winds 67, 70
True-Life Adventure series 127

U

Universe of Energy 16, 59, 114
Utilidors 44, 45

V

Vanishing Prairie, The 127, 128
Victory Through Air Power 10, 20, 21, 28, 54,127
Von Hagen, Lulu May 24, 112

W

Walker, E. Cardon 39
Walsh, Bill 124-127, 130
Walt Disney Christmas Show, The 125
Walt Disney Presents 86, 113
Walt Disney Productions vii
Walt Disney's Enchanted Tiki Room 68-69, 89, 97, 98, 108, 116
Watkin, Lawrence 124
Watts, Steven vii, xi
Weber, Kem x
WED Enterprises vii, 118
WEDway PeopleMover 98, 114
Westward Ho the Wagons! 36, 126
Wheeler, Lyle 20, 33, 108
White Wilderness 128
Who Killed Cock Robin? 27, 48
Williams, Roy 126
Winnie the Pooh 108
Winnie the Pooh and the Blustery Day 115
Winter Olympic Games 37, 139
Wonderful World of Color 86, 128, 132
Wonderful World of Disney 113
Wonders of China 114
Wonders of Life 71
World of Motion 53, 114, 133
World Showcase 9, 13

X

Xerox drawing-transfer technology 7

Y

"Yo Ho (A Pirate's Life for Me)" 116, 119

Z

Zorro 16, 20, 28, 34, 89, 108, 116
Zorro building 12, 34

ABOVE: A gathering of Imagineering legends celebrate their eternally youthful spirit at a 1990 photo shoot for the Walt Disney Imagineering in-house magazine. From left to right: Marty Sklar, Marc Davis, Ken Anderson, Claude Coats, Leota Toombs, X Atencio, John Hench, Sam McKim, and Bill Martin.